# Improvements That Increase
# the Value of Your House

Hubbard H. Cobb

# Improvements That Increase the Value of Your House

139600

**McGraw-Hill Book Company**

New York   St. Louis   San Francisco   Auckland   Düsseldorf   Johannesburg
Kuala Lumpur   London   Mexico   Montreal   New Delhi   Panama
Paris   São Paulo   Singapore   Sydney   Tokyo   Toronto

Library of Congress Cataloging in Publication Data

Cobb, Hubbard H, date.
    Improvements that increase the value of your house.

    Includes index.
    1.  Dwellings—Remodeling.  I.  Title.
TH4816.C63        690'.8        76-5834
ISBN 0-07-011487-0

1234567890  KPKP  785432109876


The editors for this book were Robert A. Rosenbaum and Beatrice E. Eckes,
the designer was Elliot Epstein, and the production supervisor
was Teresa F. Leaden. It was set in Melior by University Graphics, Inc.

Printed and bound by The Kingsport Press.

# Contents

# Preface

In today's inflationary market an older house is usually a far better buy than a new one. You are likely to hear this opinion echoed by almost anyone familiar with current housing costs: architects, lenders, and even some builders.

This situation is quite a switch. Until recently the American way was to build or buy a new house if you needed a bigger or better one, but the high cost of land, materials, and construction labor has now put new houses beyond the reach of most prospective buyers. As a result, more and more of us are taking a second look at the houses we already live in and are putting money and time into expanding or changing them to suit our needs. If we want to buy a house and we look at both new and older houses, it is soon apparent that the top value is in older houses even if we must invest money to make them meet our requirements.

For this reason the home improvement industry is booming. The way things look at this time, the chances are that the boom will continue for many years, for there are tens of millions of houses in the United States that need modernization. What's more, every minute there are forming new families and new combinations of families that will either have to settle for an existing house if they are unable to buy a new one or live in an apartment, a condominium, or a mobile home.

The trouble with any sort of boom is that it encourages us to let down our guard and assume that no matter what we do, we can't lose. We've all seen this happen countless times in the stock market, real estate developments,

vacation land, and other endeavors. It can also happen in home improvements.

Sound, reasonable improvements that will add true value to your house
are a good investment, not only in comfort but in financial security. The
wrong kind of improvements—those that are overpriced, shoddily done,
idiosyncratic, or poorly planned—not only won't add to the property value
but can even detract from the original value. How to make sure that the
improvements you make are sound ones that will benefit you in terms of
both comfort and monetary value is what this book is all about.

HUBBARD H. COBB

# Improvements That Increase the Value of Your House

# 1. Which Improvements to Make

The term "home improvement" can cover a lot of ground. An improvement can mean anything from a fresh coat of paint or a new screen door to the addition of a wing as large as the original house. It may include work that must be done to keep the place from falling apart or just to keep it habitable, putting on a new roof, getting rid of termites, or replacing leaky pipes. It can mean enclosing a porch to create more living space, adding a bathroom, building a garage, or putting new tile on the kitchen floor. Or it can mean remodeling a whole house or putting in an apple orchard.

But do not assume that every improvement is going to add to the resale value of your house. As you are going to find out in this book, what, if anything, you get back will depend on the kind of improvement you make, how well it is executed, and whether you make it at a reasonable cost.

For example, the kind of improvements you may have to make to keep the house habitable and comfortable—a new roof, a fresh coat of house paint, termite control, insulation, storm windows—won't add much if anything to the resale value because a buyer will naturally assume that the roof is tight, the paint is in fair condition, the place is not infested with termites, and insulation and storm windows are provided. But improvements of this sort, called "basic improvements," will very definitely make it easier to sell your house at a fair market price. In one respect, therefore, money you spend will come back to you if and when you sell the house. And one thing is sure, if you don't make basic improvements, you will find that their lack often detracts more from the resale value of your house than it would cost to have them made.

Some months ago some young friends of ours asked us to take a quick look at a house they were interested in buying. It was a very attractive piece of property, and the price wasn't bad. But we had to point out to our friends that the roof was shot and should be replaced at once, there was a serious moisture problem in the basement, the house was not well insulated and lacked storm windows, and, all told, they'd probably have to put $3,000 or $4,000 into the place just to make it habitable. The couple decided that if so many obvious things were wrong with the place, probably a lot of other things that were less obvious also were wrong; so they decided not to buy the house but to keep looking until they found one that was basically sound. You will, of course, find buyers willing to take on a house that needs a good deal of basic work, but most of us do expect a house to be in a livable condition.

There is one type of improvements—we might call them "ego improvements"—that won't add value to your property and may even be a decided handicap when it comes time to sell. These are the expensive and highly personalized projects that are so dear to the hearts of many homeowners: a basement remodeled into an "olde English" pub, a Roman-size marble bathroom complete with sauna and gym, an Olympic-size swimming pool, a monster backyard brick barbecue. If you have the need and the money to make such improvements, that's your affair, but don't expect a prospective buyer to give you an extra nickel for them. And it's possible that he or she may want you to come down a bit on the price to cover the cost of getting rid of them. Ego improvements are a form of overimprovement, and this is something you want to avoid.

## Overimprovement

Overimprovement simply means putting more money into a house than you can ever get back when you sell it. It is the commonest mistake of homeowners who make major improvements and is something you want to be careful to avoid unless, of course, you expect to live in the house for a good many years or are willing to absorb the loss if you have to sell.

Overimproving is very easy. The first way to overimprove is to put so much money into a house that it becomes the most expensive house on the block or in the neighborhood. Most people buy neighborhoods rather than individual houses. And they look for the least expensive house in the most expensive neighborhood they can afford. There are plenty of exceptions to this rule, but it is a good rule to keep in mind. We've seen many families that have bought a tacky house in a fashionable area when they could have bought an infinitely better house for the same money in a less desirable section. What they really were buying was the address.

What this means is that if you have a house with a market value of, say, $35,000 in a neighborhood of houses in the $50,000 range, you are in a good position to make extensive improvements and get your money out. Even if you put $10,000 into the house, it's still $5,000 below the market value of the houses around you. On the other hand, if your house has the same *present* market value, $50,000, as other houses in your neighborhood and you put $10,000 more into it, you are overpriced in comparison to the other houses. Although you may find a buyer who will be willing to pay the $60,000 you require to get your money out, there is no guarantee that you will. And certainly it's going to take a lot longer to find such a buyer.

Of course, there are determining factors other than the market value of houses in the same neighborhood. Older readers may remember the dire predictions when developments similar to Levittown on Long Island, New York, began to spring up shortly after World War II. Their little houses on concrete slabs were selling like hot cakes to young families for around $8,000, and people said the developments would be the slums of tomorrow. Yet in spite of the low market value of these houses, owners started to put in more money—adding wings, lifting roofs to create more rooms, and so on. As the families and their income expanded, so did their houses. The improvement business in many of these areas became so brisk that several firms moved in and became specialists in expanding and improving that particular type of development house. The net result was that you might find a house to which nothing had been done next to a house with $10,000 or more worth of improvements, and if the improved house was sold, it was sold for the asking price. So here are cases in which the original market value of the houses was not as important as the fact that they were well built to start with and were located in the right place at a time when a population explosion was beginning to create the housing shortage that is still very much with us today.

The rule of not spending a lot of money to make yours a considerably better mousetrap than your neighbor's applies primarily to the typical suburban community. When you get into rural and semirural areas, it's often a different matter. The market value of a house may be little if at all affected by the market value of the house down the road (assuming that it is not located in the town slum).

Another way to overimprove a house is to put a lot of money into the wrong place. In other words, it's not always the amount of money you put into a house that makes it overimproved; it's where you put the money.

Here's a good example. Some years ago my wife and I were house-hunting. We wanted to be near salt water but not too far from the railroad station. And the house had to be within our price range, which had a $45,000 top. We went with a broker to look at a place that sounded great. We were told that the owner had recently put $10,000 into improvements but now had to sell because he had been transferred to another part of the country. The location was beautiful, and the outside of the house was pretty good, but the inside was a disaster. There was a tiny living room without a fireplace, and adjoining it was another small room that wouldn't even be adequate as a dining room for two people. The house had only one bath (upstairs), worn linoleum flooring, and numerous cracks on the walls and ceilings.

We were wondering where the $10,000 worth of improvements had been spent, and then we got to the kitchen and found out. There it was—all $10,000 of it. The owner was a kitchen nut. He, not his wife, had put in an entire stainless-steel kitchen, complete with an island sink and a magnificent gas-fired built-in barbecue with a 6-foot-long hood and a stainless-steel bar. In short, he had overimproved the kitchen, and he had overimproved it in such a fashion that it would have been exactly right for a short-order lunch counter, which was not exactly what Betsy and I had in mind.

The $45,000 asking price was in line with that of other houses in the area, but what this seller had to offer was not. He had put the money in the wrong place as far as most prospective buyers were concerned. The logical thing to have done would have been to rework the interior to make a good-size living room with a fireplace, put in some decent-size windows to take advantage of the view, fix up the kitchen modestly, and maybe add another bath. While we were willing to put some money into the house, we would have had to put so much into doing some rather basic improvements that we would have ended up with a totally overimproved house, for the style of architecture and the general area did not warrant the expenditure.

This is a rather typical case of overimprovement of one area of a house, and it's very common. You'll find houses in which too much money has been put into kitchens, bathrooms, swimming pools, landscaping, or something else that struck the fancy of the owner. But people don't buy a house because it has an expensive kitchen, a fancy bathroom, or a study paneled in solid oak. They buy the total house, and if you overimprove one area at the expense of all the others, you will not get back much, if any, of your money.

Buyers are much more realistic than they are often given credit for, especially by sellers. If a family is able to afford a house in the $40,000 price range and the members have had a chance to look over a few houses, they know pretty much what to expect and what not to expect. They don't expect the house to have a kitchen and a bathroom that would be typical of a house in the $150,000 price range. They expect a kitchen and a bathroom that would normally be found in a $40,000 house. As a matter of fact, when they do find certain areas that have obviously been overimproved, they are likely to mutter, "Am I supposed to pay extra for this souped-up kitchen or that bathroom that gives me the creeps?"

While it's possible to overimprove just about any area or room in a house, there are certain locations that seem to lend themselves most readily to overimprovement. Kitchens are the most likely to be overimproved, as are bathrooms. Basement recreation rooms also get out of hand; we've seen such rooms in which, by the time the job was over, the owner had invested $25,000. Landscaping is something else to watch for, as are swimming pools, for although a pool at a reasonable price can be a sound investment, an overpriced one is not.

Recently we saw in a home magazine an attic that had been remodeled into bedrooms for the kids. These must have been very rich kids because that remodeled attic looked as if it had cost around $20,000. So it appears that you can overimprove even an attic.

## Cost

How much you get back on any improvement project depends on how much you have spent on it. If you can make a worthwhile improvement at a low or reasonable cost, you'll get back all your money and perhaps more to boot. But if you have not been careful and the project has cost more than it's worth, you won't stand much chance of getting back your investment.

Spending more money than a project is worth is a form of overimprovement. And it's a very common one at that. If you have been stuck with a contractor who has charged you twice as much as he should have done to add a second bathroom, that's your loss. If your project has cost more than it should have cost because you have kept changing your mind and the plans during the course of the work, that's your loss. And if you have used the most expensive materials and products available, the chances are no one will pay you extra for them.

If you are making any kind of improvement with a view toward getting your money back, you must be as careful in the way you spend those home improvement dollars as you would be if you were making your living by buying old houses, fixing them up, and then selling them for a profit. The professionals who do this for a living watch every penny. They use the least expensive materials that will produce good results. They shop for the best price on labor, and they plan the job in advance to avoid second-guessing once work gets under way. If you want to get back your home improvement dollars, you must be just as careful as the pros.

## The Neighborhood

It is not just what you do and what it costs that determine how much any given improvement will add to the resale value of your house. Much depends on the house itself and on the neighborhood. As we mentioned earlier, the neighborhood is often the key to how much you can safely invest in a house. It is the condition and value of the other houses around yours that may be the deciding factor on how much money you should spend.

Not all neighborhoods are the same. Some are very stable, some are deteriorating, and others are in the process of being revitalized. Take the time to look over your neighborhood to see into which category it falls.

## Stable Neighborhood

A stable neighborhood may be a relatively new suburban development or a community that has been in existence for thirty, forty, or more years. The basic characteristic of a stable neighborhood is the similarity of the houses in style, size, age, and general price range. You can find neighborhoods such as these all over the country with houses in the $30,000 range or in the $100,000-and-up range.

These neighborhoods are comfortable and attractive to live in. Here, as we mentioned, the attraction is the area, not the house. These are not the most fertile fields in which to sow big money on improvements unless your house lacks a feature that is common to most of the others: a garage, a second or third bathroom, a family room. On the other hand, these are prime examples of areas where exterior maintenance of houses and grounds is essential. If a house is allowed to run down, it will stand out like a sore thumb. These are the places where you've got to keep up with the Joneses. But don't get too far ahead of them if you want to get your money back.

## Deteriorating Neighborhood

Any block with a mix of houses, some small and some very large and of different ages and architecture, can and often does decay to the point at which it is no longer inviting to home buyers. Large old houses, even if they are in good condition, are not attractive to most families because they are simply too big and require too much money for maintenance. So, in time, they either begin to decay for lack of upkeep or are turned into rental units. And when a block is peppered with rental units, the character of the neighborhood has changed. It may still be OK to live in, but it's not necessarily a good place to buy into—rent, yes, but buy, no.

Deterioration can also set in when a large number of houses in the same neighborhood are owned by older people who live on relatively modest fixed incomes. Even if the older people have the desire to maintain and improve their property, they may not have the strength to do the work or the

Dramatic change is evident in this 1905 San Francisco home. The earlier photograph (top) shows the house many years ago. The building was completely remodeled and refurbished from floor to ceiling, inside and out (bottom). The walls of the "new" house are random redwood; the railing and door, solid redwood. This is a classic example of a location making it worthwhile to spend a lot of money to improve a house. [*California Redwood Association Photographer: Phil Palmer Designer: George Rescalvo*]

additional funds to have it done; so houses go unpainted, porches begin to sag, grounds are not maintained, and things in general begin to decline.

Some years ago we had an opportunity to observe a home improvement promotion venture in Cleveland, Ohio. The idea was that the local home improvement industry would take over one house in a run-down block, fix it up, and thus inspire other residents on the block to do the same. It was a good idea, and when the chosen house was finished, it really sparkled. All the residents on the block were invited over for an "open house" so that they could see what they might do with their own property. All they could do, alas, was to look and admire, for the vast majority were living on fixed or modest incomes. Even if they had been given the improvement free, the additional real estate tax they would have had to pay on the improved property would have been more than they could handle.

## Neighborhood Ready for Revitalization

Usually this is a neighborhood in which the houses have some historic value but which has been allowed to deteriorate until it has become a virtual slum. Examples of such neighborhoods are to be found in the Georgetown area of Washington, D.C., the Society Hill section of Philadelphia, blocks on New York's West Side, and blocks in Brooklyn, Providence, Chicago, San Francisco, and many other major and minor cities. But this process also develops in small towns and villages. We know of one little community that had badly deteriorated over the years and then came to life when a large company decided to build a plant in the general area. Suddenly there was a great demand for housing—any kind of housing. Families began to buy some of the run-down old houses and fix them up, and soon the entire community changed from a rural slum into a highly desirable area.

What is it that revitalizes a neighborhood? Well, there may be many influences, but frequently the catalyst is that young or middling-young professional families need space, and often the only way they can find space they can afford is by buying an older dwelling and fixing it up. Very often there will be enough space so that a rental unit or two can be included to help carry the overhead. And once one family has taken over a old place and fixed it up, the chances are it won't be long before friends and friends of friends buy into the same area and do the same. Pretty soon they've started a trend. Architects, artists, writers, doctors, lawyers, and teachers who need the facilities usually found in large cities, such as museums and libraries, are the people most likely to take over these old urban dwellings and fix them up.

Factors that help revitalize sections in rural and semirural areas may be

You find houses of this sort (left) on the fringes of many towns and cities. If the area is coming back as a desirable place in which to live or work, putting money into a house can pay off. The major alterations to the exterior of this house were removal of the old porch, changing the location of the front door, and applying new siding and shutters (right). [*Bird & Son, Inc.*]

recreational facilities (there are parts of northern New England that were depressed until skiing became popular), a highway that makes commuting to a nearby city feasible, or simply the circumstance that a locality is the only place where reasonably priced housing is available.

If you have courage, vision, and plenty of energy (and some knowledge of what is about to happen), this is the way to get back all your home improvement dollars and a few more to boot.

## Appraising the Quality of Your Neighborhood

Since the neighborhood can be such an important element in establishing the market value of property and therefore the amount you may safely invest in what you have, you'll be wise, before you spend any substantial sums on your house, to analyze your neighborhood and see how it stacks up.

Real estate appraisers have about twelve key areas which they consider in judging the quality of a neighborhood. They rate these areas as good, average, fair, and poor. The twelve areas are the following:

1. Employment stability
2. Adequacy of shopping
3. Convenience of schools
4. Quality of schools
5. Recreational facilities
6. Level of taxes
7. Adequacy of utilities
8. Neighborhood compatibility
9. Protection from adverse influences
10. Police and fire protection
11. General appearance of properties
12. Appeal to market

These points are not listed in the order of importance, for each buyer will naturally put greater emphasis on one point than on another. For example, a family with school-age children will often put greater emphasis on the quality and convenience of schools than on any other single item. We know of many families with school-age children that settled for a less expensive and less attractive house than they might otherwise buy just because there were outstanding schools in the area. We have also known families that had to reduce their standard of living drastically to afford a house in a good school district that was really beyond their means.

Others may place greater emphasis on employment stability or on the level of taxes, but on the average they take all twelve points into consideration. And so, for that matter, will a bank in determining how much money it will give on a mortgage loan, which is a key factor when it comes to selling.

So you, too, should take all these items into consideration when you plan a major improvement, for if you can give only a fair or poor rating to many of them, you may not be able to get back all your improvement dollars when you sell.

Let's discuss these points in greater detail.

1. *Employment Stability.* Are jobs available in the area to attract families to move into it, and will the jobs last? This isn't an important consideration if you own a house in a typical suburban bedroom community from which a large number of people com-

mute to a metropolitan center for work, but it can be a very important matter in smaller cities and towns where many people, both white- and blue-collar, are dependent on relatively few industries for employment. What can, and often does, happen is that one large outfit will go out of business and move to another area. The net result is that a lot of houses go on the market at the same time, and there is a drop in property values. Communities that are highly dependent on defense or other government contracts are particularly vulnerable to sudden changes in property values. It takes only a cut in the defense budget or hanky-panky in Washington that takes a contract away from one outfit and gives it to another in some other part of the country to push such a community into a decline.

You should also be cautious about areas with old factories, for these are probably antiquated and unprofitable. Many companies close old factories and build new plants, generally at new locations, leaving the old locations with an unemployment problem on their hands.

Good sources of facts and figures on employment in any area are local chambers of commerce, the state labor commission, and publications such as *County Business Patterns* issued by the U.S. Department of Commerce, which are available at most public libraries.

2. *Adequacy of Shopping.* It's obvious that today people expect to be able to shop locally without having to drive halfway across the county to buy a pair of shoes for the kids or a loaf of bread. A convenient shopping center or district is a definite plus, but how much of a plus depends on the character of the shopping center. If it's full of discount houses, fast-food chains, bowling alleys, and the like, it will lend a less favorable tone to the general area. It will not be an attractive shopping area for higher-income families. On the other hand, if it contains some smart shops, a branch of a leading department store, and a good supermarket, it will be attractive to more affluent buyers.

3. *Convenience of Schools.* Most parents don't like the idea of long bus rides for their children, especially the younger ones. And they don't like the idea of any of their children having to stand outside before dawn in winter waiting for the school bus. If you are not familiar with the school bus schedule in your neighborhood, call the office of the school superintendent to obtain it.

4. *Quality of Schools.* As we have said, families with school-age children are deeply concerned with all aspects of the school system, especially the quality of the schools. You may find that families without school-age children are also concerned with these matters because if the schools are poor, families with school-age children won't move into the area or, if they are already there, may be planning to move out. Often the first step in the decline of property values is a decline in the quality of the local schools (unless, of course, there are no schools at all because you are living in a planned adult community).

   One of the best ways to determine the quality of the schools in your area is to find out from the superintendent of schools what costs per pupil are allocated and how they compare with those of other schools in the state. In almost every case, the more money spent per pupil, the better the teaching staff, the better the school facilities, and the better the overall quality of the schools. You can also get a good indication of the school system by talking with school officials, members of the PTA, and other parents of school-age children.

5. *Recreational Facilities.* We know of one man who asks just one question about a neighborhood: "How good is the local golf course, and what's the waiting time to tee-off on Saturday morning?" A few years ago people did not expect to have much in the way of recreational facilities unless they joined the local country club, but today they ask about facilities for tennis, golf, swimming, fishing and boating, camping, and so forth. If there are no such facilities in the immediate area, it will not be attractive to younger families. And if the energy crisis continues, more families will be looking for these facilities close to their homes.

   Under recreational facilities you should include theaters, museums, libraries, and other cultural centers. Areas close to colleges and universities are generally very desirable because of their many cultural activities.

6. *Level of Taxes.* Your concern is how the property taxes in your area compare with those in adjoining areas, for if your taxes are excessively high compared with those of surrounding communities, it's obvious that the intelligent buyer is first going to check out sections where taxes are low. Of course, you can't, or you shouldn't, judge this point entirely on the rate of taxes: what you

get for your tax dollar also is important. But if taxes are high and property owners don't get much in return, they are going to look elsewhere. Your local tax assessor can tell you the tax rate and the way it compares with taxes in adjoining areas.

7. *Adequacy of Utilities.* In the typical suburban area buyers will expect an adequate supply of good water, a central sewer system, paved roads, and sidewalks. If any of these are lacking, they may shy off, drawing the obvious conclusion that if and when these utilities are added, property owners will be stuck with a special tax assessment to pay for them. In rural and semirural areas, where private wells and septic tanks are the rule, however, people don't expect all these amenities.

8. *Neighborhood Compatibility.* What this point means is that all the houses in the neighborhood or on the block are of about the same age, design, size, and general price range. Compatibility also applies to the age and income of the families who live there. Young families generally prefer to live in areas where there are other young families with children and with the same general interests. Many middle-aged families prefer the company of people their own age, while older people may be tired of kids, dogs, and cats and prefer a quieter block.

   You don't need an expert to help you decide on the compatibility of your neighborhood. Just walk down the street and look at the houses and the people who live in them.

9. *Protection from Adverse Influences.* What we are concerned with here is whether the neighborhood will remain as it is—a residential section of single-family houses—or change into an area of multifamily homes or have commercial establishments move in. These matters are in the hands of the local zoning board, for it has the authority to set sections aside exclusively for single-family residences and to change the regulations to allow multifamily dwellings as well as commerce and industry to come in. You can get all the pertinent information regarding the zone in which you live from the zoning board. The board can also give you some idea of whether a change in zoning that might affect your property is anticipated. Another adverse influence would be the construction of a new highway near your residential area that would increase the traffic along your street.

10. *Police and Fire Protection.* In these days, so many families are concerned about crime that a good police department and a low crime rate are major assets in determining property values. Check with your local police department to find out what the crime rate is in your area and how it compares with the rate in other sections.

   As far as fire protection goes, the key factors that concern insurance companies and the ones on which they base their rate are the proximity of a house to a hydrant and the proximity to the fire department.

11. *General Appearance of Properties.* If we make the assumption that most people buy a neighborhood rather than an individual house, it's a definite plus if all the houses on a block are well maintained—freshly painted, with well-groomed lawns and yards, clean sidewalks, and roads in good repair. By the same token, even if your house is a perfect gem and beautifully maintained, the fact that the vast majority of the other houses are poorly maintained, garbage cans are out on the sidewalks, and wet wash is hanging on the line is going to hurt you. The prospective buyer will assume that this block is running down and he'd be wiser to buy elsewhere.

12. *Appeal to Market.* You might say that this is the sum total of all the elements discussed thus far. It comes down to whether a neighborhood is so appealing in all respects that almost any buyer who can afford to live in it will want to and be willing to pay more than the going market value of a particular house.

After you've rated your neighborhood, you'll be in a better position to decide how much, if anything, to put into your present house or whether the best policy is to get out now before it's too late. But there is something else you should look into, and that is whether buyers are moving into your area, because if there are no buyers, even the best house in the best neighborhood may not easily be sold.

Activity in the real estate market has a big role in determining how much you can safely put into a house. If the market is a seller's market and likely to remain so, you can expect to get back a lot more of your money than in a buyer's market, in which a lot of houses are for sale.

The real estate market is influenced by the number and kind of people moving into an area and by the amount of housing, new and used, that is available. The local chamber of commerce can give you a lot of information on the kind of industry that is moving into the general area and the kind of people who will be requiring housing now and in the future. If the industry is the type that requires a large number of professional managers and highly skilled workers, there will be a good market for the more costly houses. If it is the type that requires large numbers of lower-paid workers, rentals and less expensive houses are going to be in demand.

You also need to know what's available in housing, and here the chamber of commerce and local real estate boards can help you out. It's especially important to learn about new construction, because new houses are the biggest competition you'll have if and when you decide to sell. Most people vastly prefer a new house to a used house, and they can generally get a new house in the same price range as a used one with a lower down payment. Check what's going on in the condominium field, for condominiums are becoming popular with young families.

If you visit a local real estate broker, you can learn the condition of the market. If the broker is loaded with listings and a lot of them are for houses in about the same condition and price range as yours, it's obvious that there is not a great demand, at least for used houses, in your area.

There is one final point about what makes a neighborhood desirable today, and that is the availability of mass transportation—buses or trains. This was not a very important factor a few years ago when gasoline was readily available at a low cost. Husbands would think nothing of driving 40 or 50 miles to and from work in their cars, while their wives had the second car, usually a large station wagon, for shopping and driving the children to and from their various activities. Today it's a bit different, and some form of mass transportation is becoming more and more important to many people. This is true even in the quite affluent areas. In Westport, Connecticut, for instance, the town recently purchased a fleet of small buses to provide local service to the commuter railroad station, shopping centers, and educational and cultural facilities. In the next several years there will probably be much more of this sort of thing as we become increasingly accustomed to conserving energy.

## Kinds of Improvements

There are roughly two kinds of home improvements, essential improvements and nonessential improvements. Essential improvements are those you have to make, or certainly should make, to keep the house in good condition and habitable. Essential improvements would include a new roof, outside painting, insulation, storm windows and doors, and necessary improvements to the existing plumbing, wiring, and heating systems. The money you spend making these improvements probably won't add much if any value to your house—a prospective buyer naturally assumes that the roof is tight, the heating system works, and the water pipes do not leak. But essential improvements will ensure that the house maintains its fair market value, and they will help you to get a fair price when you sell. For this reason they are the most important kind of improvements to make.

Chapter 26 contains a home inspection checklist similar to one that might be used by a professional house inspector who might be called in by a prospective buyer to inspect the condition of a house. The list includes all the elements and items that the inspector will look for. It would be well worth your time to study this list and be sure that your house gets an A rating in each category. If it does not, tackle these basics before you undertake any nonessential improvements.

Nonessential improvements are those things you may want to do to accommodate family needs and to make the house more comfortable, more attractive, and more efficient. If you are considering several optional improvements, the question of priority naturally comes up. You will, of course, give high priority to projects that are really necessary: a functional kitchen, a second bathroom, more storage. Once these basic needs have been met, and they should be really basic, take a breather and start thinking of further improvements as an investment first and as a convenience second. Look around you and observe what features are predominant in houses in your immediate vicinity.

For example, if most houses have a garage or carport and you do not, adding one will be a good investment. If many of the houses have air conditioning, adding a central system can be a good move. If almost every house but yours has a fireplace, a fireplace is a wise improvement.

Now all this sounds a bit like keeping up with the Joneses. In a way it is, and in a way it isn't, because you don't have to build a better and more expensive garage than the one Jones has or install a more costly air-conditioning system or build a $10,000 fireplace, not by a long shot. What you want to do is to build a good garage but at as low a cost as possible. And the same holds true for air conditioning, a fireplace, and anything else. If Jones built a fancy garage that cost $10,000 and you can get a *good* garage for $5,000, you both have garages, but you won't have to add $10,000 to the selling price of your house to get your money back. You just have to add $5,000. Remember the rule that people buy neighborhoods and that they buy the least expensive house in the most expensive neighborhood they can afford.

## Checking the Real Estate Ads

Another clue to what kind of improvements seems to be important in your area is the ads in the real estate pages—not the ads inserted by private individuals who want to sell their houses but those placed by the large and busy real estate brokers. Because brokers are in daily contact with home buyers, they know what buyers are looking for and their ads will point out as many of these features as possible. Since they try to cram as much into a small ad as they can, they stress what they consider to be the most popular sales features of a particular house. If you find a lot of ads for houses in your general price range that stress family rooms, a family room would be a wise addition to make. If a majority point out that a house has two or more baths, air conditioning, a swimming pool, or a fireplace, these are obviously improvements worth considering.

The demand for certain features can vary, of course, with the section of the country. A screened-in terrace would be popular in Florida and other areas where insects are a problem but not in the Southwest, where they are not a nuisance. Swimming pools are naturally most popular where the climate enables them to be used for several months of the year, as opposed to the far northern sections, where, without a heater, they can be used only in July and August.

## What Others Are Doing

Some months ago, the trade publication *Building Supply News* made a nationwide survey to find out what kinds of improvements homeowners were making. Here is the listing, and it may help you decide which of several improvements you should make first.

*Additions and Major Remodelings*
1. Added garage
2. Added carport
3. Added driveway
4. Added terrace or patio
5. Enclosed porch or breezeway
6. Added on room or rooms
7. Expanded attic into living area
8. Put room in basement
9. Added fireplace
10. Added bathroom
11. Added in-ground swimming pool

12. Remodeled kitchen
13. Remodeled bath

*Improvement and Maintenance Projects*
1. Installed floor tile
2. Installed carpeting
3. Installed wall tile
4. Installed wall paneling
5. Installed new heating system
6. Installed air conditioning
7. Installed additional circuits
8. Installed built-in range or oven, or both
9. Installed new hot-water heater
10. Installed exhaust fan
11. Installed additional insulation
12. Installed lighting fixtures
13. Put on new roof
14. Put on new gutters
15. Installed exterior siding
16. Installed storm windows
17. Installed awnings
18. Installed exterior shutters
19. Installed fence
20. Installed outdoor lighting
21. Installed burglar or fire alarm
22. Installed shelving
23. Did interior painting
24. Did exterior painting
25. Did wallpapering
26. Installed garage door
27. Installed garage door opener
28. Installed exterior doors

Don't make the mistake that many homeowners do and expect that every dollar you invest in improvements is going to add value to your house. Many improvements, of course, will make it easier to sell your house at a fair price. There is no doubt that a house that is in tip-top shape is going to be very attractive to a buyer. But the fact that you have installed new siding or a new roof or put down a new kitchen floor probably won't increase the market value of your house to any great degree.

The improvements that are most likely to add substantial value are the more extensive and more costly ones. Among these are putting on an addition, adding a second bath or downstairs powder room, renovating an old kitchen, and similar improvements with a wide and general appeal.

There are other extensive improvements that probably won't add any value to your property. These are the highly specialized or personalized improvements that have a very limited appeal. Among these would be a photographic darkroom, a greenhouse, a sauna bath, a very personalized basement game room, and extensive, exotic landscaping.

# 2. Building Codes, Taxes, and Insurance

## Building Codes and Zoning Regulations

You should be familiar with local building codes and zoning regulations before you spend any of your money or much of your time planning an improvement that involves changes in the house structure. You want to make this study before you start in order to be sure that there are no regulations that prohibit what you want to do or that might make the improvement so expensive that it would not be a practical investment.

You can get detailed information on building and zoning regulations from your local building department or building inspector. The building department is usually located in the city or town hall.

Building codes are local regulations that deal with all aspects of construction: the type and size of materials approved for use, the qualifications and licensing of the men who do the work, the quality of workmanship, and all areas of construction that bear on the health and safety of the individual or the community at large. Zoning regulations have to do with the use of land: what proportion of the property can be devoted to a structure and for what purpose the structure may be used. If you want to put an addition on your house or if you want to use some of the space for a rental unit or for an apartment for your in-laws or parents, you will be involved with local zoning regulations.

You cannot ignore these codes and regulations because you must obtain a building permit from the building department before you can begin work on a project. Before you obtain a permit, you must submit plans and specifications to the building department. And before you can legally use the completed project, you may have to get a certificate of occupancy from the building inspector after he has inspected and approved the work.

## Building Codes

Practically every community has some form of building code. In heavily built-up areas codes are comprehensive and cover every aspect of construction. In rural areas they are generally not comprehensive and may require only that you use accepted methods of construction and have plumbing and wiring done by a licensed mechanic.

Most building codes are not concerned with routine maintenance and repairs. For example, you generally do not need a building permit to paint the inside or outside of a house, replace a worn gutter, or install storm windows. Some codes do, however, specify the type of roofing you may use. And almost every code will have something to say if you make any changes in the house structure: enclose a porch, remodel the kitchen, or make changes in the house wiring or plumbing.

While most codes today are reasonable, you still find communities where they are very unreasonable, and unreasonable codes can run the cost of an improvement right through the roof. Some communities have codes that do not permit the use of flexible plastic-coated electric wiring if you want to add another circuit. Instead, they require the installation of rigid metal conduit. This costs several times as much as the flexible type in terms of labor and materials. Many codes do not permit the use of plastic pipe even for drainage systems but require far more costly cast-iron or copper pipes.

Many codes are written so that if you make a change, you must bring the entire system up to existing standards. We know of one community whose code requires that if any change is made in the existing plumbing system, the entire plumbing system must be modified to conform to present code requirements. In other words, if you were going to replace a bathroom fixture in your house, it might be necessary to replace the entire sewer system. On the other hand, if you left the old fixture alone, the outdated system would not have to be changed.

A good local builder or contractor will be familiar with local building codes (he should know them if he wants to stay in business); so if you bring him in early to give you an estimate on the proposed project, he will base his figures on doing the work in accordance with the codes. But if you haven't reached this stage or plan to do the work yourself or be your own contractor, check with the building department. Show the building inspector or building official the rough plans of the project and a list of the materials you plan to use. The inspector can tell you whether there are any regulations that are going to make the proposed project unnecessarily complicated or expensive.

On any project that involves changes in the house structure or the wiring, plumbing, and heating, you will have to get a building permit before starting work. And to get a permit you must first fill out an application that describes the purpose of the change and the approximate cost. You may also have to provide detailed plans and specifications for the project. If you use a contractor, he can do all this for you and obtain the permit, but it is still your responsibility to be certain that you have a building permit before the contractor begins work.

It is also your responsibility to see that the building inspector approves each phase of the work as required by the code. The code may, for example, require inspection and approval of foundations for an addition, of rough wiring and plumbing for the addition, and, finally, of the completed job. And if you fail to get the inspections made as required, the omission can cost you money. For example, if you must have rough wiring inspected and approved and you don't have the inspector over when the wiring is exposed, he may insist that sections of the wall and ceiling material be removed so that he can check the wiring. A good local builder or contractor will know when to get the building inspector over to approve each step of the work, but if he doesn't, it's your responsibility to see that he does.

When the project of improving an area or room has been completed, the building inspector will check it over and, if he finds all the work satisfactory, issue a certificate of occupancy. Until you have a certificate of occupancy, you can't legally use the area or room.

## Zoning Regulations

If you are going to put an addition on your house, build a separate structure (a garage, for example), or put in a swimming pool, the building department will check a survey map of your property and the site on the property where the proposed addition is to be located. Local zoning regulations will specify the amount of setback, the distance that any structure can be set to the actual lot lines or boundary lines of the property. If your proposed addition or structure is going to occupy more space than is allowed, you won't get a building permit.

You may also be denied a permit if you plan to create a rental unit or a living unit separate from the main house in an area that is zoned exclusively for single-family dwellings. In many resort areas, there are regulations that forbid you to winterize a summer house for year-round occupancy, especially if the property is near water or wetland or marsh areas and the house has a septic system instead of being connected to a municipal sewer system. Zoning regulations also may prevent your adding a two-story extension to a one-story house or may state the distance that a front-yard fence must be set back from the street or sidewalk.

## Appealing Denial of a Permit

If you are denied a building permit because the proposed project does not conform with zoning regulations, you can appeal to the zoning board for a variance that will permit you to go ahead with the project. The board will give you a hearing so that you can state your case. At the hearing other interested parties, your neighbors in particular, can express their opinions on whether they feel you should be allowed to go ahead with the project.

The strongest basis for an appeal is a hardship plea, but such a plea can be open to a wide range of interpretations. You might consider it a hardship if you were denied a permit to winterize a summer cottage so that you could rent it during the winter months. The zoning board, however, may not consider this to be a true hardship but simply a way for you to increase your income. A board may turn down your application to convert space into a rental apartment but may grant permission to someone else who wants to make a downstairs apartment for a close relative who cannot climb stairs.

A zoning board will rely quite heavily on how your neighbors feel about the proposed application; so if you decide to appeal to the board, first talk with your neighbors, especially those who own land adjoining yours. Convince them, if you can, of the merits of your appeal and also encourage them to come to the hearing or give you a letter to the effect that they have no objection to what you plan to do.

You can have your attorney make your appeal, or your attorney can be on hand when you make it yourself. Whether having an attorney does much good is hard to say. In most cases it is the merit of the case and not the manner of presentation that counts.

If the board does not grant you a variance, you can go to court and attempt to get the decision reversed. But you should face the fact that unless you can prove that the board is being unfair in its enforcement of existing regulations, you aren't going to get very far with your case.

Do not get involved in a project that takes your time or your money because someone—a real estate broker, builder, or remodeler—has told you that you'll have no trouble in getting a building permit or a variance. The only way to be sure is when you see the official papers allowing you to go ahead with the project.


## Insurance

You should be concerned about two areas of insurance when you make improvements: your own fire insurance policy and the policy issued to the firm doing the work that protects you from property damage and liability.

## Fire Insurance

You do not want to wait until an improvement has been completed before you increase the amount of fire insurance on your house. As soon as you know the scope of the work but before it begins, get in touch with your insurance agent. Explain to him what you plan to do, what the approximate cost will be, when the work is to begin, and when you expect the job to be completed. He can then arrange to have your insurance increased to cover you as the work progresses. If you wait until the improvement has been completed to get additional coverage, you can be in for a lot of trouble. If the work is well along and you have a fire, the total replacement value of your house may exceed the amount of your coverage. That would mean that you would not collect the full amount.

## Property Damage and Liability Insurance

You also want to make sure that the firm which is doing the work has adequate insurance to protect you if there is damage to property or if someone gets hurt because of any acts or omissions on the firm's part. Most large firms will have enough insurance to protect them as well as you if there is property damage or injury during the course of the work. They have learned from sad experience that every job involves certain hazards and that there can be damages and injuries no matter how careful they may be. They also know that they'll need substantial protection for claims that might range well over $100,000. But many small firms don't have sufficient coverage. If they won't tell you the amount of their coverage, ask them for the name of the company that carries their policy and check with it.

Don't rely on the amount of liability insurance in your homeowner's policy. It's probably adequate for normal needs but not when construction is going on.

## Real Estate Taxes

Sad to say, any improvement that increases the market value of a house will ultimately mean an increase in real estate taxes. There are, to be sure, some very progressive communities that give homeowners who make certain improvements on their property some relief from added taxes for a period of time. Unfortunately, this relief usually applies only to dwellings in deteriorated neighborhoods in which the community wishes to help residents and owners revitalize their dwellings. Since the energy crisis, several states are providing a tax incentive to encourage owners to insulate, install storm windows, and adopt other measures to reduce consumption of heating energy. In years to come, we hope to see more of this practice, which is eminently sensible in the long run. But for the most part now, when you spend money to improve, you'll also have to spend money to pay the added tax.

Everything other than routine maintenance and repairs that you do to improve a house will increase its market value in the eyes of the tax assessor. You may have difficulty convincing a buyer that a certain improvement adds value, but you'll have even more trouble trying to convince the tax assessor that it does not. Adding more living space by building an addition, finishing off a basement or attic, or enclosing a breezeway or porch is going to raise your taxes. So will adding a fireplace, modernizing a kitchen or bathroom, or installing a deck or swimming pool.

And it's hard to keep improvements a secret from a tax assessor. In most communities you must get a building permit from the building department before you may make any improvements that involve the structure of a house. When you fill in the permit application, you or your contractor will have to give an estimate of the cost of the work. The building department passes this information on to the assessor, who not only knows you are making an improvement but what the improvement is going to cost.

The tax assessor is very much concerned with an improvement's cost, and he will take this figure into account when he determines the value of the improvement. For example, if you add a second bathroom with ceramic tile on the walls and floor plus deluxe plumbing fixtures, the assessor will put a higher figure on the project than he would if you had just painted the bathroom walls and used low-cost plumbing fixtures. Both bathrooms may be the same size and contain the same number of fixtures, but because one has cost perhaps half again as much as the other, it's going to add more to the tax bill. This is another good reason for keeping the cost of your improvements down and not overimproving: the more money you spend, the more it's going to cost you in taxes.

The cost of the project is not all that is used to determine how much a certain improvement adds to the value of the house. There is "Catch-22." This means that even if you do all the work yourself and therefore spend relatively little on labor, the actual cost won't count as much in determining the additional tax you pay as the results of your labor. Does this sound contradictory? Well, it is.

There can be a good deal of variation in how certain improvements are assessed, depending on the community and even on a particular tax assessor. If you are about to make an improvement and want to keep your tax as low as possible, it might be wise to visit your local assessor and find out what changes you could make in your plans to reduce the assessment. For example, it might be wiser from a tax point of view to paint the masonry walls of a basement than to cover them with wallboard or plywood. And you might save a good deal if you left a portion of your attic as unfinished storage space rather than finishing off the entire area. We know one man who spent hours designing and building a wood deck for an aboveground swimming pool that could easily be disassembled so that it would not be considered a permanent improvement.

## Keeping Records of All Costs

It's going to pay you in several ways if you keep very detailed records of every nickel you spend on any home improvements and repairs from the time you take title to your property. Good records will come in handy in your dealings with the Internal Revenue Service when you sell your house, they'll be useful sales tools in helping you get the best price when you sell, and they can help you determine the amount of fire insurance you should have and aid in backing up your claim if the house is damaged by fire.

The best kind of records consists of receipted bills that describe in detail the scope of the work involved. Canceled checks show that you paid some-one to do something, but only an itemized bill stamped "Paid in full" will show exactly what was done and by whom. If a contract was involved, hold on to this, too. The best place in which to keep these records is a safety deposit box.

It's suprising how much money you can spend on improvements over the years and not realize the total unless you keep detailed records. Most of us remember and may even keep records of big expenses, but we don't bother with all the little items, and these can add up. And don't forget the cost of materials used on do-it-yourself projects. These, too, can add up, and often they are paid for in cash at the local building supply, hardware, or paint store.

## Records for Tax Purposes

When you sell a house, you can deduct the cost of any improvements you have made from the price you receive when you sell. This can be important, because if you sell a house for more than you paid for it—and it's pretty hard not to do so in this age of inflated real estate prices—the profit you make is considered taxable. Of course, if you buy a house within a year or build one within eighteen months, either of which costs as much or more than the sum you received for the house you sold, the profit is not taxable. Otherwise, if there is a profit, you will have to pay a capital gains tax.

But if you have made improvements and have kept a record of your costs, the costs can be deducted from the selling price along with broker's fees, legal costs, and other expenses involved in the actual sale. For example, suppose you paid $35,000 for a house five years ago and cleared $40,000 when you sold it. Then, instead of buying a more expensive house than the one you just sold, you buy a condominium for $35,000. On this basis, as you bought a new house for less than you got for your old one, you would have to pay a capital gains tax on $5,000, the difference between what you paid for the house and the net amount you received when you sold it. But if you have made $5,000 worth of improvements during the time you have lived in the house and have records to prove it, you would not have to pay any tax on the $5,000.

It's also wise to keep complete records of major amounts spent on routine maintenance and repairs. These would include items such as outside and inside painting, a new roof, and repairs to heating, wiring, and plumbing. Repairs of this sort are not deductible, but sometimes they are of such a nature that all or part of the cost can be credited as an improvement rather than a repair. Suppose, for example, that the old paint on the wood siding was in such poor condition that you decided you would be better off to cover it with aluminum or vinyl siding than to strip off all the old paint and apply fresh paint. Painting would be considered routine maintenance and would not be deductible as an improvement, but applying siding could be considered an improvement and therefore would be deductible.

One kind of repairs you can deduct consists of those you make to help sell your house. These repairs must be made within ninety days of the date the house is sold and must be paid for within thirty days after selling. This is a very important point to keep in mind, for it means that you deduct many of the things you might wish to do to your house to make it more attractive and to help get the top price for it. If you are selling the house through a real estate broker, you would be wise to get a letter from him stating which repairs he feels are essential to make in order to get a fair market price for the house.

## Records to Use When You Sell Your House

A folder full of itemized bills for all the money you have spent over the years on improvements will help you and your broker establish a good selling price for your house. They will also make very effective sales tools. Even a relatively unsophisticated home buyer will be impressed if you can show records of when various improvements and repairs were made, the amount of work involved, and the total cost. These records can be particularly valuable in the critical areas of the house that buyers are especially concerned about, such as the amount of insulation in walls, roof, and so on, the condition of the roof, wiring, and heating.

Detailed bills along with any guarantee on materials and workmanship are also useful in providing you and your broker with answers to questions about the condition of the house. For example, we had a new well put in a few years ago, and the licensed well driller sent us a log when the job was completed. The log states the exact depth of the well, the type of soil and rock involved, the diameter and length of the steel casing, and the rate of flow in gallons per minute. If we ever sell the house and a buyer asks us or our broker about the well, we'll simply show him the log. This will be a lot more reassuring to the buyer than if we just tell him "It's a fine well—never had trouble with it," or something to that effect. And if he does buy the house and the well runs dry, he can't say that we or our broker misrepresented the condition of the well.

## Records for Insurance

When you make an improvement in your house, you increase its value as far as your fire insurance coverage is concerned. You should increase your coverage to include the amount involved in making the improvement. But you also need to have records to show how much the improvement actually cost you.

# 3. Planning and Materials

The most successful improvements are those that are carefully planned. And the more extensive the improvement, the more important it is to take the time to plan carefully. Not only will the end result be better, but you will also save money. A major cause of improvements' not turning out as expected or costing far more than they should is lack of planning and failing to specify the materials to be used.

## Planning Improvements

Before you can even begin to draw up a rough plan for a project, you need ideas, and few of us are creative enough to be able to come up with a whole bunch of practical ideas out of nowhere but our heads. We need stimulation and source material; so it is often very helpful to see what others have done with similar projects. We can then adapt those ideas to suit our purposes, reject them entirely, or come up with some brillant amalgam. And some of the ideas can tell us what not to do.

Even if you are going to get plans from an architect, designer, or contractor, you should have your own ideas to discuss with them. If you don't, you are apt to end up doing whatever these professionals suggest, which may or may not be right for your way of living or appeal to your tastes.

As soon as you start thinking about any change or improvement, start collecting ideas on the various ways in which it might be handled. One place to start is with friends and neighbors. We, for instance, are thinking about building a carport in the next couple of months, and the plan we are going to use is adapted from a storage shed some friends down the road built a year or so ago.

You can pick up good ideas by driving around residential areas. This is especially helpful if the houses are similar to yours in size and design. You may see an addition that pleases you or even a color scheme for the exterior. We have a friend who is a house painter, and he carries a color camera in his car and takes pictures of interesting color schemes. He uses these to help his customers decide what colors they wish to use.

Home and shelter magazines have lots of interesting ideas, some of them far more elaborate or expensive than you may have in mind but nonetheless useful as a starting point. Home and real estate sections of newspapers are useful, too, and so are advertisements by manufacturers of building products, home furnishings, and so on. Many of these firms offer booklets that contain suggestions about how to make the best use of space for various projects (and of their product), and you can crib from these. There are also many excellent books that deal with specific jobs: kitchens, fireplaces, swimming pools, terraces and decks, fences. These are usually well illustrated.

Keep a file of all your ideas and pull it out when it comes time to sit down to plan the job with an architect or contractor. It will be a great help if you can show rather than describe exactly what you want. And if you have an example of what you want, there is less chance of ending up with something else than if you depend on words to describe the item.

## Rough Plans

You can begin to plan a project on your own by drawing up rough plans that include all the basic elements. You'll want to do this even if you are going to have professional assistance with the final plans because it will help you to see which approaches are good and which ones are not. Make up a lot of rough plans, each slightly different from the others.

All you need to draw rough plans is some ¼-inch graph paper, a ruler, and a pencil. Let each square on the paper represent 1 foot, and half a square 6 inches. Because these are just rough plans, they don't have to be accurate down to the last inch.

Start by drawing lines to represent the basic dimensions of the room. Then indicate the approximate size and location of existing doors and windows or of doors and windows to be added. Take measurements of some of the major items that may be included in the room—sofa, beds, chairs, dining-room table, plumbing fixtures, kitchen cabinets, and appliances—and draw them on the plan to approximate scale. Take out your idea file and add any ideas that you want to include: a corner fireplace, built-ins, and so on. Save only those plans that you particularly like, and use them as a starting point to develop the final plans.

You should have complete plans and working drawings for any extensive improvements such as putting on an addition, remodeling a kitchen, making an attic room, enclosing a porch, or making a finished room out of a garage. If you don't have complete plans and working drawings, there is no way of being sure exactly how the job is going to turn out until it has been finished. And then it's too late unless you want to pay extra to have some of the work ripped out and redone.

We have had several sad experiences in making improvements with just a rough sketch on the back of an old envelope instead of a complete set of plans. We added a large deck to the rear of our house, and because we thought that the contractor understood exactly what we wanted, we didn't bother with plans. Well, he didn't really understand what we wanted, and it cost several hundred dollars extra to make the necessary changes after the work had been completed. On the other hand, we once completely remodeled a kitchen, even moving it to a different location, and this time we had complete plans, and the job turned out perfectly. And it was perfect without any changes in the plans.

Good plans and working drawings must be detailed, and they must be specific. They must show the exact location and size of windows and doors and the location of electric light switches, wall outlets, and lighting fixtures. They should indicate the exact location of plumbing fixtures, radiators and registers, cabinets, and stairs.

## Where to Get Help with Plans

If you are completely satisfied with your rough drawings, you can turn them over to a draftsman, who can produce finished plans and working drawings. A draftsman may not be a licensed architect or engineer, but he usually does have extensive knowledge of these fields so that he can catch major errors in your plans. You'll find draftsmen listed in the Yellow Pages, or your contractor or remodeler can probably give you a name or two.

But before you turn your plans over to a draftsman, it's smart to check them with your contractor. It may be that your solution is a very expensive or impractical one. Get the contractor's opinion and the approximate cost before you spend money on final plans.

*Architects.* Architects are the very best persons to go to with your rough plans. They can advise you if the plans are good or if something better can be developed. They can help you to include your ideas in the plans and add some good ideas of their own. And they can take rough drawings and put them into finished shape. *See also* section "The Architect" below.

*Contractors and Remodelers.* The larger firms of contractors and remodelers often have design departments that will help you develop plans. In many cases there is no charge for this service if you have the work done by the firm that designs the plans. A decided advantage in using such a design service is that you can get a pretty good idea of your costs early in the game.

Many remodelers have stock plans for certain improvements such as additions, attic and basement rooms, and garages. Some of these designs are fair, but a good many are ordinary—about what you would expect of plans designed to be adequate for everybody. But it can still be better to use an ordinary stock plan than no plan at all. At least with a stock plan you'll have some idea of what you are getting, but if you have no plan, you'll be taking a chance, and in the building field a chance is not worth the risk.

*Building Supply Houses.* Some of the larger and more progressive building supply firms, especially those that specialize in home improvement supplies, can often provide help in drawing up plans. And if you take them a set of plans, they can give you a pretty good idea of the cost of all the materials that will be required.

*Kitchen Designers and Others.* Kitchens are so popular that there are firms that specialize in them for both new and remodeled rooms. These firms can handle all aspects of the work, planning as well as execution. Some of them are good and really will take the time to design a custom kitchen, but others just use stock plans and adjust them to fit the required space.

You can also get some help with kitchen planning from local gas and electric firms, as the larger ones often have home economists on their staffs to assist customers. And your local cooperative extension service may also have a home economist who can help you.

Most kitchens are planned for women by men who never have to spend much time working in them. If you want a kitchen that is the most practical from the standpoint of the person who is going to have to work in it, get help from a woman rather than a man.

## Materials and Specifications

Plans can tell a good deal about the way a job is to be done, but they don't tell everything. They usually do not include all the materials that are to be used or the exact way in which the work is to be done. To cover these two important areas you need a list of materials and specifications that cover the manner of installation.

## List of Materials

Before the work begins, you want a list of almost every item to be used on the project, right down to the type and size of hinge to be used on a kitchen cabinet door. About the only items you need not be particularly concerned with are those used to erect the basic structure. It's not necessary to specify the brand of wood to be used for the wall studding or roof rafters or the brand of plywood to be used for the wall and roof sheathing. But you do want to be concerned with any item that will show when the work is completed.

You should be closely involved in the selection of all the items and make sure that you have approved them. If you don't bother to select or at least approve what is to be used, you'll get what the architect or contractor decides you should have. And what they select is not always what you want or might wish to pay extra to have. Don't leave anything to chance, because in the building game chance usually means that you are going to be the loser.

We once neglected to select the style of wood molding to be used in a room that we renovated, and we have paid dearly for this neglect. The stuff the contractor installed is far too ornate for the style of the room; it was very expensive and is miserable to paint.

Insist on seeing samples of all the items to be used or at least pictures of them supplied by the manufacturer. If color is involved, as it is in many items, be sure that you see color pictures.

Many architects and contractors have samples of some of the items that you'll use, and you can also see them at building supply houses and at hardware stores, lighting fixture shops, and plumbing supply firms. If you can't find a sample, at least see a picture of an item. Architects and contractors have a good deal of literature supplied by manufacturers that shows items. And many architects and contractors have a set of *Sweet's Catalogs*. This set of large books contains specifications supplied by many manufacturers. They are arranged by category. This makes it easy to thumb through one section dealing with a particular item, windows, for example, and select the brand, style, and size that you find the best.

One thing that most manufacturers' literature and specifications don't give is the price. And the cost of a particular item can be a big factor in helping you decide whether or not you want to use it. Your contractor should be able to give you prices on most items and also tell you if there is another item that will do just as well but will cost less. But don't make a substitution until you see what you are getting.

A good list of materials should contain the brand name, the model number if there is one, the size, and the color. If you were putting on a family room addition, your material list might be as follows:

1. Roofing
2. Siding
3. Windows
4. Gutters
5. Outside doors and hardware
6. Color of exterior paint or stain for siding
7. Color of exterior paint or stain for trim
8. Material for interior walls and ceilings
9. Interior doors and hardware
10. Interior trim for doors, windows, baseboard, etc.
11. Flooring

## Specifications

Specifications are detailed instructions on how the work is to be done. They help ensure that the work is done correctly, and they also help prevent misunderstandings between you and the contractor or workmen.

When an architect handles a major project, he often draws up detailed specifications to cover all aspects of the work. He may even specify the exact mix to be used for the concrete foundations, the number of coats of stain to be applied to kitchen cabinets, or the thickness of the mortar joints between the bricks of a fireplace. The architect has learned from experience that you can't be certain that anything will be done exactly as you want it unless you spell it out in writing and in great detail.

Few of us can afford to have an architect draw up complete specifications for a home improvement project. But that doesn't mean that you must get along without any specifications.

The manufacturers of most major building products supply specifications with their products. These are very good and are often picked up word for word by an architect when he writes his own specifications. If a manufacturer's specifications are followed to the letter, the product will be properly installed. Even when separate specifications are not included, most manufacturers provide detailed instructions for use and application. On the back of every label on a container of paint are detailed instructions for proper use. If these are followed by the painter, the job should turn out well. Your agreement with a contractor or any workmen installing a product should have a clause to the effect that all products and materials are to be installed in strict accordance with the manufacturer's directions. And be sure that they are.

## Selection of Materials

Important points to keep in mind when selecting materials and products for any improvement job are availability, cost, quality, and general acceptance.

### Availability

If you can't get certain materials or products when they are needed, the work slows down. This usually means that costs go up. Many builders and remodelers have told us that the main reason why jobs don't get done on time is that some key material is not on hand when it is needed. If the men have to sit around doing nothing while they wait for a substitute to show up, you can be pretty sure that it will be you and not the builder who will be paying them for this wasted time. And lack of specified materials can mean substitutions that may turn out to be not what you wanted or cost more than what you originally specified.

Your safest bet is to specify materials and products that are generally stocked by local sources: lumberyards, appliance stores, and so on. If a particular item must be ordered specially, you can be in for a long delay. And when it does arrive, the chances are that it won't be exactly what you ordered or will have been damaged in shipping.

A year or so ago we were involved in a project that called for a certain type of window that had to be shipped halfway across the country. When the windows finally arrived, six weeks after they were expected, more than half the units had been damaged in transit. A friend of ours once ordered some special ceramic tile for a bathroom, and when the tile arrived, it was in the wrong color.

Among problems you can run into from time to time are shortages of certain critical materials. These shortages are often due to a lack of the energy required for manufacturing. A shortage of natural gas, for example, can create a shortage in glass, toilet bowls, and other items that require gas for manufacturing. Certain shortages are simply due to demand outstripping limited supply. A few years ago cedar siding and cedar shingles were almost impossible to find because large amounts of cedar were being exported to Japan. At the time of this shortage a builder we know had to drive all over the state trying to line up enough bundles of shingles from different lumberyards to finish a house he was building. Local shortages can also be caused by the natural reluctance of many building supply dealers to tie up a lot of money in stock when construction in their area slows down.

Although there is nothing you can do to solve the problems of shortages, there are things you can do to reduce their impact on your project. First, as soon as your plans are complete and you know what materials and products you'll need, check out their availability. Your builder or remodeler should be able to tell you which of the items you have selected are readily available in your area and which are not. Or you can check them out yourself at lumberyards, appliance and electric stores, and so on. If there is any question about the supply of certain materials, decide right then and there what you will use as a substitute if it is necessary. The time to select a substitute is before the job gets started, not after it is under way. Once work has begun, there is pressure to keep it going, and the result can be that little attention is given to selecting a good substitute if it should be needed.

When we were renovating a kitchen, we received a call at our office from the foreman of the job, who said that the exhaust fan we had ordered had not arrived and the work was being held up. The foreman said he'd run down and pick up a fan from a local supply house, and we told him to go ahead. We ended up with a very inefficient kind of fan that not only could not remove heat and odors from the kitchen but let in a blast of cold air each time the wind blew from the east.

If you find that certain materials are in short supply, you'll be wise to buy them right now and store them until you are ready for them. This is also a smart move if your builder or supplier tells you that there is going to be a substantial price increase on a certain item in the near future.

## Cost

Unless you are doing the work yourself, your primary concern on the cost of materials is their cost *installed* and not the cost of the basic material. Some materials may cost less than others but require so much labor at around $10 an hour that by the time you've finished the job the cost is higher than if you had used the more expensive but laborsaving product. For example, a prehung door costs more than a door plus the wood to build the frame, but when you add the cost of the labor it takes to build the frame, the prehung door turns out to be the less expensive of the two. Prefinished plywood paneling costs more per square foot than common pine boards, but by the time you add the cost of labor to install individual boards, the amount of waste involved, and the extra cost for finishing, prefinished plywood turns out to be something of a bargain. Stone takes so much more labor to lay than brick that even if you have enough stone on your property, it will end up by costing you more to build a fireplace and chimney out of the stone than out of the brick that you would have to buy.

The only way you can make an intelligent comparison between materials is to find out how much they cost installed, not just the basic cost of the material. And only your builder, remodeler, or the man doing the work can tell you this.

Secondhand and used materials are seldom much of a bargain unless you are doing the work yourself or will make the materials ready for use. By the time you've paid a carpenter to pull the old nails out of a load of two-by-fours and clean them up for use, it will have cost you more than if you had bought new lumber. The same holds true for used bricks. You can often get them for very little, but it takes a lot of time to chip off the old mortar before the bricks can be used.

## Quality

Because the cost of labor is such a big factor in any improvement job, it just doesn't make sense to use any but good-quality materials. For example, it costs just the same for labor to install low-quality asphalt shingles as it does to install top-quality shingles that will last twenty-five years or so. And the difference in price between low-grade and top-grade shingles is relatively small.

But it is sometimes hard to resist the temptation to try and save on materials if you are working on a tight budget. Last winter we had a carpenter come in to build a bookcase storage wall. We priced pine shelving and found that select material would cost close to $1 a foot while common shelving was only about half that price. As we were going to paint the wood anyway, we decided to use the common pine. This was a mistake because after the shelves and cabinets had been completed and painted, the wood began to warp. We had to replace several shelves and all the doors for the base cabinets. By the time we paid for the extra labor, we would have been better off to use the higher-priced select-grade pine.

## General Acceptance

Unless money is no object, a home improvement project is no place in which to test new materials and new products. If you are having the work done for you, it is far better to use materials and products with which your builder and his men are familiar and which they know how to handle efficiently. If you ask them to use materials with which they have never worked before, you'll be paying extra in labor to educate them.

It is important, too, if you have any thoughts of selling the house, to remember that well-known products will be more acceptable than unknown ones to a potential buyer. One way a lot of buyers judge the quality of a house is by the products used in it: roofing, kitchen appliances, flooring, plumbing fixtures, heating systems, and so forth. If these are products and materials with which they are familiar, they feel reassured about the entire house. But if they find few if any products and materials they have heard of, they begin to wonder about the quality of the house in general.

Builders and subcontractors generally use products and materials that do have wide acceptance. In fact, you may have difficulty in getting them to install anything else. Most of the problems occur on do-it-yourself projects, on which one is often inclined to shop around for bargains in off-brand materials, and with shady home improvement operators who add to their profits by using low-quality materials.

With a great many of the products used today it's very important to employ those that have a wide acceptance in your area because sooner or later you'll have to have them repaired or serviced, and if you can't get anyone to service them or if replacement parts are not readily available, you're in for a lot of headaches. And you'll be surprised at the number of manufactured items there are in the average house these days. Besides the obvious ones such as kitchen appliances and heating systems, there are such items as windows, flooring, roofing, siding, cabinets, and bathroom plumbing fixtures. If these items require repair or replacement, you must be able to reach some local source that stocks the necessary parts.

## The Architect

A residential architect who is experienced in remodeling and improvements (not all of them are interested in this sort of work) can be a good person to have on your side for major improvements such as adding a wing or making extensive changes in the interior or exterior, or for helping you decide which of several choices would be the most effective or practical to solve your problem. While the fact that you use an architect probably won't increase the actual value of any given improvement, you will almost certainly get better results than if you have no professional help, and you may get the whole project done for less money even after you have paid the architect.

Of all the people involved in construction, the architect is the only one who has had extensive formal training not only in design but also in related areas of construction—building techniques, knowledge of materials, and so forth. It doesn't take much if any formal training to call yourself a contractor or a designer or an interior decorator, but before anyone can use the title "architect," he or she must have taken and passed a rigid course in architecture at an accredited college, passed a state examination, and worked for a specified number of years with a practicing architect before being licensed by the state to practice on his or her own. An architect is a professional, just as a doctor or an attorney is, and as such is subject to rather rigid regulations.

While all architects are "registered" architects (licensed by the state in which they practice), many also become members of the American Institute of Architects (AIA), which is a professional organization. They are then entitled to use the initials AIA after their names. Although the fact that architects are members of the AIA does not necessarily mean that they are any better in their profession than nonmembers, they may be, since there are certain requirements for membership.

The architect can develop a better design, both in appearance and in function, than someone without his or her training and experience. This alone is an important consideration, for a poorly designed project (and many projects are not only poor but quite awful) can be worse than no improvement at all. But an architect can do more than just produce a good design. He or she can often show you how to get better results for less money through creative design and the use of lower-cost materials or laborsaving materials.

Some years ago we saw a good example of what an architect can do along these lines. A family had a large, rather formal house of stone that had been built around 1920. They wanted to put on a two-story addition at the rear to serve as a large family room with bedrooms above. The logical choice was to build the addition of stone, but when they got an estimate on a stone addition, it was far higher than what they could pay. They consulted an architect, and he designed the addition of vertical wood siding stained gray rather than of stone. The addition was quite contemporary as compared with the main house, but when the architect showed the owners a color rendering of how the house and addition would look together, they saw that the two blended in perfectly. And the cost of the addition with wood siding was a fraction of what a stone structure would have cost.

## Cost of an Architect

Most of us seldom consider using an architect on an improvement because we believe it will be too expensive. This is not necessarily the case. Many architects will take on a job on a consulting basis at so much per hour. The average hourly rate is around $25. With this arrangement you can get professional help where you may need it the most, in the area of design and concept. It might take an architect only a couple of hours to inspect your house, find out what you need, and then tell you what he considers to be the best solution to your problem. And with a couple of hours' more work he may be able to design some rough plans that you can develop further yourself or have your contractor work up into final form. This is probably the most sensible way to work with an architect on the average major improvement or expansion.

Not long ago we saw a story in our local newspaper about a family that had a relatively new split-level house but needed a lot more space than it contained. As the owners couldn't find a larger house that was suitable or that they could afford, they decided on an expansion program. The trouble was that the design of the house just didn't seem to lend itself to the addition of a wing. The owners wasted a lot of time talking with various contractors in trying to devise a solution and finally consulted an architect. He came up with a rough sketch that involved raising the roof to create what amounted to almost a full third floor, and this is what they went ahead with.

Not every architect will consult with you on an hourly basis; so you may have to shop around to find one. You can get the names of architects who do this sort of work by checking with local architects, consulting the local chapter of the AIA, or writing to the American Institute of Architects in Washington, D.C.

If a large amount of work is involved, as in designing a new house or making extensive alterations in an existing dwelling, the usual arrangement is for the architect to receive as his or her fee a certain percentage of the total cost of construction, usually around 25 percent. In other words, if you spend $5,000 on a project, the architect will charge you around $1,250. But you will be getting quite a lot for your money. This fee will include consultations with you to discuss the proposed work, making rough plans and sketches of ways to achieve the desired result, producing working drawings, making a list of materials and specifications as to how the work is to be done, helping you to select a contractor, and supervising the work. In short, once you have approved the plans and the materials to be used, you can leave town and stay away until the architect tells you your house has been finished.

## Working with an Architect

The most important thing that you must tell an architect is how much money you have to spend on the project and for him. If you are going to work with an architect on a consulting basis, tell him how much you can afford for the project and how many hours of his time you can afford. At $25 an hour you can run up quite a bill with an architect if you waste a lot of his time in idle chatter or in having him draw up one rough plan after another for your consideration. It's not only the time he spends with you that you'll be charged for but also the time he and his associates spend in their office working up plans and sketches. If you can afford to spend only $100 for architectural services, tell the architect so at the very beginning so that he can know what areas of the project to put his time into.

Whether an architect is working on a consulting basis or on a fee basis, you must tell him exactly how much you can spend on the improvement. It's not always wise to tell a contractor how much you can put into a job because the chances are he'll figure the job so that it comes to this amount or maybe a bit more. But an architect is different, and you must tell him how much you can spend. If you don't, he'll waste his time and your money coming up with all sorts of designs that you can't possibly afford.

We know of one young couple that bought a run-down old farmhouse and called in an architect to work up plans for a complete restoration. He spent hours with the couple discussing all the things they wanted done to the house and then went to work and developed plans that the couple were delighted with. But when the estimates began to come in from contractors, they were not so delighted because the low bid was for around $23,000 and the couple had a budget of less than $7,000.

## When to Use an Architect

We know some people who use an architect for everything, even for selecting the color for the roof of the garage. But these people happen to be very rich. If you aren't rich, it would be a waste of money to use an architect where an architect is not essential, as in remodeling a bathroom or kitchen, designing rooms for the attic, enclosing a porch, or planning the layout for a central air-conditioning system. You can do plans for these projects yourself, with your contractor or with the firm that installs the air conditioning. But we would use an architect where we needed professional help in design and concept: an addition, a major change in the house interior, or cases in which we could not find the perfect solution to our problem.

# 4. Financing

If you can't or don't wish to pay for an improvement out of your income or savings, you will have to borrow the money to handle the job. And this is what most of us do to finance an extensive piece of work. Obviously, you will have to pay interest on borrowed money, and sometimes this interest can be pretty high, up to 15 percent. It's not uncommon to end up paying as much in interest as you did for the actual cost of the improvement. The interest, of course, can be deducted from your income tax, and this does help.

Another factor that can make the interest you pay a bit more palatable is that building costs have been going up at a rate of between 10 and 15 percent a year, which means that a job that costs $1,000 today could cost at least $100 more next year and several hundred dollars more than that in five years. Although the government is trying to slow the rate of inflation, it appears, as of this writing, that you will be better off financially to borrow the money to make essential improvements now than to wait a year or so until you've saved up for them. This is rather a crazy way to operate, but that's what inflation does.

## Obtaining a Home Improvement Loan

The first way most of us think of to get money for such projects is a home improvement loan. Such loans are promoted by banks and other lenders. In fact, it is almost impossible to miss seeing the billboards and advertisements in trains, buses, and newspapers.

If a lender feels that your income is adequate and your financial status stable, you can get up to $10,000 on this type of loan and have up to ten years to pay it back. You'll pay somewhere around 14 percent interest in monthly installments. If you borrow, say, $5,000 for a five-year period, your monthly payment will be around $114.59.

Home improvement loans are not hard to get even when money is tight, as it is now. Lenders like them because they carry a good rate of interest—higher than that of a mortgage loan, for example—and run for a relatively short time. Equally important is the fact that this type of loan is a low-risk one as far as the lender is concerned because it is secured by the equity you have in your house: a lien on the property in the case of a commercial bank and a second mortgage in the case of a savings bank. In either case, the lender feels comfortable about the loan, for he knows you'll try hard to come up with those monthly payments so as not to risk the loss of your property.

If you decide that a home improvement loan is the best way to finance the work, you'd be wise to go first to the bank that holds the mortgage on your house. The bank will probably give you as good a deal as you can get, and it's usually a lot easier to get a loan from someone who knows you and at a place where your credit is established. The bank will also be inclined to help keep you from getting in over your head because that monthly payment, when added to all your other fixed expenses, can knock the family budget into a cocked hat if you're not careful. A complete stranger may not care whether you have enough money left over to feed the kids, but your local banker conceivably could care. A little, anyway.

Some contractors and remodelers can provide financing for a job, but unless it is impossible for you to get a loan from some other source, we suggest that you avoid this route. Aside from the fact that you'll pay a higher rate of interest (1 to 2 percent more than if you get the money from a bank), you are likely to find that your loan actually comes from a commercial lender in another part of the country who doesn't care whether the job is successful or a miserable botch and who is likely to turn a deaf ear to any pleas about a bad job or, if you get into a jam about making payments, any requests for a delay until you can get things going again.

## Increasing Your Mortgage

Although increasing a mortgage made sense a few years ago, it's not a very good idea today. First, you may not be able to do it even if you want to because mortgage money is tight and any lender in his right mind would prefer to lend money on a short-term, high-interest improvement loan to putting his limited funds into a long-term, low-interest mortgage loan. Second, you will be paying the prevailing rate of interest, which is considerably higher than what you have been paying on the older mortgage. Let's say, for example, that your present mortgage is at 6½ percent and you have an unpaid balance of $15,000. If you want to borrow an additional $5,000, you'll end up with a new mortgage for fifteen or twenty years at the current rate of interest, which is around 9½ percent, maybe more. And this applies even if you have an open-end mortgage. If you don't have an open-end mortgage, you will have to go through many of the same legalities, including a title search, that you went through when you acquired the original mortgage. If the loan is for a sizable amount, it could cost you $1,000 or more just to have the mortgage rewritten.

## Borrowing on Your Life Insurance

If the loan value on your policies is sufficient, this is the simplest and least expensive way to get money for your project. You don't have to fill out a long credit application to get money from your insurance company, and it doesn't ask and doesn't care what you want the money for. Spend the money for a new roof, a swimming pool, or bets on the ponies—it's all the same to the company. Most important, the interest rates on such loans are very low: 5 to 6 percent.

Obviously, borrowing money on your life insurance reduces the amount of protection you have by the amount of the loan unless or until you pay it off. However, if you have used the money for a worthwhile improvement, you've added this amount to the value of your house; so while your insurance is less, your house is worth more, and the total value of your estate has not changed.

There are some disadvantages to borrowing on your insurance. First, the interest is payable once a year, and unless you've put aside the money to pay this, it can strain a family budget that is already bursting at the seams. You'll have to come up with $300 in a lump sum if you have borrowed $5,000 at 6 percent, for example. If you don't come up with $300, that sum is added to the original $5,000; so your policy has decreased in value by that amount too. You can see how, over a period of years, you could end up with hardly any life insurance at all if you kept missing the interest payments. In the last couple of years, some insurance companies have been trying a new tack, billing you for the interest payment at the time you pay your premium, whether annually, semiannually, or quarterly. Although this hurts at the time, it is actually a good idea, and more companies may follow suit. Your interest payments are, of course, deductible from your income tax.

## Obtaining a Secured Loan

This is another low-interest type of loan, but you have to put up security in the form of your savings account passbook or of stocks or bonds. If you use your passbook, you can get a loan up to the amount of money you have in your account while still drawing interest on it. You pay the bank 2 percent of that interest. You can't, of course, use the money in your account as long as the loan is outstanding.

Commercial banks will also take stocks or bonds as security on a loan. They will give you a certain percentage of the current value of the securities, which remain in their possession until the loan is paid off. Interest will be payable at fixed intervals, and, of course, if the market plummets, you'll have to come up with more securities or more money.

# 5. Getting the Right People to Do the Work

If you were to ask a group of homeowners who had recently made improvements what they would do differently if they were to do the job over again, the chances are that a majority of them would say, "I'd get another contractor from the one we used to do the work," And if you had the time to listen to their long tales of woe, you'd probably agree with them.

Make no mistake about it: the single most important element in any improvement is getting the right kind of people to do the work. Even with the very best people you can expect a few disappointments, delays, and misunderstandings. But if you get the wrong sort of people, you'll be in for a lot of trouble. At best the project will take what seems to be forever to complete, it will cost more than you should pay, and it may not turn out exactly as you expected. At worst you can end up spending a lot of money, not getting much in return, and then spending more money on legal fees. So no matter how small or how large the job, take the time to find the right people to do the work.

Finding the right kind of people is not easy. There are, of course, plenty of honest firms and workmen who do home improvement work. The trouble is that not all of them do first-class work, and many of them do not have much experience in home improvement projects. And you do need someone with a lot of experience in this field. Making improvements is very different from new construction. There are many builders and contractors who are first-rate when it comes to building a new house but don't know beans about home improvement work. One of the first questions you should ask anyone bidding on your job is "How much experience have you had making improvements in my style of house?"

## Where to Find the Right People

You can get the names of local general contractors, builders, home improvement contractors, and remodelers as well as names of individual workmen such as carpenters, plumbers, masons, and electricians from the Yellow

Pages, but this doesn't tell you much about them other than their names, addresses, and telephone numbers. Some larger firms advertise in local newspapers, but just because someone advertises doesn't mean he is experienced or reliable. Many states require contractors to be licensed, and to get a license a contractor must meet certain minimum requirements, but the fact that he has a license does not necessarily mean that his price is fair or that he is very reliable or does outstanding work.

It's easy enough to avoid getting involved with a dishonest firm. This subject is covered in detail below under the heading "Home Improvement Gyps." But it's another matter when it comes to finding really good people to handle your job.

We've always found the best way to get good people is to ask around. We ask friends and neighbors who have had work done recently. We ask the local bank, local real estate brokers, the hardware store, and the lumberyard for the names of local firms they have worked with or have been doing business with for a number of years. We once got the name of a very excellent builder because we happened to drive past a job he was working on and were impressed by the quality and speed of construction.

A very good source for names of good home improvement people is the local better business bureau. The bureaus have an arbitration program that we'll discuss below in detail under the heading "Arbitration." Builders and contractors are encouraged to precommit themselves to arbitrate any differences they may have with a customer. You can get a list of the firms in your area who have precommitted themselves to arbitration from your local bureau. This can be a valuable list of names because it seems safe to assume that a firm that agrees in advance to arbitrate any differences is probably a firm that won't do the kind of work that might require arbitration.

It's always best to use local firms that have been in business at the same address or in the same general area for a number of years. The home improvement field is attracting a lot of new people, and while some of them are good, many don't have much experience in this field. Lack of experience can be a handicap for you.

Also look for firms that belong to recognized trade organizations such as the National Association of Home Builders or the National Home Improvement Council. It's also a good sign if the firm is a member of the local chamber of commerce, Lions, Rotary, or similar national organizations.

## Estimates

The first thing you want to know from anyone you are considering is "How much is it going to cost?" Now there are a couple of ways to express cost in the building game. First, there is a rough estimate. This is what you will get if you don't have final plans or have not selected materials for a job but want some rough idea of what you may have to pay. For example, if you call a builder on the telephone and tell him you want to put on an 18- by 24-foot addition and this is all the information you can give him at this time, he can give you a rough estimate of the cost based on the number of square feet involved and what he considers to be the going rate per square foot for a standard addition. This is obviously a very rough estimate because there are so many unknown factors that will influence the final cost. But at least you will know that you are talking in the $8,000 range and not in the $4,000 range, which you had hoped would be the case.

It is only after you have final plans and have selected all the basic materials and the builder has carefully inspected your house that anyone can come up with an accurate estimate of the final cost. This is the reason that you should never fall for advertisements that say "We'll finish your attic for $3,000." No builders in their right minds can tell you what it will cost to finish your attic until they've seen what sort of attic you have.

You must remember that an estimate is just what it says: the amount that someone with experience estimates it will *probably* cost to do a certain piece of work. Sometimes the final price will be exactly as estimated, but more often it will be higher. We've never heard of a final bill that was less than the estimate, but it probably has occurred some time.

We recently had our house painted and were pleased to find that the final bill matched the estimate made five months before the work was done and before the price of the paint we used went up almost $1 a gallon. And a couple of years ago we had to drill a new well and put in a new deep-well pump and tank, and the final bill from the plumber was only about $5 over the estimate. But when we put in a downstairs powder room, the plumbing costs ran around $150 above the estimate because of problems involved in installing the vent.

The value of any estimate depends on the qualifications of the person who makes it. If you get an estimate from someone who has had a lot of experience with home improvement work, the estimate should be reliable. If, on the other hand, you get an estimate from someone who is not familiar with home improvement work, the estimate isn't worth much of anything.

Some home improvement firms send salesmen to estimate the cost of a job, and many of them don't know the first thing about home improvement work except how to sell a job. You don't want to put much faith in an estimate you get from an inexperienced person. The best kinds of estimates are those you get from people who really know what the job involves. Many larger firms employ trained estimators to figure the cost of a job. With smaller outfits, it's usually the boss who comes around to estimate on the work. We know of one very large builder who has several trained estimators on his staff, but he uses them to figure new construction. When it comes to home improvement work, the builder does the estimating because the builder has had more experience in this field than the estimators.

There are some concerns that will give you a firm estimate or a firm bid in writing and hold to this figure. But these are hard to come by because in home improvement work, especially in older houses, unknown factors can run up the cost. For example, you may start out to make some changes in the house plumbing system (remodeling the bath or adding another bathroom, for example), and then the plumber discovers that although the exposed pipes are made of copper, the stuff in the walls and in the floor is old galvanized-iron pipe that will have to be replaced. Replacing all the pipes is going to add considerably to the cost of the job. Our experience has been that when you do get a firm estimate, it's going to be on the high side, because contractors or workmen must add an amount large enough to cover themselves if they should run into an unexpected situation.

Many firms will write up a contract stating the price for the work but adding that if some unexpected situation arises, you will pay extra for the labor and materials involved plus a certain amount to cover overhead. This is a reasonable way to handle matters if you assume, of course, that the contract and original price cover the new work to be done.

If you get estimates from several firms, make certain that all are based on the same work. You can't make a fair comparison of estimates unless each one is based on exactly the same work, using the same quality of materials and products. The best way to ensure getting a fair comparison is to give each builder, contractor, or remodeler a set of plans for the project and a list of all the basic materials and products you want to have included. If you are going to depend on the builder to suggest materials, then each firm should list the materials and products it intends to use.

Assuming that you get three estimates based on the same job with the same materials, you then must decide which one to accept. The logical choice would seem to be the low estimate, but if it's considerably lower than the other two, watch your step. It could be that this estimate is based on cutting a lot of corners, such as substituting less expensive and poorer materials for those specified or doing the work with a lot of semiskilled labor. Or it may be that after the contract has been signed and the work begun, the builder will announce that he has run into an unexpected situation that is going to cost you extra. Now this can put you into a real bind, especially if it is impossible to do the work without paying extra to correct the situation. We heard of a family that signed a contract with a firm that made a low estimate to finish off an attic. After the work had begun, the builder announced that the ceiling joists were undersized and, although the room could be completed, the floor would sag unless the joists were reinforced. The family didn't want a sagging attic room; so it paid extra to have the joists reinforced. The chances are that a better builder would have checked the joists and included the cost of reinforcing them in the estimate.

The high estimate you get on a job, on the other hand, may sound as though it would provide for a top-quality job and include dealing with the majority of unexpected situations. This is not always the case. A high estimate may simply mean that it was offered by a firm that didn't particularly want the job but figured that if you were willing to pay enough, it would be worth its while, or by a firm that has such a high overhead or inefficient operation that it must charge an arm and a leg on every job.

That leaves you with the middle bid, which is probably the safest choice, all other things being equal.

But whichever estimate you select, if you have three estimates, you do have a realistic picture of what the job is worth, which is not always the case if you simply get one estimate and go along with it. You'd be surprised at the number of homeowners who do just this. They call in somebody, get an estimate, and, if they have the money, give the go-ahead. Only when the job has been completed and paid for will they begin to check around and find out that they've paid far more than the job is actually worth.

One last point about estimates: a lot of small builders and individual workmen, such as carpenters, plumbers, and electricians, won't give estimates for love or money. They work on a time-and-materials basis. This means that you pay them so much per hour and for the materials needed for the work. We'll discuss this arrangement under the heading, "Time-and-Materials Basis."

You'll have better luck getting good people to estimate on a job and do the work in a reasonable length of time if you can arrange to have the work done during the slack season. In most sections of the country this means late fall and winter. Spring, summer, and early fall are the most difficult times to get good people because if they are good they'll be busy. And good people are usually busy regardless of what you may read or hear about poor conditions in the new home construction field. Good people, especially if they are good at improvements, are always busy.

Of course, if you have a project that involves outside work—roofing, siding, exterior painting, building an addition—and you live in an area where winters are severe, you can't put off the work until the cold weather.

But on inside jobs winter is the ideal time to get good people to do the work. Most builders, contractors, and remodelers are happy to have a lot of inside work lined up for the winter months because that means they can keep their crews busy when it's impossible for them to work outside.

## What Sort of People to Use

There are a lot of different kinds of firms and people who do home improvement work. Which one you select depends more or less on what kind of work is involved but also on which outfit appears to be the best.

### Builders and General Contractors

These firms are equipped to handle all phases of any building operation. Builders may not have representatives of all the specialized trades in their employ, but they will have their own crews and their own subcontractors to do specialized work such as plumbing, heating, and wiring.

Builders or general contractors can estimate or bid on an entire project. They will supervise and coordinate the work and be responsible for the job being done in a satisfactory manner. They will be the only ones you have to deal with no matter how many different trades may be required on the job.

Firms of builders and contractors come in all sizes. Some are very large organizations with 100 or so workers on the payroll. These outfits may be involved in new housing developments and in commercial and industrial work as well as in remodeling and home improvements. Others are pretty much one-man organizations. The boss usually is also a carpenter, and he may have a full-time helper; he subcontracts all the work he and his helper can't do themselves. We have such a builder in our area. He has one helper, his brother-in-law, but he's very good and can handle just about any size of project from repairing a porch floor to building a new house. For the past few months he's been busy building a bank.

On major projects, such as renovating an entire house or putting on an addition, there are several advantages to using a large builder or contractor. That's assuming, of course, that the firm has experience in home improvement work. Many of the larger firms have their own design departments to help you develop plans for your project and to aid in selecting the materials to be used. They may even show you ways to save money and still get the results you want. There is often no charge for this kind of service if the builder does the job. We've seen some excellent additions that were designed for the owner by the design department of a builder.

Another advantage in using large outfits is that they usually have well-trained and experienced estimators who can make very reliable estimates of costs. In fact, it's usually only large builders who will make firm estimates. They are able to do this not only because of very accurate estimating but also because of their volume of work. If they make a firm estimate on a job and something unexpected turns up, they won't make their usual profit, but this doesn't knock them out of business. Working on the law of averages, sooner or later they'll hit a job that works out better for them than they expected. This will more than make up for their loss on the previous job.

Some years ago we had a large building firm remodel a house for us. We had a firm estimate, and the unexpected was the rule rather than the exception. When the job was finally finished, the builder told us that he hadn't made a nickel on the project. But he wasn't crying. The job had kept his crew busy over the winter, had helped pay the overhead, and had taught his estimator a few good lessons in what you can expect to find inside the walls of a very old house.

You will also find that large builders are more professional in their business dealings than small outfits. A first-rate big builder will draw up a contract that will list in detail everything the firm will do and also what it won't do. For example, if you are making a room in your attic and state that you'll do the painting, the builder will note in the contract "Painting to be done by owner." If you state that you'll supply certain materials (lighting fixtures, for example), there will be a note to this effect. And if you make any changes during the course of the work, a good builder will confirm these in writing along with the added cost.

Once a large outfit schedules a job, it goes along at a pretty good clip because such a firm operates on a tight schedule and must move the job along so that it can get to the next one. The firm may bring in half a dozen workers; so it's only natural that the work will take less time than it would with a small contractor who only has one helper.

One disadvantage in using a large builder is the cost. Any large firm has a high overhead and will probably charge you more than a small contractor who has his office in the kitchen of his home, drives to work in a beat-up pickup truck, and leaves all the bookkeeping to his wife. And it is not very easy and can be costly to make changes in a plan after the work has started if you use a large building contractor. You generally have to get in touch with the office (the people on the job often are not allowed to make any changes unless they have authorization from the office), and this can mean that by the time the office has ordered the change, the work has been completed as originally specified. There will be an extra charge to rip the work out and do it over again.

It's a simple matter to make changes if you use a small builder because he'll probably be on the job at least a part of each day. And he can tell you right then and there how much extra it is going to cost. If you are at home and the builder isn't quite certain about a particular item, he can check with you right away and do the job the way you want it done. We have always enjoyed working with small builders more than with large firms because we like to be involved in the project as much as possible. But not everyone feels this way.

A small builder won't be of much help in developing plans for a project except in the way he is used to doing the job. He'll use the materials he is familiar with and those available at his favorite lumberyard. He's a hard man to pin down to a firm estimate, and if you do pin him down, he'll be sure to leave himself an out in case he runs into problems.

Small builders also are not the most reliable people in the world. They may tell you they are going to start work the following Monday and not show up on that day or another day that month. Often, they'll get the job under way and then disappear for a few days or even weeks. Most of them have a lot of jobs going at the same time, and they'll go to the customer who is squeaking the loudest. And if you don't squeak, nothing may happen.

A couple of years ago we decided that it might be a good thing to take a portion of the attic and make it into a home office. We called a small builder we know, and eventually he came over, took a look at the space, and made a list of some materials he'd need to get started. We ordered the materials (studding, gypsum wallboard, etc.), and when they were delivered, we called up the builder. He said he'd be over the following week. Well, he didn't show up that week or the week after. We called him over a weekend, and he said he'd start the following Tuesday. He didn't. As we were not in any great rush to have the study finished and as we didn't have a great deal of money tied up in materials, we decided to wait and see just how long it would take him to show up if we didn't call him again. Well, it's been more than two years, and he hasn't shown up. We've used the materials for other jobs. Now and then we run into the builder at the bank or the post office, and he'll say "I'll be over pretty soon to do that attic for you." Maybe he will, and maybe he won't, but it's fairly certain that if we don't call him, he never will show up.

## Home Improvement Contractors and Remodelers

Firms of this type would seem to be the logical choice for improvement and remodeling work. Sometimes they are, and sometimes they aren't. It depends on the work involved and the kind of firm you're dealing with.

Many firms calling themselves home improvement contractors are roofing and siding outfits. They can be a very good choice for these particular jobs because they are specialists, and if they are good, they can reroof or reside a house quickly, efficiently, and generally at a better price than you would get by calling in a general contractor for the job. But while they are good in their special fields, they are not the ideal choice for other, more general kinds of improvement work, and many of them don't do such work. Some, however, will take on work that they are not necessarily qualified to handle and then subcontract it to carpenters, plumbers, masons, and so on. This is not a particularly good arrangement for you.

Other home improvement contractors and remodelers are set up in the same fashion as a builder or general contractor except that they specialize in home improvement work and don't do much new construction. Some of these firms are very good, and some are not. Just because a firm calls itself a home improvement contractor or a remodeler does not necessarily mean that it is good in this particular field. The firm may very easily be a building outfit that moved into home improvement work because there wasn't enough new building going on in the area to keep it going. It's just as important to check the qualifications of a home improvement contractor or remodeler as it is to check on whether a particular builder or general contractor is qualified to do home improvement work.

There are some home improvement and remodeling firms that are first-rate. People we know had a very good experience with one of these firms. They owned a large colonial house about 200 years old and wanted to raise the roof of a shed dormer at the rear to create a larger room. They got in touch with a home improvement contractor, who came over, gave them a firm estimate on the work, and said that he'd start the following Monday. Sure enough, on Monday his crew arrived, and two days later the job was completed. Not only was it done exactly as the owners had specified, but the contractor left the place spotless. There wasn't a speck of dust in the room or a splinter of wood on the grounds by the time the crew had finished cleaning up.

## Specialists

For certain improvement jobs you are generally better off dealing with a specialist than with a builder, home improvement contractor, or remodeler, for the chances are that such a firm will call in the same specialist to do the work and charge you for the specialist's services. For example, if you need to have the house painted, you call in a painter and don't bother with a general contractor. The same holds true if you want to install central air conditioning, a new heating system, a new driveway, or another electric circuit. You call in the people who specialize in this type of work. Or at least you do if you want to save money. We know of some wealthy people who call in a general contractor to handle everything connected with their house. If a door hinge squeaks, they call their contractor, who sends over an employee to add a drop or two of oil. And then the contractor sends a nice healthy bill for the time and effort involved.

## Using Someone You Can Get Along With

Your dealings with a builder, remodeler, or specialist will be much easier if you select one who is interested in trying to do the kind of job that pleases you and with whom you believe you can get along. And let's face it, some builders are not easy to get along with. Some are extremely aggressive, and others are just plain rude. Some are unreasonable, others are temperamental, and many are unavailable once the work has started. We know of several builders who do good work, but we wouldn't use them on a bet because they are too unpleasant to deal with. And you've got to assume that no matter how well a job has been spelled out in advance, there are bound to be areas where a certain amount of give-and-take is necessary between the home-owner and the builder. If it isn't present, the job is not going to turn out very well.

## The Contract

Your agreement with a builder, contractor, or remodeler should be in writing and in considerable detail, for it covers not only the money involved and the method of payment but also the scope of the work, the materials and products to be used, and general specifications.

First, the money should be considered. The contract should state the full amount involved and the method of payment. You never should pay for work until it has been completed, although it is common practice these days for a builder to ask for a 10 percent payment in advance to get the work started. But 10 percent is the most you should pay in advance. The balance of the money should be paid in installments as the work progresses. The final payment, and this should be for a considerable sum, should not be paid until the job has been completed to your satisfaction. For your protection, there should be a clause whereby you can legally withhold this final payment for, say, thirty days, which gives you time to make sure that the work has been done satisfactorily and the builder time to correct any work that has not been properly done or work specified that has not been done. The final payment should not fall due until the job has been passed by the local building inspector and you have received from the inspector a certificate of occupancy. If you don't have a clause in the contract giving you the legal right to withhold the final payment pending approval of the work, you can get into a legal hassle with the builder and maybe end up with a mechanic's lien on your property. We'll discuss this type of lien later in this chapter.

If you have a reputable builder, you shouldn't have any difficulty in arranging a payment schedule that offers you the maximum protection. A good firm has the capital and credit not to require a large payment in advance of the work, and it can also get along without the final payment until you've had ample time to inspect the work and it has done what's necessary to make the work right. But when you find a builder who wants a large sum of money in advance to get the work started and wants the final payment the day the job is finished, watch out. This can only mean that the builder's credit is bad and your money is needed to pay cash for materials. Or maybe the builder needs your money to pay for materials and labor on a previous job. And the builder may want that final payment the day he finishes work because he knows that once you've had a chance to inspect the job, you won't pay him.

The contract should describe the scope of the work in detail as well as the kind of materials and the brand of products to be used. These may be included on a separate specification sheet that is attached to and included in the contract. There should also be a statement to the effect that if it is necessary to make a substitution for any materials or products, the contractor will notify you to that effect and tell you what materials and products are available and the cost as compared with what was originally specified. In addition, the contract should cover the following areas:

1. The builder or contractor has all the necessary insurance to protect you from any liability that might result from the work: accidents to the builder or to the workers on the job or accidents or property damage to others caused by the work. You can generally assume that a large and reputable firm will have the necessary insurance coverage, but if you are working with a single individual or a small firm, ask for the name of the company that has insured it and check with the company to make sure that the individual or firm has adequate coverage.

2. The builder or contractor should state that all necessary building permits will be obtained and that all the work will be done in strict accordance with local building regulations.

3. The builder will take all necessary precautions to protect grounds and other areas of the property from damage during the work and will repair or replace any property damaged through the builder's fault. Also, the builder will remove all debris from the site after the work has been completed and leave the premises "broom clean."

4. Finally, there should be a clause indemnifying you against liens (mechanic's liens) as well as a statement that any disagreement or dispute will be settled by arbitration.

## Mechanic's Lien

If people supply either labor or materials to improve your property and are not paid within a reasonable length of time, they can put a mechanic's lien on your property. A lien is a legal hold or claim against the property so that the property becomes security for the debt. The lien is recorded on the deed to the property and is not removed until the debt has been paid or some agreement on payment has been reached. The creditor then signs a release to remove the lien. If there is a lien on your property and you sell the property, the amount of the outstanding debt will be taken out of the proceeds. Once a lien has been recorded on the deed, the creditor can get a court judgment requiring the property to be sold so that the creditor can be reimbursed. Some states require that the owner of the property be informed before a lien is put into effect, and if the owner is not informed, the lien cannot be applied. In other states no advance warning is required, and the creditor can slap a lien on the property at any time.

The ability to put a lien on property gives a contractor, worker, or supplier of materials a very powerful weapon. For example, suppose you have had some work done and do not find it satisfactory or decide that the bill is far more than the estimate you received. You decide to withhold payment until you can reach some satisfactory agreement with the contractor. Well, unless you have an arbitration clause in your contract (and few contracts do have such a clause), the contractor can put a lien on your property. You can, of course, go to court to get the matter settled, but in the meantime there is a lien on your property, and you'll have court costs to add to the expense of the improvement you have had made.

You can also get involved with liens through no fault of yours other than dealing with the wrong kind of outfit. Suppose that you have a contractor do some work on your house and you pay him in full but that he has not paid for the materials he used or for some of the labor involved. If the supplier or the workmen can't get their money out of him, they'll turn to you, and if you refuse to pay them, they can slap a lien on your property. This puts you in the position of possibly having to pay twice for the job, once to the contractor and again to the people who supplied the materials and did the actual work.

It's easy to run into this situation if you deal with a fly-by-night outfit that sells jobs and then gets local subcontractors to do the work. The outfit collects the money from you and then gets out of town, leaving a lot of unpaid bills for materials and labor. You end up by paying these bills or by getting involved with liens.

The same situation can arise if you use a contractor who is in bad financial shape. He may pay for the materials and labor used on a previous job with your money, or he may put the money to his personal use. In either case, if the people who supplied labor and materials for your job don't get their money in a reasonable length of time, they are going to turn to you for it. You can, of course, take the contractor to court, but this is going to cost you money, and if the contractor has gone broke or left town, suing him isn't going to do you much good.

One way to protect yourself against liens is not to pay the contractor until the contractor has provided you with a waiver signed by all the subcontractors and suppliers. The waiver says in effect that they have either been paid in full or that you are released from any legal claim by them. This is called a ''no lien'' clause and should be part of your agreement with the contractor. The trouble here is that you have no way of knowing if the contractor has really obtained waivers from everyone involved in the project. The contractor can, for example, get a waiver from one supplier, but not from all those that supplied materials, or can give you waivers from a few subcontractors and not from others.

The best way to avoid problems with liens (aside from paying your obligations on time) is to deal with local people with good reputations. If you have any doubts about their financial condition, have your attorney check their credit or ask your local banker. Bankers generally know which contractors are having serious money problems.

You want to watch out for liens from suppliers if you are acting as your own contractor and working with people on a time-and-materials basis. Open an account at a major supplier—the local lumberyard, for example— so that materials will be charged to you and delivered to your house. In this way you'll not only be sure that the major supplier is paid but that the materials you pay for go to your job and don't end up someplace else. For supplies required from sources with which you do not have an account, have them delivered COD.

## Arbitration

Even if you have the best builder in the country, it's possible that you can have a dispute over some aspect of the work. If you are both reasonable individuals, the chances are that you can settle your differences without your getting involved in a lien or having to go to court. But sometimes no matter how good your intentions, you can't settle your differences between yourselves. And if you happen to have a less-than-ideal builder, there are almost sure to be disputes, which can be very unpleasant.

No matter whom you use to do the work, it's smart to have a clause in your contract that commits both you and the builder to settle any differences by arbitration. This means that if the builder's final bill is higher than the estimate and you feel that it isn't fair, you can have the matter arbitrated. Or it may be that you feel that the workmanship wasn't good or that the builder failed to do all that was required in the contract. Whatever the problem, instead of getting stuck with the higher cost or the poor-quality work, you arbitrate the dispute rather than taking it to court.

One recogized method of arbitration is the mediation-arbitration program developed by the better business bureaus. If you have agreed in advance to arbitrate and you have a dispute, you get in touch with your local better business bureau, which arranges for a hearing. At the hearing you and the builder have the chance to state your cases to a group of impartial individuals. They may even visit your house to see exactly what was done and what was not done. They make their decision on the basis of the facts and what they believe to be a fair method of settlement. There is no charge for this service, but you and the builder must agree in advance to abide by the decision of the arbitration panel.

## Being Your Own Contractor

You can save 15 percent or more on an improvement project if you act as your own contractor, for 15 to 20 percent is the amount the average contractor or builder will add to the basic labor and material costs. This covers overhead and gives the builder a profit. Of course, some builders tack on a lot more than 15 to 20 percent either because they have a very high overhead or just are able to get away with overcharging. But most of them work in this 15 to 20 percent range. This markup usually applies regardless of the amount of work involved. For example, if you call in a builder or contractor to have a carpenter sent over to put in some bookshelves, the job is going to cost you at least 20 percent more than if you go out and get a carpenter on your own to do the job. The same will be true if you call in a builder or general contractor to install additional electrical outlets, put down a black-top driveway, replace plumbing fixtures, or paint a room. So when you have only one trade to deal with, it is obviously smart to work directly with the person who will do the actual work.

But being your own contractor on a project that is going to involve several trades—carpentry, plumbing, wiring, masonry—is a different matter. You will save a good deal of money by being your own contractor on a big job like adding a wing to the house, but it will give you a lot of headaches and take a lot of your time.

First, you've got to line up all the different people to do all the different kinds of jobs involved. You've also got to work out a schedule and coordinate the work so that all the workers do their parts when they are supposed to. Nothing is more irritating, and often more expensive, than to have work back up because one or more persons have delayed or not finished their segments of the job. This is where the major problem arises for the amateur contractor. You don't have the same control over the subcontractors as builders or general contractors do. They do enough business with an electrician, for example, so that when they say "Get over tomorrow and finish the wiring," the electrician does so. But in your case, if there is a more important job to be done, the electrician will do that and let your job hang for days or even weeks, thus holding up your carpenter, plumber, or other specialist who is waiting for that piece of work to be completed. And if the plumber or carpenter hangs around all day waiting for the electrician, charges for waiting time can eat up all that you've saved by being your own contractor.

Another problem you run into concerns materials. From time to time certain essential materials are in short supply and often are not available at your local building supply house. Builders or contractors usually have many sources for materials, and they are favored customers because they buy in volume. If the supply house can find a scarce item, it gets it for a builder, but it probably will not get it for you.

Still, being your own contractor can be a very satisfying experience. We've handled major projects working with a builder and being our own contractor, and while it was a lot easier working with the builder, we like the kicks you get out of doing the job on your own.

Don't forget, by the way, that if you are your own contractor, it will be your responsibility to get the necessary building permits and see to it that the completed work is checked out and approved by the building inspector. And you had better check with your insurance agent to be certain that you have all the necessary insurance to protect you from any claims resulting from injury to persons or property due to the work involved.

## Time-and-Materials Basis

If you work with an individual workman, the chances are that he'll work on a time-and-materials basis. This means that you pay him so much per hour and for the materials used on the job. Sometimes he'll give you a rough idea of how many hours the job may take and about how much the materials will cost, but don't try to pin him down to a firm estimate on the total cost. He won't give it because he may not know the cost himself.

If you get a good man who knows his job and puts in a good hour's work, this is not a bad arrangement and can be a lot less expensive than jobs on which you get a firm bid. But you must have very good people because if you don't, the costs can go sky-high. We once had a built-in desk and storage wall done by a carpenter with whom we had never worked before but had heard was good and who charged only $6 an hour. Well, he was good, and he didn't charge much per hour, but, Lord, was he a slow worker! That built-in took weeks and weeks, and every week we paid him his $180 (he liked to work only thirty hours a week). By the time the job was finished, that built-in had cost us close to $700.

And that brings up another problem connected with doing a big project on a time-and-materials basis. Most of the people that we have worked with this way like to be paid every week, and this means that unless you've received an improvement loan in advance, you're going to pay them out of your own pocket. This can become quite a strain. If you have two carpenters working at $10 an hour and they both put in forty hours, you have to get up $800 for every week they work for you.

## Using Nonprofessionals

One way to save on the cost of many projects is to use nonprofessionals for some of the unskilled work or even for semiskilled jobs. Skilled labor runs more than $10 an hour in most parts of the country; so if you can get the same work done just as well by an amateur for $4, $6, or even $8 a hour, you can save a lot of money.

For example, in our area there are a group of schoolteachers who earn extra money each summer by painting houses. They do an excellent job at far less that it would cost to get a painting contractor to handle the same work.

We've found many high school boys who are willing to work and work hard at $2 and $3 an hour, and they've done good jobs at painting, masonry, and even rough carpentry. One of the best we had put down a flagstone walk for us. That was a mistake because he decided he liked masonry and took a full-time summer job with a mason at a better hourly rate than we could afford.

## Home Improvement Gyps

In the home improvement field there have always been a certain number of shady characters, willing and able to fleece the unwary homeowner. Their job may be a bit more difficult today because of recently enacted consumer legislation, licensing requirements for contractors in many states, and efforts on the part of reputable home improvement contractors and better business bureaus to expose the methods of these gyp artists, but they are still around. And they always will be around as long as there are naïve homeowners willing to be sheared.

You have to hand it to these crooks: they are very clever. As fast as consumer legislation is passed, they go to work to find some way to get around it. The federal Truth in Lending Act, for example, allows a homeowner three days in which to cancel a contract if he or she has a change of heart after signing it. So what does the home improvement crook do? He tells you after you have signed the contract that by a stroke of good luck he'll be able to start work on your project the very next day. And if you let him start work before you've had a chance to study the contract and cancel it, you are stuck with him unless you want to go to court and prove that you never said he could start work before the three-day cooling-off period had expired. Starting work the day after signing the contract is called "spiking the job."

The home improvement crook is almost as adaptable as the cockroach. As soon as his activities in a certain field are exposed and people get wise to him, he moves onto something else. Some years ago the furnace racket was a big thing. At one time or another the crooks have been active in termite control, blacktop driveways, aluminum storm windows, basement waterproofing, and roof coatings. At the present time they seem to be very active in home swimming pools. And when people get wise to them in this area, they'll move to something else. We bet that the next thing they'll be into will be solar heat.

The naïve (the greedy or the not very bright) homeowner makes an ideal victim for anyone who has a good sales pitch and is on the prowl for a fast buck. The gyp artist knows that the homeowner has at least one good financial asset, the equity in his or her house; so if he can get the homeowner to sign a binding contract and put some labor and materials into the house, he is going to get his money regardless of how the work turns out. In too many cases, the law still works for the gyp artist and not to the advantage of the homeowner.

Our shady friend also knows that for most people the house represents their largest investment and that many owners can easily be frightened into making unnecessary repairs and improvements to protect this investment.

All it takes is some scare tactics and a good sales pitch to convince many homeowners to buy something they don't really need. There used to be many crooks in the termite control business. Often all they had to do to sell an expensive and useless job was to come around and show a homeowner an insect, almost any insect, and say that it was a termite they had seen on the property.

The home improvement crook is an expert in human nature and knows that most people are always looking for an easy solution, a "miracle product." This could be a "space age" coating to waterproof basement walls, a "wonder plastic" that makes outside paint obsolete, or a coating for roofs that costs a fraction of a new roof and will last forever, or almost.

One of the commonest kinds of home improvement rackets is called "bait and switch." You'll find this going on in all parts of the country and sometimes with well-established firms that should know better. It is the most difficult home improvement racket to control through consumer legislation because there is a fine line between trying to con a customer and trying to sell him an item that is better but more expensive than what was advertised as a special.

The way the bait-and-switch technique operates is that the firm offers something at a very low price. Then, when you come in to buy, the firm immediately switches you to something far more expensive. The way a dishonest firm does this is by telling you that the advertised special is no good. The salesman will naturally tell you that the special is no good in strict confidence. He'll make you believe that he is on your side and wants you to get the best value for your dollar.

You've probably seen the ads for some of these bait-and-switch deals in local newspapers or heard them on the radio or TV. They'll offer a special price for this week only or for this month for just about everything: basement game rooms, kitchen remodelings, finishing off attics, dormers, garages, aluminum siding, swimming pools.

Another trick of the home improvement crook is to come around and say that he can give you a good price on certain improvements because he has a crew working in your neighborhood. This is a common approach for the blacktop driveway and termite control crooks.

Another common game is to tell homeowners that they can get a special price on an improvement if they allow the installation to be used as a model to sell other homeowners in the area. Just as a formality the homeowners must sign some papers, and often these turn out to be a binding contract; so the homeowners end up by paying the full price for a shoddy job they don't really need.

Another character in the home improvement field whom you want to avoid is known in the trade as a "commission merchant." He is a hotshot salesman who generally has an office and a fancy showroom. He has a book full of color pictures to show the wonderful work he does: kitchens, bathrooms, swimming pools, basement game rooms. Once he has sold a job and got a client to sign a contract, he goes off and hunts up some subcontractors to do the work. He doesn't do anything except sell, and he has no trained crew of his own. But he makes a good living selling low-quality jobs at a very fancy price. This is obviously a miserable setup for homeowners because not only do they pay a lot more than a job is worth, but the quality of workmanship and materials will be shoddy since the commission merchant is obviously going to hire subcontractors who will do the job for the least amount of money. Needless to say, once the job has been completed and you find it not satisfactory, your chances of getting matters fixed are dim. The commission merchant may have closed up shop and moved to the next town, and the subcontractors who did the work don't care one bit that you are not a satisfied customer.

No one needs to be taken in by any of the shoddy people in the home improvement field. It's easy to protect yourself if you just use common sense and remember that in this world there are few if any real bargains.

1. Never buy a home improvement job from a door-to-door salesman. Your antenna should go up the minute you get a knock on the door or a phone call from anyone who is offering any kind of improvement or repair service. And you've got to keep turning the salesmen down because they may keep on trying every few months or even years until you finally give in. Each year we get a call from some outfit that wants to sell us aluminum siding at a special price. We keep saying "No," and the outfit keeps on calling.

2. Be careful of any home improvement outfit that uses a salesman to sell a job. Most reputable contractors and builders don't use salesmen to drum up business. Their rule is "You call us. We don't call you." The minute you get involved with a salesman, you want to watch out. He is going to work hard to sell you the most expensive job he has to offer. What's more, no matter what he promises, the job is probably going to end up by costing you more money than if you used a firm that does not employ salesmen. Someone has to pay the salesman's salary, and that person is going to be you.

3. Be leery of any outfit that promotes, either by advertising or verbally, any improvement job with a price tag: "A finished attic room for under $1,200"; "Your dream kitchen for just $2,999." No

reputable contractors will give an estimate on a job until they have seen the house and know what the work is going to involve. Most of these ads with a price tag are bait-and-switch rackets, and you want to stay clear of the firm that offers them.

4. Never sign a sales contract or any other printed form until you've read it over carefully. And you'd be wise to have it checked out by your attorney or the lender who holds the mortgage on your house before signing. Some homeowners have signed what they were told was a credit application or an application for a building permit that turned out to be a sales contract as well. And some people have signed a completion certificate before the work had even begun.

5. If you do get pressured into signing a contract and if your house is the security for the money involved, you can, within three business days, cancel the contract and get your money back by putting your request in a letter and getting it to the contractor.

6. Don't sign a completion certificate or make the final payment on a job until you've had a chance to inspect it carefully to be sure it was done in accordance with the terms of the contract. Also, don't make a final payment until the work has been approved by the local building inspector and the inspector has issued you a certificate of occupancy.

7. If you feel that you have been had or are about to be had, don't sit around and worry. Get in touch with your state department of consumer protection or the state attorney general and your local better business bureau.

8. The best way to avoid problems is to deal with reputable established local firms. If you have any doubts about one, you can check with your department of consumer protection, attorney general, or better business bureau.

9. Don't look for bargains in the home improvement business because there are none. Each contractor must pay about the same amount for the same quality of materials and the same amount for skilled labor. The only difference in price will occur because one outfit is more efficient than another, does not have the same high overhead, or does not want as large a profit.

# 6. Do It Yourself?

One sure way to cut the cost of any improvement job is to do some or all of the work yourself. On many projects 75 percent of the cost will be for labor; so if you supply the labor, you can get the job done at a bargain price. Even if you supply only some of the labor, the unskilled portion, you can save a good deal on any major improvement.

But before you tackle a project on your own, be sure that you have the skills to handle it well, for a botched-up job isn't much fun to live with, can be costly to correct, and definitely won't add value to your house.

Every do-it-yourself project requires a little talent, a certain amount of skill, and a lot of patience. And make no mistake about the patience. Magazine and newspaper articles, as well as advertisements for various building products, tell you how easy it is to build a deck, put down floor tile, install kitchen counter tops, or convert an attic into a bedroom, and it is—if you are a pro and do it every day for your living. But none of these jobs are easy for an amateur. We just don't have that many opportunities to develop all these specialized skills. Some of us do pick up such skills faster than others so that, by the time we have had a little practice, we can turn out a fairly first-class job. But others of us are slow learners, and sometimes it's not until we come to the last piece of floor tile or the last section of wallboard that we've really got the hang of the job.

You also need a lot of perseverance to follow through on a major project. Some neighbors of ours recently remodeled their kitchen. Working evenings and weekends as well as on their vacation, they took the better part of a year to complete the job. We know of couples who have spent an entire summer building a screened-in porch. A lot of other families have started similar projects and, after several months, have given up and called in a professional. Often they have ended up by paying about as much as if they had started the job with a pro.

The do-it-yourself jobs with the best chance of success are probably those in which time is not of the essence and the work will not disturb the normal routine of the house. For example, making a room in the attic is a good project because unless you are in desperate and immediate need of the room, it won't make much difference if you take a few weeks or a few months to finish the job. The same holds true of jobs like finishing off a basement, enclosing a porch, or even building a garage. You can putter along at your own rate of speed and not bother anyone. It's when you get involved in major projects in critical areas of a house such as the kitchen, bathroom, and living rooms that amateurs are likely to get into trouble, because there is pressure to get the job finished. This pressure can lead to sloppy workmanship, bad tempers on everyone's part, and a lot of frustration for all. You often end up by calling in the first pro you can find who will finish the job for you, regardless of what it might cost.

We do-it-yourselfers need a lot of time. It's safe to assume that any job will take about two or three times as long as you figure it should. Some jobs take especially long if only one person does the work. Our theory is that if you have two people on a job, it doesn't make the job go twice as fast—it makes it go three or four times as fast. For example, if there are two people, it's a relatively easy job to get a 4-foot by 8-foot sheet of wallboard into place, position it just right, and then nail it to the framework, but if there is just one person on the job, this little operation can take four or more times as long. Just having another person to hold the end of a piece of lumber while you measure it for cutting or nailing is a tremendous time-saver as well as a morale booster. We have a high school boy who comes over every Saturday or Sunday to do various chores, and we hold off on a lot of projects until he arrives because we have found that while we can do them alone, it's much easier and faster if Mike is there to lend a hand.

And there are certain jobs that are literally impossible for one person to handle alone. It's going to take at least two people to set even a lightweight sliding glass door in place, fit roof rafters into place for an addition or a garage, or build a retaining wall out of railroad ties. And it takes a whole bundle of friends or neighbors to help you fit the liner into an aboveground swimming pool.

Physical strength and stamina are also factors in how long it takes to complete a job. We know people who can come home at night, grab a light supper, and work four or five hours on a project and do good work. There are others who can work only an hour or so before they are so tired that they have to stop. If you have a lot of muscle, you can toss up masonry blocks all day Saturday and not feel any strain, but if you are the relaxed-muscle type, a few hours of this work will send you right back to the sofa or hammock—or the bed board.

Another factor that will determine how long a job takes, or if you can do it at all, is whether you have the right tools and know how to use them properly. For example, if you are going to do any sort of cabinetwork—make kitchen cabinets, built-ins, and the like—it's essential to have either a radial saw or a tilting arbor table saw. Aside from the fact that doing cabinetwork with hand tools will take almost forever, it also requires far more skill than most of us have. A table saw makes the job go much faster, and you can turn out good work with less skill than you'll need if you use hand tools. First, however, you must master this power equipment before you can expect good results. And it takes time to acquire the necessary skills. You read some of the advertising copy for power saws, and it sounds as if having one will make you a master cabinetmaker overnight. That's hogwash. It takes a lot of practice and a lot of wood before you can turn out first-class work.

You will also waste a lot of time if you don't have all the specialized tools you need to complete the work. You may get started on installing a kitchen exhaust fan on a Saturday, and by Sunday you discover that what you need to finish the ductwork is a pair of tin snips. It may not be until the following Saturday that you can take the time to buy a pair or find someone who has a pair that you can borrow. We have a pretty fair set of woodworking tools, but when we get into areas like plumbing or wiring, we usually find that at some point we don't have the right tool to finish the job. Then we either make a mess of things trying to do the job with the wrong tool or let it remain unfinished until we decide whether to rent or buy the tool that's right.

## Planning the Job

A big reason that a lot of do-it-yourself projects take forever and often turn out poorly is that few of us take the time or trouble to draw up detailed plans before we start. This means that we waste a lot of time trying to figure out how to get out of the spot we've worked ourselves into or, even worse, having to undo the completed work because it did not get off to a proper start. It's even more important to have a complete and detailed plan on a project that you are going to do yourself than to present a blueprint to a professional. Skilled and experienced professionals, whether they are carpenters, masons, plumbers, painters, or electricians, are like good chess players: they anticipate their moves so that when they start, they know fairly well where they are going to end up. They don't necessarily need a drawing to tell them—they just know. We amateurs don't have the experience to work in this fashion. Maybe we don't need a plan to keep us from painting ourselves into the corner of a room when we paint the floor, but we certainly do need a plan on any construction job. We don't want to start paneling a room and find when we get to the door frame that we have a gap of about ¾ inch between the paneling and the frame.

Often a contractor who has been called in to salvage a do-it-yourself project will tell us that one of the main reasons for the trouble was that the job was never planned; like Topsy, it just grew as it went along.

## Which Jobs to Do

We've handled a lot of do-it-yourself projects in our day, everything from building a house to extensive remodeling. We've tried just about every-thing—some jobs with success and some with not so much luck. Here, for what it's worth, is a list of some of the commoner projects you might consider doing yourself. We've graded them on how much skill we feel they require: moderate, high, and very high. And we've added comments that might help you to decide which jobs you feel you want to do and which ones you will let someone else handle for you.

1. *Interior Painting.* Moderate skill. A latex paint is easier to work with than an oil paint, and the job goes faster if you use a roller instead of a brush. Figure that it will take you two working days to do the average room if you don't have much preparation work such as fixing cracks and filling holes.

2. *Painting the Outside of a House.* Moderate skill. This job is more difficult than painting indoors, however, and it can be risky if you have to work from a high ladder. Allow yourself two weeks to paint the average-size one-story house. This should be enough time to prepare the surface and paint the siding, windows, shut-ters, doors, and trim. The best time to do this job is in late spring or early fall, when the weather is neither too hot nor too cold.

3. *Removing Exterior Paint.* Moderate skill. Allow plenty of time for this job, which can seem almost endless even if you use an electric paint scraper, about the best tool for the job. Working evenings and weekends, you will require a month or more to strip a one-story house.

4. *Hanging Wallpaper.* Moderate skill. You must know what you are doing on this job; so get from your dealer an instruction sheet or

booklet that tells you how to prepare the wall and lay out the job. It's a big help to have a second person on this job. Unless you are very good at this work, don't try to paper ceilings.

5. *Installing Floor Tile.* Moderate skill. However, this job is not so easy as it is often made to seem in advertisements. Get complete instructions that not only cover the actual application of the flooring but tell you how to prepare the floor over which the tile is to be applied.

6. *Hardwood Flooring.* Moderate to high skill. Hardwood floor tiles that are set in cement are easier to work with than strip flooring that must be nailed in place.

7. *Refinishing a Hardwood Floor.* High skill. It takes time to learn how to use the heavy-duty floor sanders you rent for stripping off the old finish and smoothing the wood. While you are learning, you can mess up the floor. Moreover, handling large sanders takes a lot of muscle.

8. *Installing Sheet Flooring.* High skill. It takes a lot more skill to install solid vinyl or linoleum than tile. It is especially difficult in a kitchen or bathroom, where the material must be fitted and cut around cabinets, fixtures, and pipes. You'll be better off using tile, but if you do use the sheet material, have a helper.

9. *Plastic Brick or Stone Wall Coverings.* Moderate skill. One person can handle this job alone, and if you have good instructions, it's not very difficult.

10. *Ceramic Tile.* High skill. Tile that comes in sheets with a special backing and can be installed with a special adhesive is easier to use than individual tile, but this is tricky work, and it will take a lot of time and patience to do a good job.

11. *Prefinished Plywood Paneling.* High skill. You may have to spend a good many hours getting the wall in condition for the application of this material. And you'd be wise not to try to do the actual installation alone.

12. *Insulating.* Moderate skill. It's easy enough to insulate an attic floor with batts, blankets, or loose fill if there is no flooring over the joists. If there is and if you don't want the insulation material to blow into the floor, the floor boards will have to be ripped up, and this can take a couple of days of hard work. If you are using

blanket insulation between roof rafters or on the underside of a floor, have someone around to help.

13. *Plastering.* Very high skill. This job looks easy when you see it being done by a pro, but it isn't. Don't try it. Use gypsum wallboard, which does just as good a job and is a lot easier to install.

14. *Installing Gypsum Wallboard.* High to very high skill. Applying wallboard to a wall frame is not very difficult, but getting it on a ceiling is. Have someone to help you get the boards in place and nailed down. Once this has been done, you can handle the taping and cementing yourself.

15. *Removing a Non-load-bearing Partition.* Moderate skill. This can be a very messy job, especially if the covering is plaster on lath. Be prepared for a lot of mess and dust. Wear a mask and goggles to keep dust and dirt out of your eyes, nose, and mouth. And go slow because you never know what may be inside the wall: wiring, plumbing, etc. Take the wall covering off both sides first, and then take the framing down piece by piece. It's nice to have help on this job.

16. *Removing a Load-bearing Partition.* Very high skill. You must provide support while you are taking down the wall and eventually replace the support with a heavy wood or steel girder. Don't try to tackle this job yourself unless you have had a good carpenter or contractor explain exactly what must be done.

17. *Framing an Interior Partition.* High skill. Not only do you need to know what you are doing here, but you had better have some help.

18. *Hanging a Door.* High to very high skill. Using a ready-hung door is easier than doing a job in which you must first build a frame and then get the door to fit and hang properly, but it still is not easy. And you'll probably spend the best part of a day getting a ready-hung door finished. Have a helper on this job.

19. *Installing an Outside Door.* Very high skill. This job is hard even in new construction, and it is very difficult if you want a door put in an existing wall. You must first make an opening through both the interior and the exterior wall covering, then frame the rough opening, and finally install the finished door frame and door. You really should have a carpenter on this job.

20. *Installing a Window.* Very high skill. This job presents the same situation as installing a door. You had better use a carpenter.

21. *Installing an Attic Skylight.* High skill. The job is not as hard as installing a door or a window if you can reach the underside of the roof easily. Be sure to get a unit designed for do-it-yourself installation and accompanied by good instructions, and have a strong helper.

22. *Installing Subflooring.* Moderate skill. You can use tongue-and-groove boards on this job or ¾-inch plywood. The boards are easier if you are doing the job alone, but if you have a helper, plywood is your best bet.

23. *Framing an Attic Room.* High skill. You'll need a helper on this job, and don't try to rush it because it will take far longer than you have figured it should.

24. *An Attic Dormer.* Very high skill. This job must be done in a hurry unless you live where it never rains or snows. It's a complicated project, and you'd be wise to leave it to a contractor or get a carpenter to help you with it.

25. *Installing Ready-made Kitchen Cabinets.* High skill. Have a helper on this job, and don't plan to use the kitchen the same day that you start putting in the cabinets.

26. *Building Kitchen Cabinets.* Very high skill. Don't attempt this job unless you've had a lot of experience doing cabinetwork.

27. *Installing a Kitchen Exhaust Fan.* Very high skill. This is one of the jobs that is more complex than it sounds. You must make a hole through the wall, get wiring to the fan, and install the ductwork. If you are good, it will take a day's work to do the job.

28. *Installing Recessed Lighting Fixtures.* Very high skill. In an existing house this can be a miserable job because it involves cutting holes in the ceiling, getting the wiring to the holes, and then hanging the fixtures. In new construction it's a lot easier. We recently gave three "high-hat" recessed light fixtures to the Lions Club's auction rather than try to put the fool things in ourselves.

29. *Reroofing.* High to very high skill. This is a practicable do-it-yourself project if you have a one-story house, the roof is not very steeply pitched, and you are putting asphalt shingles over a

single layer of asphalt or wood shingles. It's another matter if you have a two-story house, the roof is very steep, or there already are two layers of roofing that must be ripped off. We'd call in a roofer to deal with such a complex job.

30. *Installing Gutters and Downspouts.* High skill. Even if you use lightweight aluminum or vinyl gutters, you'll need a helper and a couple of good ladders. You'll also need complete instructions because while this job may look easy and sound easy, it's not easy if you do it right. And on a two-story house the job is very tricky.

31. *Installing Exterior Siding.* Very high skill. You must know what you are doing if you use vinyl or aluminum siding, for if the work is not done right, the siding will buckle and bulge. Wood clapboard is easier to handle, but you'll need a helper. The best siding for the amateur is wood shingles.

32. *Masonry Fireplace.* Very high skill. Even if you use a metal factory-built unit which will be enclosed in brick or stone, the job is tricky and takes a great deal of time. This job might be all right to tackle in a vacation cabin, but otherwise leave it to a professional.

33. *Prefab Fireplace and Stoves.* Moderate to high skill. Because these units don't require a foundation or masonry and can be used with a metal prefab chimney, you can install them yourself. Be sure to have complete instructions and a helper, and figure on two full days' worth of hard work.

34. *Laying Bricks.* High skill. Building a walk or terrace of brick set on a bed of sand is easy, but laying up a wall with mortar so that it will look right takes skill and patience. Get some practice with brick before you build anything where appearance is going to count.

35. *Laying Masonry Blocks.* Moderate skill. Blocks are easier to work with than bricks, but they are heavy, and you need muscle to toss them up on a high wall.

36. *Laying Stone.* Very high skill. Stones are much more difficult to lay up properly than bricks and far more difficult than masonry blocks. It's very slow work, and you'll need a lot of stone for even a modest-size wall.

37. *Pouring a Concrete Slab.* Moderate skill. The only practical way to handle this job is either to have premixed concrete delivered to the site or to rent a concrete mixer. In either case, you need at least one helper.

38. *Electric Wiring.* High skill. Most communities require you to use a licensed electrician to make any changes or additions to the house wiring. If you are able to do the job yourself, get a book on the subject. Sears, Roebuck has a good one.

39. *Installing Water Pipes.* High to very high skill. Be sure that local codes allow you to do this sort of work. Plastic pipe is much easier to work with than metal and doesn't require a lot of special tools, but it still takes a certain amount of know-how to handle pipe properly.

40. *Replacing Plumbing Fixtures.* Moderate to high skill. If it's not necessary to make changes in the plumbing, this job isn't very hard, but have a helper.

41. *Installing Exterior Window Shutters.* Moderate skill. If you have a one-story house and use plastic shutters, this is a relatively easy job. Wood shutters are heavier, and it helps to have two people on the job. For second-story windows you should have a helper.

42. *Installing Combination Storm Windows.* Moderate skill. The trick here is to make accurate measurements so that the units will fit properly. And it helps to have an assistant even on units for first-floor windows.

43. *Installing Weatherstripping.* Moderate skill. Even if you use the adhesive-back foam type of weatherstripping, this job takes a lot longer than you expect it to.

44. *Fences.* Moderate to high skill. Whether you are using metal chain link or wood, you'll need a helper on this job.

45. *Aboveground Swimming Pools.* High to very high skill. Even little pools for kids are not easy to assemble, and installing big family-size units is a major project. You'll need at least one helper to get the framework set up and four or five good strong friends or neighbors to help you set the vinyl liner in place. And don't figure that you can start this job on a Saturday morning and have the pool ready for a dip that evening. It can take four or five days of solid work to get the pool set up.

46. *In-ground Pools with Vinyl Liners.* Very high skill. Once you've dug the excavation, you'll have a good many weeks of work ahead, and you'll need a strong helper every inch of the way.

47. *A Wood Deck.* High skill. You'll need a helper to install the foundations and get the framing in place. Applying the decking is the easiest part of the job. It can take a good part of your summer vacation to complete a fair-size deck.

48. *Installing Awnings.* Moderate skill. Aluminum and reinforced glass fiber units are not very hard to install, but you'll need help. Canvas types are considerably more tricky.

49. *Installing Overhead Garage Door.* High skill. You may have to put in some time adjusting the door opening to accommodate the door, and you'll need a couple of helpers to aid in setting the door in place.

50. *Automatic Overhead Garage Door Opener.* High skill. Get a model that is designed as a do-it-yourself project, and figure that with a helper it will kill a weekend before you have finished the job.

# 7. Improvements to the Interior Floor Plan

It is a dismal fact that a great many houses, even some new, expensive houses, are not particularly well planned. We've seen very expensive houses that were supposed to be well designed but contained basic flaws. Our favorite example is a house that was designed and built as a showcase for a leading manufacturer of building products. It was supposed to be the ideal house, but a woman who visited it when we did pointed out that if you wanted to take the garbage outdoors from the kitchen, you had to march across the living room. Then you had to walk outdoors clear around the house because there was no back door. And we've seen countless front-to-back split-level houses in the high-priced bracket in which one bathroom was set smack in the center of the second level and opened onto a balcony so that anyone going in or out of the bathroom, clothed or unclothed, was in full view of people in the living room on the lower level.

There is no doubt that making changes that involve partitions can create a good deal of mess and confusion. We lived in our house while we were reworking half the upstairs floor and can speak from experience. There is no nonmessy way to remove an existing partition of plaster and wood lath and build a new one of gypsum wallboard. But the end results generally justify what the job costs in money and confusion.

Many of us never get around to undertaking the major improvements that should be made to the interior layout of our houses. Sometimes it's not just that this sort of improvement, which usually involves changes in the inside partition walls, can be costly and create a good deal of mess and confusion while the work is in progress. Probably a big reason that we don't make changes to improve the floor plan and traffic pattern is that we get used to putting up with all the inconveniences.

The floor plan may be irritating, but out of sheer inertia we accept things as they are. We accept the fact that the work area of the kitchen is also the main traffic lane from one part of the house to the other. We accept the fact

79

that it is necessary to go through one bedroom to reach the bathroom or that the front door opens smack in the middle of the living room. We know that the floor plan is not good and doesn't really work. However, we usually are not conscious of all the shortcomings until we get around to selling the house. Then it is usually a potential buyer who, not too gently, begins to point out all the flaws and may even wonder in a loud voice how we have ever been able to put up with such a poor arrangement. And, of course, if there are enough serious flaws, the buyer won't buy the house.

If you have serious flaws in the layout of your house, correcting them will add to its value. Improvements of this type may add 15 percent or more to the value of your house. And improving the floor plan will make it easier to sell your house and at the same time make it more comfortable and convenient for you and your family.

## Bathrooms

The rule with bathrooms is that it should be possible to get to a bathroom from all areas of the house without having to go through a bedroom. The one exception is a house that has a master bath off a master bedroom and a second bathroom to serve the other bedrooms. But if there is just one bath and it can be reached only by going through a bedroom, you have a problem area. It would be worth taking space from the bedroom to create an entry hall with a door leading off it into the bathroom.

Having a lavatory or powder room opening directly into the living room or dining room is another poor arrangement. You may be able to change the location of the door to the lavatory so that it opens onto some other area or put up a partial partition or other form of room divider in front of the door so that the lavatory can be reached more or less inconspicuously and sound is somewhat deadened.

## Bedrooms

In many older houses you still find an arrangement that requires you to go through one bedroom to reach an adjacent one. For obvious reasons, this is a poor setup and one well worth correcting if the job is at all feasible. It is especially important to correct this fault if the house has only three bedrooms, the minimum number for the average family. Many buyers figure that if you have to go through one bedroom to reach another, the house is not truly a three-bedroom house but a two-bedroom house. If you have this sort of arrangement, it would be worth shaving a few feet off each bedroom to create a short hall to serve both rooms.

## Too Many Small Rooms

This is another problem you often encounter in older houses. There may be several small rooms—parlor, sitting room, study, dining room—but none large enough for today's needs. Here it often pays to remove a partition to make one large, comfortable room out of two small ones.

## Doors

A number of doors opening into one room is not a good arrangement. Each door reduces the amount of usable wall and floor space and restricts furniture arrangements. And a lot of doors produces a very confusing traffic flow through the room or rooms. You may wish to close one or more of the doors that are not essential.

One reason that you find so many doors in older houses is that they were necessary for heating. Before the days of good central heating, one had to depend on doors to allow heat from the parlor stove or gravity warm-air furnace to flow to the other areas of the house.

As you go through your house, you'll probably spot many areas where closing off or changing the location of a door or removing or changing the location of a partition will make the area more attractive and comfortable. Changes in doors are not particularly complicated, but before you become serious about changes in partitions, find out how practical it will be to make them. The type of partition you are dealing with holds the answer.

## Bearing and Nonbearing Partitions

There are two types of partitions in a house: bearing partitions provide support, whereas nonbearing partitions do not. All outside walls are bearing walls, for they support the roof and the floors. But there are also bearing partitions that provide support to the floor. Nonbearing partitions can be removed without harm to the house structure. Bearing partitions can also be removed, but some other means of support must be provided to carry the load. The general rule is to install a steel or wood girder to carry the load, but this can be a fairly large undertaking and will increase costs considerably. If possible, try to improve the interior of your house by removing or changing the location of nonbearing partitions and leave bearing ones alone.

There are several ways to tell if a partition is bearing or nonbearing. One is to get into the attic or attic crawl space and note in which direction the floor joists run. Load-bearing partitions always run at right angles to the floor joists, while nonbearing partitions often run in the same direction as the

Three "before" views (above) of chopped-up interior space that was cleared out and restructured into an airy multipurpose family room, kitchen, office, and dining space (opposite, top). The plan shows which partitions were removed and where a steel girder and a new U-shaped kitchen were installed. The old kitchen was at the rear of the house overlooking a broad river, but an outbuilding and small windows obstructed the view. As shown, the view was opened up by clearing away a useless shed and installing double-pane insulating-glass sliding doors. A newly constructed wood deck further extends the living space and makes the view part of the whole experience. The slate-color laminated plastic used on counters in the kitchen was also used on the counter top in the office area. The mantel was made from leftover maple butcher block used in the counter around the range. The entire floor was covered with charcoal-color vinyl tile. [Photo: Hartford Courant]

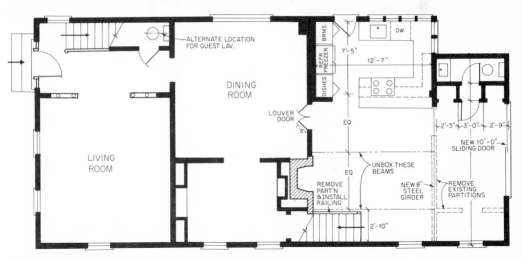

ALTERNATE LOCATION
FOR GUEST LAV.

DINING
ROOM

LIVING
ROOM

LOUVER
DOOR

1'-6"

REMOVE
PART'N
& INSTALL
RAILING

2'-10"

BRMS

REFR
FREEZER

DISHES

7'-5"

12'-7"

DW

EQ

EQ

UNBOX THESE
BEAMS

NEW 8"
STEEL
GIRDER

REMOVE
EXISTING
PARTITIONS

2'-3"  3'-0"  2'-9"

NEW 10'-0"
SLIDING DOOR

This compact laundry center can double as a sewing area while keeping all aids and accessories in neat storage cabinets and drawers. Such a center might be installed in the basement, on the first floor adjacent to the kitchen, or on the second, or bedroom, floor of a two-story house. The convenient second-floor location saves a lot of toting of soiled and clean clothes up and down stairs. [Photo: Westinghouse Electric Corporation]

floor or ceiling joists. Another way to get an idea of whether a partition is a bearing one is to see if it runs continuously (with the exception of door openings) through the center or near the center of the house, since bearing partitions are usually set to provide support at about the midpoint of the floor above them. Any competent carpenter or contractor can tell you which are bearing and which are nonbearing partitions after a quick inspection of your house.

Although it is generally easy to remove a nonbearing partition, things may get complicated if there is something inside the partition. There is almost sure to be electric wiring, but this is no great problem. Water pipes, sewer lines, and heating lines are another matter. You'll have to pay for reworking and repositioning the pipes, and this can be costly.

Friends of ours were remodeling an old house and doing a lot of the work themselves. They began to rip down a partition between the living room and the dining room to make one large room. To their dismay, they found, almost in the middle of the wall, the main sewer line, a cast-iron monstrosity. Their plumber told them that it would cost about $750 to remove and reposition the pipe; so they just encased it in wood, added a couple of similar columns to balance things, and let the job go at that.

In any event, before you begin to make plans on how to improve the interior arrangements of your house, find out which partitions are feasible to move or remove and which will make the job very expensive. Needless to say, there are seldom big problems connected with adding a partition, just with removing existing ones or changing their location. Incidentally, no problems are involved in cutting a new doorway through a bearing partition. Here the top of the door opening can be framed to provide the necessary support.

# 8. Attics

If you have a full attic, this is a natural and convenient place to turn to if you need more living space. And an attic can provide good living at about half of what it would cost to put on an addition with the same amount of space. A full attic can provide finished space for two comfortable bedrooms plus a bath, with enough unfinished space left over for storage. Many families have converted their attics into family rooms, complete with prefab fireplaces, or into recreation rooms for the children. And an attic makes a good quiet spot for a den, study, or home office.

The only kind of attic that is practical to use as a living area is the full attic and not the attic crawl space. In a full attic there will be sufficient headroom from the floor to the peak of the roof to create comfortable rooms. Crawl space may have only 6-foot headroom or less. It is possible, of course, to raise the roof to get the necessary headroom, and many homeowners have done just this. But raising the roof can be a very expensive operation, and it may spoil the architectural lines of the house. Before you spend money to raise a roof, it would be smart to check and see how much more money, if any, it will take to get the required added space by putting on an extension.

## Access to the Attic

If the attic space is to serve as good living space, you need good access to it. You should have an honest-to-goodness flight of stairs. The folding stairs so often used for unfinished attics are not really suitable for attic rooms. They may be fine if the attic is to be used only as a recreation area for the children, but they are not satisfactory for adults. And if it is feasible, the attic stairs should be reached without having to go through a bedroom.

## Utilization of Space

When you start to plan your attic room, you must keep in mind that not all the space is usable. The ceiling of finished attic rooms should be at least 2 feet below the peak of the roof. This space is necessary to provide adequate ventilation for the area between the ceiling and the underside of the roof. If the roof has a very steep pitch, there may not be much actual ceiling in the room. Instead, there will be long, sloping walls separated at the top by a short, flat ceiling. Another way to handle this problem is to leave the ceiling open right to the peak. You would leave the supporting rafters exposed, insulating between them and then covering the insulation with gypsum board. You still must ventilate the space on the cold side of the insulation to prevent condensation, but this can be done with a ridge vent or with vents along the eaves. Leaving the rafters exposed makes a very attractive room, more contemporary-looking than the narrow-ceiling look.

Whichever way you treat the ceiling, you still won't have headroom out to the eaves. The general rule is to come in from the eaves to a point where a 4-foot-high knee wall running the length of the room on both sides can be erected. This space can be used for storage either by building cabinet doors into the walls at convenient intervals or by building in drawers to take the place of chests of drawers and other furniture.

If you are going to use the space for two bedrooms, these should be arranged so that they can be reached separately from a landing off the stairs. This means some wasted space. If you plan to install a bathroom, that may well be the governing factor on how to utilize the space. Your best bet, as far as costs go, is to put the attic bathroom directly over the bath or kitchen below. This arrangement cuts installation costs to a minimum.


## Dormers

A fine way to get more headroom and additional floor space in the attic and at the same time obtain natural light and ventilation is to install a shed dormer. A shed dormer is a continuous dormer that can, if you want, run the entire length of the attic. It can increase the amount of usable space by one-third or even more. You can have windows running almost the entire length of a shed dormer or install only the windows needed to provide cross ventilation and light to one or more of the attic rooms. Needless to say, the more windows you use, the more the dormer is going to cost.

Installing a dormer is a roof-raising operation. It will make a decided change in the exterior appearance of the house. And the change may not

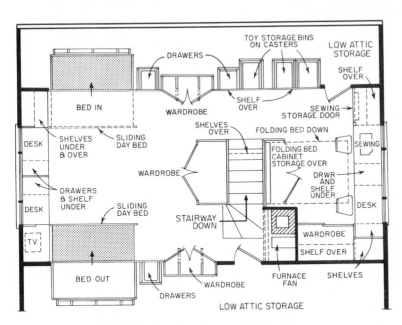

(top) Snug study, play, and sleeping quarters for two children was created out of a typical unfinished attic. The desks were built of softwood plywood, as were the storage units, shelves, and drawers, which utilize space under the roof eaves. The roof was insulated with mineral wool, then covered with ⅜-inch plywood. Picture windows were installed at each gable end. (bottom) Plan for the attic showing the location of the stairs and various built-ins. [American Plywood Association]

always be for the better. For this reason, it's always best if a shed dormer can be placed at the rear rather than at the front of the house.

Although putting in a dormer is a major project, it can often be done quickly and with a minimum of fuss. And if the dormer roof is to have sufficient pitch, it's not even necessary to remove the existing roofing and replace it over the dormer. The way many contractors install a dormer is first to prefabricate all the necessary new framing right on the floor of the attic. Next, the roof rafters are cut and sometimes hinged at the top so that the entire section of roof can be jacked up and the prefab framing panels set in place. A good contractor can handle the entire operation in one day so that by the time the crew quits, the dormer is in place and the roof and sidewalls are weathertight.

If you don't want to install a shed dormer, you can install individual dormer windows. These won't supply the added headroom and floor space that a shed dormer will, but they do provide natural light and ventilation. And as they do not make the drastic change in the house that a shed dormer does, they can be used on either the front or the rear of the house and sometimes on both sides.

## Windows and Skylights

The average attic generally has two small windows, one at each end. These seldom provide enough natural light and ventilation. Even if you install a shed dormer, you'll want to increase the size of the attic windows to provide better light and ventilation. And if you are not going to put in a dormer, it's absolutely essential to have larger windows.

But even two good-size windows at each end of the attic won't give you good ventilation, especially if the attic is to be made into two rooms or a single room is to be constructed at one end. Even if the attic is well insulated, it tends to be warm and stuffy in hot weather; so cross ventilation is essential for any living area. If you don't want to add a dormer, you may want to consider installing a "blister" type of ventilating skylight, which can be installed for around $300, as opposed to a $2,000 dormer. One or more skylights that are set in the roof and are opened with a crank can provide good ventilation and light.

## Insulation

If the attic rooms are to be comfortable in summer as well as comfortable and fuel-conserving in winter, the walls and ceilings must be insulated. The chances are that there already is insulation in the attic floor. That insulation will not be of any use for the attic rooms, but you might as well leave it there.

Minimum windows in the attic (left) were enlarged to create a cozy room for a child (right). The rafters were completely closed in, and the roof was insulated. The wood windows are encased in vinyl and glazed with insulating glass. [Andersen Corp.]

It won't do any harm and may even act as a sound barrier and so help reduce the impact of sounds made in the attic that come through the ceiling of the rooms below. Some homeowners have removed the insulation from the floor because they believed that this would allow heat from the rooms below to flow up and heat the attic. If you depend on the amount of heat that can seep up through the floor to heat your attic rooms in winter, they are going to be mighty cold rooms.

You still must insulate the attic rooms, and if you live in the colder regions such as the Northeast or upper Midwest, you should have about 9 inches of mineral wool or rigid foam insulation of equal value.

The entire attic room must be enclosed by insulation. The standard method of insulating an attic room is to run the insulation between the studding of the knee walls, then between the rafters, across the ceiling joists, and down the other side. Blanket insulation is the type most frequently used, but if you wish to leave part of the roof rafters exposed, foam boards can be used, for they are not as thick as mineral wool blankets.

Make absolutely certain that there is adequate venting on the cold side of the insulation. The specification sheets that come with good-quality insulation usually state how many inches of vent you need for a certain number of square feet of space.

Unused attic space became an attractive sitting room when the walls were insulated and a finished floor and carpeting were added. The fireplace hood and matching wainscoting were fashioned from warm-color wood paneling. The roof rafters were stained to match. [Georgia-Pacific]

## Heat

You should not depend on the heat that might flow through the attic floor or up the stairs to heat attic rooms. Even installing a floor register in an attic room so that heat in the rooms below can flow into the attic is not particularly effective. It also means that sounds in the attic will travel through the register to the rooms below and vice versa.

If your house heating system has the capacity, it may be possible to run ducts or pipes into the attic, but this can be an expensive solution. In most cases you are better off to use some form of electric heat.

## Attic Floors

One of the major complaints about attic rooms is that footsteps are quickly transmitted to the rooms below. Even if there is insulation between the

Walls of white pine paneling follow the roof slope in this attic remodeling. The framing members were stained dark to make an interesting contrast. An attic finished in this fashion makes a handsome, dry, and less dusty storage area. If insulation and heat are added at the same time or at a future date, the space can be used as living quarters at short notice. [*Georgia-Pacific*]

ceiling joists of the attic, sound still will come down. And don't let anyone try to convince you that if the ceilings of the rooms under the attic are covered with acoustical tile, it's going to help. It won't. Acoustical tile will absorb some of the sound made in the room where it is used, but it will not stop the passage of sound from an overhead room.

The very best way to keep attic sounds from coming to the rooms below is to use wall-to-wall carpeting on the attic floor. Carpeting is the ideal attic flooring. The next best thing is the cushion type of floor tile. The very worst kind of flooring to use is hardwood, which creates a lot of noise because it is so dense. Another drawback to hardwood or even softwood is that it takes a lot of nailing, which can cause cracks in the ceiling below.

If there is no rough flooring in the attic, ½-inch sheets of plywood can be laid down. These will serve as a base for either carpeting or tile.

## Walls and Ceilings

Gypsum wallboard makes a good material for attic walls and ceiling as it is inexpensive, can be papered or painted, and has wide acceptance. But there are other materials that can do very nicely in this location. If you are making the attic into a family room or study, you might consider using wood paneling, either rustic or of another type.

## Fire Exit

If an attic is going to be used as a sleeping area, there should be exit from the attic rooms besides a single flight of stairs. Some building codes require you to provide a suitable fire exit, but even if they don't, you should do so. And it's especially important if the attic rooms are to be used by children.

The best fire exit is a second flight of stairs. The most practical and least expensive way to add stairs is to put them on the outside of the house. A flight of outside stairs not only makes a good fire exit but enables one to go to and from the attic rooms without passing through the house.

If you don't want to pay for a flight of stairs, buy a good-quality chain fire escape ladder. This should be stored near an attic window large enough to allow someone to climb out. And it's important that anyone sleeping in the attic be familiar with the use of the ladder.

# 9. Basements

A basement can furnish you with a lot of extra living space for far less than it would cost to put on an addition or even to finish off an attic if the attic needed a shed dormer to provide adequate space. One important point to keep in mind when you are sizing up a basement for possible living space, however, is that while it can provide low-cost space, the space is not always the best kind for all purposes or for all people. There are people, including ourselves, who just don't like spending much time underground no matter what the surroundings.

Now this doesn't mean that basement space can't serve a lot of useful purposes. It can be useful, very much so. For one thing, the basement is usually the only area in a house with enough floor space to handle games such as table tennis, billiards, and darts. It's probably the best place for the rock or jazz group, and it can be a great spot for a workshop, hobby area, or indoor play area for the kids. It can also be an appropriate location for a den, study, or home office, for it can offer a lot of peace and quiet. And it's the ideal place to build in a lot of storage space, which is an asset for any house.

But those expensive, tricked-up basement rumpus rooms, complete with wood paneling, a custom-designed floor, and a built-in bar with sink, that were so popular a few decades ago are no longer in great demand. Today there has been a change in attitudes; people prefer their living space, family rooms, for example, above ground, where they can have fresh air, sunshine, and a view. It could be that such elaborate basement rooms lost their appeal at about the time that most of us stopped building or thinking of building home bomb shelters and decided to take our chances above ground. Or maybe expensive basement rooms just went out of style like the sleeping porches and breakfast nooks that were so popular a few decades before.

Moreover, the average basement is generally not suitable for bedrooms. As a matter of fact, some building codes prohibit using a basement for sleeping

A depressing sight indeed is this "before" picture of a basement laundry area (top left). Remodeling was accomplished by the use of plastic-finished hardboard for the ceiling, main walls, and door and perforated hardboard for the end walls. Inadequate wiring was replaced, and a new resilient floor was installed in the laundry area (top right) and hobby-sewing room (left). The remodeling was relatively inexpensive because no changes were made in the window placement. Lighting is concealed in the suspended ceiling. [*Marlite Paneling*]

purposes, and others require that if you do so, there must be enough windows to provide natural ventilation, that there be some means of exit from the sleeping area other than the one flight of stairs to the floor above, and that fire-resistant materials be used throughout.

There is one type of basement that does offer good possibilities for general use. When a house is built on an incline, part of the basement, usually the rear, is at ground level, You can really go to town with this setup if you are willing to spend the money. What you can do is open up the wall with sliding glass doors or a window wall and build any kind of room that pleases your fancy or fills a need: bedroom, family room, kitchen–dining room, home office with a separate entrance. Such improvements are a definite plus for any house.

## Wet and Damp Basements

Some basements, of course, are not worth fixing up or can't be fixed up unless you are prepared to spend a lot of money that you will probably never get back. At the top of the list are leaky basements, in which groundwater seeps through walls, floor, or the seam where walls and floor meet.

There are many reasons for a wet basement and an equal number of ways to correct the problem. If you are lucky, the water running into your basement after a heavy rain may be coming from the downspots. If this is the case, all you have to do is to put down some drainpipe and connect it to the end of the downspout so it will carry the water 8 or 10 feet away from the house. Or the problem may be the fact that the ground around the basement walls was not properly graded so that water collects in low spots and eventually gets into the basement. Grading the earth around the house so that it slopes gently away from the basement walls for a distance of 8 feet or so may do the trick.

When water flows into the basement through the seams between the walls and floor, the standard treatment is to pack these seams with a waterproofing compound. The old-fashioned cure is to cut out the cracks with a cold chisel and then fill with hot tar, but new products on the market are equally effective and don't require enlarging the crack or seam. You can get these products at most hardware stores.

When water seeps through the walls, you have a major problem. There are many brands of waterproofing compounds that can be applied to the inside surface of the walls. Sometimes they work, and sometimes they don't. Success depends not only on how well the waterproofing compounds are applied but also on the amount of hydrostatic pressure.

The most effective way to waterproof walls is from the outside. It's also the most expensive or takes the greatest amount of work. To waterproof from the outside it is first necessary to dig a trench all around the house right down to the footings that support the basement walls. This can mean a trench 8 or 10 feet deep and wide enough so that a man can get into it and work on the basement walls. After the trench has been dug, the exposed walls must be cleaned and any cracks patched. Then a membrane waterproofing material is applied to the walls. Finally, drainpipes are set at the base of the trench along the footings to carry any water that might collect here away from the house. This operation can cost several thousand dollars, and if it isn't done right, you've tossed the money away. If you are going to hire someone to do this kind of work, get the best outfit in your area. And don't try to do it yourself unless you are prepared for a lot of work and are sure that you can do a first-class job.

Many homeowners don't want to bother to waterproof their basements or wish to go to the expense. Instead, they rely on a sump pump to remove any water that gets into the basement. Depending on a sump pump to keep a basement from turning into a swimming pool when there are heavy rains is fine if you don't plan to invest a lot of money in fixing up the basement. But if you are going to want to put down flooring, finished walls, and so on, it is not a good solution. We know of plenty of families that have had expensive basement game rooms and used a sump pump to keep them dry; then one day when it was raining cats and dogs, the power went off and so did the sump pump, and all their expensive furnishings and materials were ruined by water.

Some basements don't leak but are uncomfortably damp. Dampness is not a very serious condition and can usually be corrected without much difficulty or expense.

Basements in newly constructed houses, especially if the walls are made of poured concrete, are often damp because of the large amounts of water used in mixing the concrete. After several months, the water in the walls will evaporate, and the basement will become dry. Evaporation of the water is speeded if the heating system in the basement is running.

In other cases, the dampness is due to condensation of water vapor in the air as it strikes the cold masonry walls and floor. This can often be corrected by improving ventilation in the basement. It can also be corrected by insulating these surfaces so that the warm, moist air cannot come in direct contact with the cold masonry; this can be done when the wall and ceiling materials for the finished basement room are installed. Electrically operated dehumidifiers can be used to remove excessive moisture from a small basement area, but you should not count on them to dry out an entire basement.

## Structural Considerations

Some basements are designed and built so that all or at least a good portion of the total area can be readily and economically converted into usable living space. These basements have a good number of operable windows to provide natural light and ventilation. There is also direct access to the outdoors. All the mechanical equipment—heater, hot-water heater, electrical service—is grouped in one small area. There are a minimum number of vertical posts that support the floor girder, and these are placed to provide a maximum amount of clear floor space. The ceiling is clear of pipes, ducts, and so forth, so that a finished ceiling can be installed easily. These are the sort of basements you see pictured in magazines and newspapers with before-and-after photographs showing how a family converted its basement into a delightful game room with a hammer and saw for just a few hundred dollars.

There are other basements that don't lend themselves readily to fixing up. We have such a basement in our house. It's nice and dry, and it opens onto a backyard terrace; so it would be ideal to make into a family room. But the problem is that it is so cluttered with water pipes, sewer lines, electrical cable, posts, and so on that there just isn't enough headroom or clear floor space to do much with. And the cost of repositioning all those pipes and cables and reworking the floor framing to eliminate a few of the posts would cost more money than the results would justify. So we shall continue to use the basement as we have in the past, for a workshop and storage area.

## Low-Cost Basement Improvements

The least expensive way to improve a basement is with paint, and this is something you can probably do yourself. It won't cost much more than $100 for all the paint you'll need.

Painting is a very good approach if you just want to make the basement into an attractive play area for the children, a place for table tennis, billiards, or other games, or even for informal living. And a clean, bright, and tidy basement with a lot of obviously usable empty space can add quite a bit of value to your house, for it represents all sorts of potential uses to a buyer. In fact, conceivably it can be a lot more valuable to a buyer in an unfinished state than if you had finished it, for it represents all sorts of wonderful possibilities.

We know of one family that "finished" a basement of the type you find in a typical builder's house with paint, and the result was really fine. The owners painted everything: walls, floor, ceiling joists and the underside of the flooring, posts, heating ducts, water and sewer lines, and even the smoke

Random-width hardboard paneling in a wormy-chestnut grain covers the walls and suspended ceiling in this basement home office (center, bottom), which was once an old coal bin (top). The generous use of lights concealed in the ceiling compensates for the lack of windows. The paneling, which comes in 16-inch by 8-foot planks, is $\frac{1}{4}$ inch thick and so could also be used for the storage cabinets. [Marlite Paneling]

pipe from the heater to the chimney. They used a lot of bright colors for items like the ducts and pipes.

You might want to consider doing something like this yourself, but be sure you use the right kinds of paint. Most latex house paints are suitable for the basement walls. On the floor you need a concrete floor enamel. On metal you need a metal paint, and if the metal becomes warm, you need a heat-resistant paint.

## Building a Basement Room

If you are going to create a separate room in the basement, the first thing to do is to pick the location. The best spot, insofar as keeping costs down is concerned, is one end of the basement. If you put the room there, three of the basement walls will serve as walls of the room and you will have to build only one partition. If you put the room in a corner, you'll have to add two partitions, and if you build your room out from one wall, you'll need three partitions. That's going to run up costs.

You will also want to place your room where it will be close to the basement stairs and where there are existing windows and possibly a second flight of stairs leading to the outdoors. It is not difficult or expensive to install or enlarge basement windows if the walls are made of masonry block, but it is costly if the walls are made of poured concrete. And if you need to install a flight of stairs from the room to the outside and want to include an areaway to provide natural light, the cost will be around $800.

Don't make the mistake that a lot of homeowners have made and build the room larger than necessary. You may have a lot of space down there in the basement, and you may not be paying much per square foot to turn it into a room, but you are still going to pay for every square foot of finished space. Also remember that a huge barn of a game or recreation room is not particularly inviting unless it is full of people, and it also will add to housekeeping chores.

## Basement Masonry Walls

If you live in a moderately mild climate or if your basement masonry walls never become damp because of condensation, you can leave them alone and just apply a coat of paint. But the general rule for basement rooms is to cover the masonry with some form of wall material such as gypsum wallboard, hardboard, or plywood. This gives the room a finished appearance and also reduces the noise level somewhat.

The commonest method of securing wall material to the masonry is first to

When remodeling basements or garages for living space, one problem is what to do with cold concrete slab floors. One solution, shown here, is to use a plywood underlayment over rigid foam plastic board (Styrofoam in this installation). Carpeting or tile may then be applied over the plywood underlayment. [*American Plywood Association*]

apply 1- by 2-inch or 1- by 3-inch wood furring strips spaced 16 inches on center. These can be fastened to the masonry with masonry nails, studs, or special fasteners that are attached to the masonry with a special mastic cement. The wall material is then nailed to the wood furring strips. This method works well if water will never leak through the masonry wall. But if water does leak, it can ruin the wall material. If you are not certain how waterproof the walls are, play safe. What you do then is to build a standard partition wall set several inches from the masonry. It's going to cost a lot extra to build the wall, but at least if water comes in, it won't ruin the finished wall.

If you are troubled with a lot of condensation on the masonry walls or if you live where winters are cold, it's wise to insulate between the masonry wall and the finished wall, at least down to the frost line in cold areas. Insulation will eliminate the dampness and also will make the room more comfortable in cold weather. Rigid foam plastic is an excellent material to use for insulating over masonry walls because it can be fastened in place with a mastic. But ordinary mineral wool blankets or batts can be used by placing them between the furring strips.

We prefer gypsum wallboard as a wall covering because it is inexpensive

This basement was converted attractively into a multipurpose entertainment, hobby, and sewing center. The sliding door and walls are made of hardboard paneling with the look of matched barn siding. The plumbing and sewer pipes are boxed in with clear pine. Plenty of overhead lighting and light-color paneling and plastic finish on tables and cabinet doors keep the area bright and cheerful. [Masonite Corp.]

and can be either painted or papered. And if prospective buyers don't like your choice of paint colors or wallpaper patterns, they know that it's a simple and inexpensive matter to change things to suit their taste. This is not the case with prefinished plywood and similar materials with a built-in color or texture.

## Ceilings

One major complaint about many basement rooms is that sounds made in them can be heard all over the house. And most of the sound comes through the ceiling. Covering the basement ceiling with acoustical tile is only partially effective in reducing the transmission of sound, for although the tile does absorb some of the sound originating in the basement, it does not prevent sound from going into other areas of the house.

The best way to make the ceiling more resistant to the passage of sound is to use a suspended-ceiling system. A wood or metal framework is suspended from the ceiling joists with special nonconductive hangers. Insulation is applied between the joists, and the framework is then covered with two layers of gypsum wallboard. Finally, acoustical tile is applied over the wallboard. This is an expensive type of ceiling unless you do the work yourself, but it is effective in helping to keep sounds from the rooms above the basement.

In any event, don't let anyone tell you that tacking acoustical tile to the ceiling joists is going to keep sound out of the house. The tile makes an attractive ceiling, but it's not soundproof by any means. Incidentally, the more fabrics and soft materials you use in your basement room, the less of a problem you'll have with sounds and echoes.

## Floors

Most basement floors are covered with either paint or vinyl asbestos tile applied directly over the concrete. Both of these result in a good low-cost finished floor and are fine if the concrete slab is warm enough so that it is comfortable in cold weather and does not sweat in warm, humid weather. But if you must deal with cold or moisture, you may want to spend more money to make the floor really comfortable the year around. One way to do this is to install indoor-outdoor wall-to-wall carpeting. Another approach is to cover the concrete with sheets of rigid foam plastic and then to cover the plastic with plywood. The plywood can serve as a base for any type of flooring you wish.

## Lighting

Unless ample natural light comes into your basement room—and we have never seen a basement room that has ample natural light—you'll need a lot of lighting fixtures. Fluorescent lamps are popular for basement rooms because they use a good deal less electricity than incandescent lights and so can be left burning day and night at little cost. We don't happen to like the kind of light you get from these fixtures, but that's our problem.

## Heat

You want to give some advance thought to heating the basement room. Most basements are kept more or less warm just from the heat that escapes from the heater, stove pipe, and heating pipes and ducts that run across the basement ceiling. But if you close off a room from the rest of the basement, it probably won't get enough heat to make it comfortable in cold weather. If it is not practical to add a register or radiator to the basement room, install some type of electric heat.

**This built-in music center is located in the basement, but a similar one could be installed in almost any area of the house. Shelves and drawers are specially made to hold records and other sound and party needs.** [*Masonite Corp.*]

## Built-ins

If you are anxious to keep your costs down and want to get back some of your investment when you sell, resist the temptation to include a lot of expensive built-ins in your basement room. Simple shelves, closets, and even storage walls are fine, but when you get into specialized items such as bars, benches, entertainment centers for TV, stereo, and everything else but the family cat, watch out. They'll cost you plenty and probably won't return a nickel for every dollar you spend on them.

# 10.  Bathrooms

## Adding a Bathroom

Adding a bathroom to your house is an expensive improvement. It can cost from $2,000 to $3,000 to add a full bath to an existing house and around $1,500 to add a half bath, but either one can be a sound investment in both convenience and resale value. Any house with three bedrooms and only one bath is not up to current standards.

But be very careful not to sink too much money into a bathroom. And it's easy to put so much money into one that you'll never get much of it back when you sell. It is especially easy to go overboard on costs if you fall into the hands of certain bathroom specialists who will do their best to sell you the most lavish and expensive bath you can afford—or maybe one that you can't afford. Buying a bathroom is like buying a new car. You can get a good one for around $3,000, but you can also spend $10,000 or even more. And the $3,000 bath is going to work just as well as the $10,000 one.

A full bath needs a minimum of 5 feet 7 inches by 5 feet 8 inches of space and should be in a location convenient to one or more of the bedrooms. It may be possible to create space by partitioning off a section of a large bedroom or to take over a small unused bedroom. In some older houses there may even be a large closet or a landing at the head of the stairs that can be used.

A half bath or powder room needs about 3 feet 6 inches by 4 feet 5 inches. It may not be quite as desirable as a full bath, but if there isn't space for a full bath, it is certainly the second-best thing. And even if there are two full baths on the second floor, a half bath on the first floor makes a lot of sense.

Ideally, a first-floor half bath should be as close to the kitchen as possible. It should be convenient to the living area, but for the sake of privacy it should not open directly into the living or dining area. In older houses there may be a pantry or back porch off the kitchen that can be used for a half bath. In newer houses the utility-laundry room is often large enough to take two plumbing fixtures. And you can often fit a half bath under a flight of stairs. We did this in our house a short time back and are very happy with the results.

You no longer have to be concerned about locating any sort of bath on an outside wall with windows because windows are not essential for a bath. You can get along with a good exhaust fan, which costs a fraction of what it takes to put in a window.

## Major Cost Factors

The cost of adding a bath will depend to a great degree on its relationship to the existing drainage system of the house. It is not a big problem to bring the hot- and cold-water pipes to almost any spot in the house, for these are small-diameter pipes that can be fished up through the walls and even across finished ceilings. But the drain and sewer lines are another matter. These are large-diameter pipes, and the horizontal runs from the fixtures to the main sewer line must have a slight downward pitch so that the water can drain out. What's more, the drain lines for the new plumbing fixtures must be vented by a line that runs right up through the house and opens above the roof. It may be possible to connect the vent system of the new bath to the existing vent system, but if not, a new vent will have to be installed. This involves running a large-diameter pipe from the new bath to the roof.

If the new bath cannot be connected to the existing drainage system, a complete new drainage system will have to be installed for the bath. This can add a good many hundreds of dollars to the cost. When we installed the half bath under the stairs, we had to run a separate vent for it up through the house; this added around $150 to the cost. Most of this sum was for labor. As a general rule the best location for a new bath in an existing house is either next to or directly under or above an existing bath or kitchen. In these locations it's usually possible to connect the bath to the existing drainage system with a minimum of labor.

About the best way to begin a bathroom addition is first to pick out as many possible locations as you can find and then to call in a plumber and ask him which one, in his opinion, is the most practical. He should also be able to give you a rough idea of the cost. But be sure that the man you call in to inspect the job is an experienced plumber or a plumbing contractor and no one else. Only an experienced plumber really understands what is involved in adding a bathroom to an existing house. A salesman for a home improvement outfit has no idea of what it's all about, and even experienced

In many houses space under the stairs is almost made to order for a half bath – powder room (top). Here a wedge-shaped marble-top lavatory, probably made around the turn of the century, fits perfectly in a fairly narrow space (bottom). A standard-size toilet fits at the other end of the space, directly under stairs. Small lavatories and toilets are available from most manufacturers of plumbing fixtures.

general contractors will call in a plumber rather than rely on their own limited knowledge and experience in this area.

## Schedule of Work

Two elements are involved in creating a bathroom: plumbing and the work required to make the room. One involves the plumber, and the other the carpenter. Both must be coordinated if you want to avoid a lot of trouble and added costs. One case we ran across a few years ago involved a bath that was being added to a house by partitioning off a section of a downstairs bedroom. The carpenter went to work and framed the room but neglected to leave quite enough space along one wall for the bathtub. The plumber had the tub delivered, spent some time trying to fit it into the space, and finally called in the carpenter to rip down an entire wall and rebuild it to the correct dimensions. Needless to say, the homeowner paid for all this wasted labor.

If you are using a general contractor, the contractor will coordinate the work, but if you are doing the job on your own and just hiring a plumber or if you are hiring both a plumber and a carpenter, it's up to you to pull things together. Here's how to go about it.

Once you have decided on the location of the bathroom, get your plumber over and select the number and style of fixtures you will use. You can't even begin to draw up a finished plan for a bath until you know the size of each fixture and how much space it will need. When you have selected the fixtures, the plumber can give you the specifications for each one. These specifications will indicate the exact amount of space that each fixture must have. The plumber should also point out the best location for each fixture. These locations should be indicated on your plans or marked with chalk on the floor. Keep the specification sheets handy, for if you do, they can save you a lot of trouble.

Draw up a rough plan of the room and indicate on it the position of the fixtures, doors, windows, and so on. Now you can get the carpenter to frame the walls, or you may be doing this yourself. In any event, as soon as the walls are framed but before any wall or ceiling material has been installed, call in your plumber. This is the time when the plumber should do the roughing-in work, which involves bringing in the hot- and cold-water lines and the drain lines so that they can be connected to the various fixtures. If there is to be a tub, it can be installed at this time. Make sure that before the tub goes in place, the walls around it are insulated. If you don't insulate the space around the tub, you'll get a lot of racket through the house each time the tub is filled. Insulation is especially important if you are using a steel or plastic tub. And while the partition framing is exposed, you should have installed the electric wiring and outlets as well as the exhaust fan if you need one.

After the plumbing has been roughed in, the work of finishing the room can be resumed. Have the walls of the bath insulated, for this will help reduce sound transmission through them. For the same reason specify a solid rather than a hollow flush door. After the room has been completed, the plumber returns to connect the water closet and lavatory.

## Reducing Costs

You can find a lot of ways to save money and still come up with a quality bathroom. A good place to start cutting costs is the selection of the plumbing fixtures. There is a tremendous range in the prices of fixtures. The deluxe models may sell for $100 (or more) more than the standard models. And you will pay around $30 extra if you select a color rather than a white fixture.

You do, however, want to buy quality fixtures made by recognized manufacturers. People recognize brand-name products, which thus add value to your property. And brand-name products, in our opinion, are much better made than the off-brand stuff that you may get for a good deal less money. We have one bathroom in our house with off-brand fixtures put in by the previous owner, and if we had the money, we'd replace every one of the fixtures. The toilet bowl is poorly designed and soils easily, the enamel on the bottom of the tub is badly pitted so that it's impossible to get it really clean, and the lavatory is so shallow that you can hardly wash both hands in it at the same time. About the only good thing that can be said about these fixtures is that they are white and not some color that only the previous owner could have liked.

Don't let the plumber or general contractor select your plumbing fixtures, for they will generally choose the more expensive models. Ask to see the manufacturer's catalog, and go over it with the plumber. Have the plumber give you the price on each model and select the least expensive one that will do the job. By the way, many plumbers will push one particular brand of fixtures, but if you know of another brand that you'd rather have, they can get it for you.

## Water Closets

Be sure you select a closet with an elongated rather than a round bowl. Round-bowl toilets are the least expensive, but the bowl soils easily. The most expensive type of toilet is a unit with tank and bowl cast in one piece. Toilets of this type are very quiet when flushed and may be worth the added cost for a first-floor bath or powder room right off the living area. And many of them can't overflow, which is an advantage if you are using carpeting on the bathroom floor. It may also be wise to pay extra for a toilet with a venting system that removes odors from the bowl. This can be a good feature for a powder room.

## Bathtubs

Tubs can be made of enameled cast iron, enameled steel, or plastic. The cast-iron tub is probably the best, but it is the most expensive and weighs a lot. You may have to reinforce the floor of a second-floor bath to handle the load. The stainless-steel and plastic tubs are quite adequate and are relatively

A handsome bathroom for a busy couple was made from a long, narrow storage room. The tub, shower, and toilet are opposite a plastic laminate–topped vanity, which has generous storage space for bathroom necessities, cosmetics, and towels. Two oval lavatories are set into the vanity, which runs the entire length of wall, as does the space-enlarging mirror above it. Imported ceramic tile was used on the floor and windowsill. [*Alma McArdle*]

light. The one problem with them is that unless the area around the tub is insulated, you get quite a racket through the walls when the tub is being filled. Plastic tubs are available as complete units that include the tub and surrounding walls. These are very good because they eliminate the problem of leaks around the edge of the tub and walls and are also easy to clean. They generally can't be used when you install a bath in an existing house because there isn't enough room to get them into the space, but they are fine if you are putting on an addition that includes a full bathroom.

## Shower Stalls

It's worth putting in a shower stall if you don't have space for a bathtub or if it's going to cost more to put in a tub than a shower. On the other hand, if you are going to install a recessed tub, adding a stall shower is a luxury that you may wish to forgo.

The most expensive type of stall shower is made of ceramic tile. Showers of this type are custom-made on the job. But you can get a good-quality plastic stall shower that will do quite well and cost a lot less money.

## Lavatories

The best lavatories are made of vitreous china, but you can also get lavatories in enameled cast iron and steel. Lavatories are designed so that they can be hung on the wall, supported by legs, or set into a counter or vanity. The counter-top units are the least expensive, but you must add the cost of the counter or vanity, which can run into money.

Lavatories come in a wide range of styles and sizes. Naturally enough, the larger the unit, the more it's going to cost. You can get a good-quality lavatory that does a fine job in most bathrooms for under $100, but you can also pay $300 and more for a deluxe unit.

## Faucets, Drains, and Fittings

You'll find that the price quoted for a plumbing fixture does not include the faucets, drains, and other fittings, and these can cost a surprising amount of money. Standard fittings for a bathtub will run around $50, and if you want the deluxe stuff, you can spend more than twice this amount. Stick with good-quality fittings, but select the standard units rather than the deluxe.

## Worthwhile Extras

You might want to consider installing a second hot-water heater to serve the new bath. This makes a lot of sense if the bath is in an addition or at some distance from the existing hot-water heater. You may find that it will actually cost you less to put in a new hot-water heater than to run lines from the existing heater to the new bath. And you certainly will want another hot-water heater if the present one is just adequate for your present needs.

When we installed our downstairs powder room, we spent $15 to have a mixing valve installed in the supply line to the toilet flush tank. With this arrangement the water flowing into the tank is warm rather than ice-cold so that no moisture collects on the sides of the tank during warm, humid weather.

## Other Ways to Save on the Bathroom

First, forget about ceramic tile for walls and floors. Tile is going to cost around $3 a square foot. If you have a recessed bathtub, the walls around it can be covered with plastic or plastic-coated hardboard, which is very durable and a lot easier to keep clean than tile. For the rest of the bathroom walls use water-resistant gypsum wallboard. This can be painted or covered with a washable paper or wall fabric. The same material can be used for the ceiling. Sheet vinyl, linoleum, and indoor-outdoor carpeting all make satisfactory bathroom floors.

## Bathroom Improvements

Anyone paying $40,000 or more for a house today expects two bathrooms or at least a bath and a half bath. As the price of a house goes up, so do expectations. In the $45,000-and-up range, the norm is two to two and one-half baths. If you live in an older house and want to bring it up to current standards, you will probably have to add at least one bathroom or certainly a half bath. Even if you don't add a new bathroom, you will probably want to improve the one you already have. And even if you don't mind the bath as it is, you'll want to improve it before you put the house on the market.

We are a very bathroom-conscious nation. Next to the kitchen, the bathroom is the first spot that a potential buyer, especially a woman buyer, will want to inspect. If the bathroom looks clean and bright, the buyer will give the house a good mark, but if it's gray and dingy with beat-up walls, cracked linoleum on the floor, and fixtures stained with rust, expect a very low mark on your house.

There are two ways to go about improving a bath. One is to rip out everything—fixtures, flooring, walls, ceilings, windows—and begin afresh. This will cost a lot of money. It may cost more than it will to add a bathroom because you've got to pay to take out all the old material before you can begin to rebuild. The other approach is to replace only those items that are beyond hope and to give what you have a face-lift.

## Face-Lifting the Bathroom

The first rule is to leave the existing fixtures unless they are cracked or the enamel coating has become chipped or badly scratched. Rust stains and mineral deposits on the surfaces of fixtures can generally be removed with special cleaners sold at hardware and plumbing supply stores.

If faucets and other fittings are worn, badly scarred, or of low quality, replace them with good-quality but standard fittings. Get a new showerhead and, by all means, a new toilet seat.

If there is a recessed tub without a shower, get a price from your plumber on adding a shower. Showers are more popular today than tub baths because they take less time and require less hot water than tub baths.

## Replacing Fixtures

If it is necessary to replace any of the fixtures, don't change the location if you can avoid it. It may take a plumber only an hour or so to connect a new lavatory or toilet if it is put in the same spot as the old one, and there won't be much of a charge for materials. But if you move the location, even just a few inches, making the necessary connections can become a major project, and that means a lot of added expense.

Always try to avoid having to replace a tub, because this is a big project, if for no other reason than the fact that you can't get a large tub through the standard-size bathroom door without removing the door frame. Sometimes old tubs have to be chopped up in order to remove them. If you happen to have one of those deep old-fashioned tubs on legs, you can either paint the outside with a coat of epoxy paint or surround it with a wooden frame and make the top of the frame water tight with ceramic tile or laminated plastic. A lot of young families love old-fashioned tubs and like them just as they are without added touches to make them look more efficient.

If you have to replace the bathtub, it will cost you around $200, plus the expense of getting rid of the old one. A new white lavatory of standard quality will cost you around $100, while a flush toilet will be around $150. You will pay these prices under more or less ideal conditions, which means that the plumber won't have to take more than a hour or so to disconnect the old fixture and connect the new one. If you decide to put the new fixtures in a different location, find out how much extra it will cost before you give the go-ahead.

Unless you are a do-it-yourselfer, you are better off to install the standard wall-hung lavatory because the drop-in type requires a built-in cabinet with a counter top, and this can further dent your budget. If you really need counter space, you can do as many ingenious people have done and shop around secondhand stores or auctions for an old-fashioned buffet or similar piece of furniture. Cut the legs of the buffet to the proper height, cut out an opening for the basin, add a similarly cut piece of laminated plastic for a counter top, and drop in the basin. After all the plumbing work has been completed, you can either paint the buffet or wallpaper it. The result, if well done, can be very handsome. If carelessly done, it can look pretty awful, so don't attempt the job unless you are fairly handy. An old-fashioned mirror or mirrored picture frame (also from the secondhand store) can be painted to match and hung above the lavatory in place of a run-of-the-mill medicine cabinet. Bathroom supplies and medicines can be stored in the cabinet or drawers below.

## Electric Wiring

You'll probably want to do something to improve the electric wiring because much of the wiring in older bathrooms, and in some that are not so old, is unsafe as well as inadequate. A bathroom is an ideal spot to receive a serious electric shock because of the presence of water and plumbing fixtures. Moist skin is an excellent conductor of electricity, while a plumbing fixture or a wet or damp floor provides a good path to the ground. If you happen to touch a "hot" wire or a faulty appliance with an open circuit in it while your hands are moist and you are standing on a damp floor or touching a plumbing fixture, the combination can kill you.

To make the electric wiring in a bathroom as safe as possible, place light fixtures, heaters, exhaust fans, and similar devices where they cannot easily be touched while one is touching or in contact with any of the plumbing fixtures. All such items should be designed and installed so that they can be turned on and off from a wall switch and not from a pull chain or switch on the fixture itself. And the plate on the switch box, as well as the plates on all convenience outlets, should be of plastic, porcelain, or ceramic and not of metal.

Because of the chance of an open circuit's occurring in one of the many electrical devices used in bathrooms these days, it's also a smart idea to have something called a ground fault interrupter installed. This little device will sense an open circuit in any appliance that is plugged in, and if there is an open circuit, it will shut off the flow of electricity before any harm is done. Ground fault interrupters can be installed in the outlet box in the bathroom or in the circuit breaker panel and wired into the bathroom circuit. They cost only about $15.

There should be at least two lights in a bathroom (ceiling or wall), and it's best if they are served by two separate circuits so that if one circuit fails, there will still be light. There should be at least one duplex outlet near the mirror or grooming area for various gadgets such as electric hair dryers, shavers, and combs.

If you have difficulty in keeping the bathroom warm in winter, you might want to install some form of electric heat: a baseboard unit or panel set into the wall. It should have its own circuit.


Walls

If the existing walls are in good condition, you can freshen them up with a coat of paint, which is the least expensive approach. Use a good-quality semigloss wall enamel which will provide a water-resistant finish that is easily cleaned and won't dull with repeated cleanings. A plastic-finished wallpaper or vinyl fabric wall covering gives a more individual look to a bathroom but costs more than paint. Both can cover a lot of sins, however, and the vinyl fabric can actually strengthen an old wall. If you use either, be sure that it is applied with a water-resistant paste. The moisture content of a bathroom is high, and even if the paper or fabric is not exposed directly to water, moisture from the air can get behind it and loosen it if ordinary wallpaper paste is used.

Ceramic tile, while practical and long-lasting, is the most expensive standard material to use on bathroom walls. If the existing plaster or gypsum wallboard surfaces are in good condition, it will cost around $2 a square foot to install ceramic tile over them. Nonetheless, ceramic tile is the accepted material to be used on walls around recessed tubs and shower stalls, and this is one area where you might consider using it.

If your water supply has a high iron or other mineral content, tile is not always the ideal material. What happens is that the grout between the tiles and sometimes the tiles themselves become stained and dingy and need frequent hard scrubbing to brighten them. In this instance, a substitute material may be better.

One excellent substitute for tile around tubs and showers is laminated plastic. This material comes in 4-foot by 8-foot sheets and in many colors and wood tones. Some friends of ours who build a low-maintenance vacation house had this type of surface applied around the shower-tub in their bathroom. They have found the material a perfect solution—very practical and truly low-maintenance.

Fiber glass panels are another excellent substitute for ceramic tile. These are sold in a complete package for tub areas and are not difficult to install.

Other materials are sold as substitutes for ceramic tile, among them plastic tile and tileboard. We consider these poor substitutes, for they try to look like something they are not, and a lot of people can easily recognize them as pretenders.

## Refinishing Ceramic Tile Walls

If there is ceramic tile on the walls and it is in poor condition (covered with hairline cracks, having missing tiles or badly soiled grout between the tiles, or of an unfortunate color), you don't have to remove the tile to improve the appearance. What you can do is to paint the tile after you have replaced the missing tiles. For this job you use an epoxy paint, which will produce a hard, high-gloss finish that is waterproof and not likely to chip or peel. It will even stand up on the tile in shower stalls and around bathtubs. In fact, it can even be used to paint the interior surfaces of a bathtub or lavatory, although constant exposure to standing water will dull the color.

Epoxy paint comes in two containers. One container has the paint, and the other the hardener, which is mixed with the paint just before use. Once the two have been mixed, you must use the paint in a matter of hours, for it will not hold overnight even if the lid of the container is placed on tight. The fumes from epoxy paint are quite toxic; so you want to have windows open to get good ventilation while you are working with it.

Before applying the paint you have to prepare the ceramic tile. First replace any missing tiles. The new tiles can be cemented into place with a liquid tile cement sold at most hardware and paint stores. Remove any loose grout from between the tiles with an awl or any sharp, pointed tool, and then regrout. Tile grout is available in ready-to-use form. Just smear it along the joint and wipe off the excess with a cloth. Let it dry thoroughly before washing.

To get a good bond with epoxy paint, the tile must be superclean and free from any film left after cleaning with a detergent or other cleaner. First, wash the tile thoroughly with a detergent and water, then rinse thoroughly, and scrub with powdered pumice stone (available in most paint and hardware stores) and water, using a clean cloth. Be especially careful to remove all traces of soap or soap film in soap dishes or recessed niches where soap might have accumulated. If you don't, the paint on these areas may peel. Rinse again, let dry thoroughly, then apply the epoxy paint. In most cases one coat will do the trick. The paint will not only conceal the color of the tile but also cover hairline cracks and other minor flaws in the surface.

## Floors

You can paint ceramic tile floors with epoxy paint, but you can also cover them with carpeting or a resilient-type floor covering—vinyl or linoleum. Carpeting is relatively inexpensive and can be very attractive. It is especially inviting in cold weather.

If the floor has previously been covered with vinyl, linoleum, or the like and the material is in poor condition, it can be painted with special paints designed for these materials. But you are better off to rip the old stuff out and apply new material.

# 11. Kitchens

Redoing a kitchen is by far the most popular major improvement project, and this makes sense, for the kitchen is the focal point of most at-home activities. An attractive, efficiently planned, and well-equipped kitchen is a decided plus for any house. It makes a sound investment in convenience for everyone living in the house as well as adding value.

However, in this particular area it is very easy to let your enthusiasm run away with your pocketbook so that you spend far more money than can be justified or that you can ever hope to get back when you sell. For this reason, it is important to approach kitchen improvements with caution.

In the average house the kitchen is the most expensive room to build, and it's also the most expensive one to remodel or change because remodeling usually involves changes in plumbing and wiring and the purchase of high-cost items such as cabinets, counters, and major appliances. The cost of redoing the average-size kitchen with new cabinets, counters, sink, major appliances, flooring, and decorating can easily run over $5,000, and you may still have to do some of the work yourself to bring the job in at this price. If you want the kind of kitchen pictured in many home magazines and advertisements, the price tag can just keep zooming.

An acquaintance of ours, a specialist in kitchen planning and construction, recently completed a kitchen for a wealthy family at a cost of $30,000. That's not for adding a wing to the house, mind you, just for redoing the existing kitchen. It is not a bit uncommon to find $12,000 and $14,000 kitchens in houses in the $40,000 and $50,000 price range. Needless to say, this is out of line with other houses in the price range, and the kitchen won't add that amount of market value to the house.

The quality of the kitchen should be consistent with the quality of the rest of the house. No one really expects to find a $12,000 kitchen in a $45,000 house, but one does expect to find a kitchen that is reasonably efficient and up to date.

"We allocated approximately $5,000 for the entire project. Of course, it would have cost more had we not done most of the improvements ourselves." Before (top, left and right) and after (bottom, left and right) pictures show what a young couple accomplished in this corridor kitchen with quite a bit of "sweat equity." The cabinets are a warm medium brown. Six feet of additional counter and cabinet space was added right up to the dining area. The old ironing board closet was made into an attractive herb and spice space by adding shelves. [Alcan Aluminum Corp.]

If you have a kitchen that is reasonably up to date, you might be wise to resist the urge to remodel it completely and, instead, consider other areas where you might spend the money to better advantage. It's not that we are against redoing kitchens, but if you also need more living space or a second bathroom, it makes a lot more sense to spend money on these improvements rather than on a kitchen that isn't really bad.

## Basic Layout

If you do decide to invest in remodeling the kitchen, put your money into the areas that will improve its efficiency and make it more convenient and not into a lot of expensive cosmetics that make it a highly personalized kitchen. We've seen kitchens that were remodeled at considerable cost and, aside from the fact that everything in them was new, they were still pretty much the same as the original kitchen with all the same faults. Children and pets still had to march right through the middle of the kitchen work area to reach the back door, there still was not enough counter space or the space was in the wrong places, the basic layout made it necessary to walk a dozen miles to prepare a meal, and a stepladder was needed to put the dinner dishes away. The heart of a kitchen is the work area. Put your planning and money here and not into frills.

Unless you are willing to pour a lot of money down the drain, don't create a highly personalized kitchen. Keep in mind that your idea of a dream kitchen is not necessarily the same as anyone else's, especially a potential buyer's. You can spend thousands of dollars to create a "colonial" kitchen, complete with a fireplace and fireplace wall made of used brick, oak beams on the ceiling, and pine paneling on the walls, but this kitchen might leave a buyer ice-cold. The buyer may prefer modern or French provincial. You are much safer to have a kitchen well equipped and efficiently planned which can easily be altered with paint and wallpaper to suit the tastes of a buyer.

## The Work Area

The essential element in every kitchen, regardless of style or size, is the work area. Here is where you have the major appliances, cabinets, and counters. Planning the work area is the most difficult and important part of any kitchen remodeling. What you do with the rest of the space, if you have it, is incidental. If you happen to have enough space, or wish to create it by removing a partition, you can have a country kitchen, a family room kitchen, or a kitchen of any other type. But it's the work area that counts, and as you'll learn, the actual size of the work area will be approximately the same whether you have a small kitchen or a huge one.

An L-shaped kitchen with a small island in the middle that can double as a serving, work, or snack area (top). These cabinets are the factory-built knockdown type designed for the do-it-yourselfer (bottom). [IXL Furniture Co.; Westinghouse Electric Corporation]

# Planning

Strange as it may seem, most kitchens are planned by men—builders, architects, kitchen designers, and remodelers. We have yet to meet one of these "kitchen experts" who ever spent much time in the kitchen except to get a cold beer out of the refrigerator or to boil water for instant coffee. But they are are the ones who decide on the kind of kitchen that is right for "Mrs. Housewife," and that's the kind of kitchen she gets.

As there is no great mystery about what makes an adequate kitchen, you can probably do a better job of planning your own kitchen than a hired expert can. Of course, at some point you may need professional help to draw the finished plans in order to be sure that each of the elements will fit properly, but for the basic plan, you are probably as well qualified to do the job as anyone.

It's a lot easier to plan the work area for a kitchen in a new house because to a great degree you can tailor the space to meet your requirements. It's a somewhat different situation when you remodel because unless you want to spend a great deal of money, you'll have to work with the space you have and with other limitations on what you can do. It costs money, for example, to change the location of a window or a door, move a partition, or change the location of the sink. If you are working on a tight budget, you must take extra time to work out an efficient layout that will not require expensive changes in the basic structure of your kitchen.

*Drawing Detailed Plans.* The first thing you must do is to draw accurate plans of the existing kitchen space. You will need a floor plan that shows the floor area and also an elevation of each wall that shows the width and height of the wall and the location of windows, doors, and the like.

You'll need a 6- or 8-foot folding or flexible rule, ¼-inch graph paper, and tracing paper for your planning. Allow each square on the graph paper to represent 3 inches; a half square will be 1½ inches. This is about as accurate as you need be for making rough plans.

Start out by making a floor plan. Measure the overall length of all walls, and draw them on your graph paper. Indicate on the plan the exact location and width of all doors and windows. Also indicate the location of fixed items such as supply and drain lines for the kitchen sink, radiators, and floor registers.

Next draw the elevations of each wall. Take measurements of the height of the walls from floor to ceiling. Indicate on the plan the exact location, width, and height of doors and windows as well as the distance between them. You should also indicate the exact location of electrical outlets, wall switches, wall registers, and the like.

Once you have plans of the existing kitchen, you can begin to make rough layouts of various ways to remodel it. Just put a piece of tracing paper over the floor plan, and draw your layout on the tracing paper. You will need to refer to the elevations from time to time, for these will tell you if your proposed layout is going to work or if, for example, there is a window that will prevent an abovecounter cabinet from being placed where you have indicated it.

Start planning by deciding which particular kitchen layout is going to work the best for the space you have. There are three basic layouts worth considering. There is the L-shaped kitchen work area, which is fine if you have two adjacent walls of sufficient length. The U-shaped kitchen has counters and appliances on three sides. The corridor kitchen has counters and appliances on opposite sides of the work area. In remodeling, you seldom encounter a situation in which any of these layouts will be perfect. The chances are that you'll have to modify any of them to some degree because of the location of doors and windows.

The one important goal you do wish to achieve is an efficient work triangle. You should try to plan your kitchen so that the range, refrigerator, and sink form a triangle and the total distance between all three points of the triangle is less than 23 feet and in any case, not more than 26 feet.

The corridor design is the least expensive to build because there are no corners. Corner cabinets cost extra, and unless they contain a lazy susan (another added cost), a lot of the storage space will be wasted or be very inconvenient to use. The L-shaped kitchen has one corner, while the U-shaped kitchen has two corners and is the most expensive design.

## Location of Major Equipment

Start your planning by locating the major pieces of equipment and appliances: kitchen sink, refrigerator, range, and so on. You should not try to make final working drawings for a kitchen until you have selected all the equipment and have manufacturer's specifications that give the exact dimensions for the models you will use. But for rough planning use the front dimensions listed below:

| | |
|---|---|
| Double-bowl sink | 36 inches |
| Single-bowl sink | 24 inches |
| Range | 30 inches |
| Built-in oven | 24 inches |

The simple walnut-stained cabinets and base of the island contrast with the lighter-looking birch veneer plywood paneling on the dining-area walls of this kitchen. The surface cooking units are set in the island. Such an arrangement is ideal for informal serve-yourself groups. [*Georgia-Pacific*]

| | |
|---|---|
| Built-in surface unit | 30 inches |
| Refrigerator | 36 inches |
| Dishwasher | 24 inches |

Begin with the sink because this is the most often used piece of equipment. It needs a central location, and, like many homeowners, you may want to place it under a window. Remember, however, that if you move the sink from its present location, there will be added costs for plumbing. Avoid island sinks for the same reason: the necessary plumbing will be very expensive.

The sink should be set so that there will be at least 15 inches between it and the nearest inside corner of a base cabinet. If you plan to install a built-in dishwasher, this should, if possible, be set on the right side of the sink. You will need 24 inches or so of space between the end of the sink and the nearest inside corner of a base cabinet to accommodate the dishwasher.

The range and built-in surface units should never be placed under a window because this can create a fire hazard with window curtains. And you should never place these appliances at the end of a wall or counter where the handles of cooking utensils may protrude into traffic lanes. It is best to have at least 10 inches of counter space between the cooking surfaces and the end of a counter or wall.

Refrigerators should be placed as near as possible to the door where groceries are brought into the kitchen. Refrigerators are made to hinge either left or right; so select the type that is most convenient for your particular layout. If possible, a continuous counter should run from the refrigerator to the sink.

Because refrigerators and built-in ovens are tall, they should not be set where they will break the flow of work from one counter to another. The best location for these two pieces of equipment is at the end of a counter or wall.

## Counter Space

Experts have figured that there should be around 14 feet of counter space for the average-size kitchen. Much more than this is a waste of money, and it's just added space that must be kept clean.

There should be between 30 and 36 inches of counter space on each side of the sink, 24 inches on the latch side of the refrigerator, and about the same amount on one side of the range or cooking surface. The material used for counter tops near the range or cooking surface should be heat-resistant unless you have a range with its own set-out counter.

## Base Cabinets

You should have around 10 feet of base cabinet frontage. The standard base cabinet is about 24 inches in depth and 34½ inches high. Stock cabinets range in width from 9 inches to 60 inches in increments of 3 inches.

## Wall Cabinets

It is fine if you can have the same amount of wall cabinets as base cabinets, but this is seldom possible because you don't want to place cabinets over the range, the sink, or the refrigerator. Stock wall cabinets are from 12 to 13 inches in depth and from 12 to 60 inches wide in increments of 3 inches.

## Checking Your Work Area

After you have made a rough plan of the kitchen, check to make sure that you have adequate space for work and access but not more than is necessary.

This sturdy-looking kitchen is completely paneled with prefinished white pine panels for low maintenance. Note the diagonal installation of the panels around the oven areas to avoid monotony and the use of wood dowels for hanging pots and utensils. The trash container in the foreground is also made of pine panels. [*Georgia-Pacific*]

You should have at least 48 inches but not more than 60 inches between base cabinets and appliances that are opposite each other. This amount gives space for work and allows someone to pass by even if the oven door is open.

## Appliances, Equipment, and Materials

Once you have a kitchen layout that seems to meet your needs, you can move along and select the major appliances, counter tops, cabinets, and all basic materials. Buy good-quality major appliances, but unless you have money to burn, don't get deluxe models, which not only are expensive but have a lot of gadgets that can get out of order.

You'll be smart if you buy your major appliances from a local authorized dealer who is known to provide good, fast, and efficient service at a fair price. We stick to one particular brand of major appliances, not because it is probably any better than another brand but because the local dealer is a whiz at service.

If you want to play it safe, stick to white appliances. Colored appliances are fine, but the color you select may not suit a prospective buyer, and even you may tire of the color after a time. And colors do go out of style. You may remember that some years back pink was a very popular color for appliances. Pink lasted just a few years and then was finished. Stick with white, and get color in your kitchen with paint and wallpaper.

It's also a wise idea to keep operating costs in mind when you buy major appliances. Electric and gas rates continue to go up, and the equipment that uses the least amount of energy can save you money. Microwave ovens, for example, are popular because they require less energy to operate than a conventional electric or gas range. A frost-free refrigerator uses almost twice the electricity that the conventional type does. However, some manufacturers put out a frost-free model with a switch so that you can turn off the defrost heater on days when the humidity is low.

## Sinks

A single-bowl sink is less expensive than a double-bowl sink, and if you are going to install a dishwasher, you can get along with a single-bowl model. Otherwise, install a double-bowl sink. If you can afford it, you may want to consider putting in two single-bowl sinks spaced some distance apart. This setup allows two people to work in the kitchen at the same time, and this is becoming a trend, especially in younger families. More and more husbands work side by side in the kitchen with their wives helping to prepare meals, baking bread, preserving foods, and so on. And the second sink is a handy place for the kids to get a drink of water or wash their hands before eating and for mixing drinks or arranging flowers.

Stainless-steel sinks are somewhat more expensive than those made of porcelain enemel. Stainless steel has the advantage that it won't chip if a heavy pan falls on it, but it can be difficult to keep clean if the water has a high mineral content. You might check with friends or neighbors who have a stainless-steel sink and find out what their experience has been with it.

## Dishwashers

In our opinion the dishwasher is one of the greatest inventions of all time, and you should install one if you can. But if you don't need or can't afford one at this time, at least leave space for it alongside the sink in a base cabinet. You can put a door on the cabinet and use the space for storage until you or the buyer of your house installs the dishwasher. There are, of course, portable dishwashers, and these work well, but they are not as convenient as the built-in units.

## Garbage Disposers

These are handy appliances, but check first to be sure that they are permitted in your community. Some towns don't allow disposers. By the way, you can install a disposer even if you have a septic tank. Just be sure that the waste from the disposer goes into the tank and not into a dry well or cesspool. A septic tank needs kitchen waste for proper operation. You may, however, need to have the tank pumped out more frequently after you've installed a disposer, which will increase the amount of sludge that accumulates in the bottom of the tank.

## Ranges

There are two basic types of ranges, freestanding ranges and built-in, or separate-oven, ranges. Freestanding ranges combine one or two ovens and top-of-the-stove burners in a single unit. The most familiar freestanding range is the counter-height unit that can be set anywhere but is generally placed between two base cabinets or at the end of a counter. There are also freestanding ranges that are designed to drop into a space made for them in a counter so that they have a built-in appearance. In addition, there are freestanding ranges with the oven set at eye level above the surface cooking units.

The freestanding range is the least expensive kind to install and is good for a kitchen that might be too small to accommodate a separate-oven range. One drawback to almost every freestanding range is that there will be a joint between the range and adjoining cabinets and counters where grease and food particles accumulate and which is very difficult to clean without pulling the range out. Another drawback is that when the oven is on, the working area around the range becomes uncomfortably warm.

The built-in, or separate-oven, range consists of two separate elements, the surface cooking unit and the oven. The surface cooking unit is set into the counter, while the oven can be placed off to one side of the work area. The oven can be set into a base cabinet, but it is much more convenient if it is placed at waist or eye level.

The separate-oven arrangement gives you a lot of flexibility in planning your kitchen, for counter-top burners can be used in a cooking island or peninsula. And you pick up a little extra storage space with a separate oven because you can use the space under the counter-top burners. But a separate oven will run up your costs because of the extra cabinets involved. And this arrangement works most effectively in a fairly large kitchen where there is enough space to place the oven at a good distance from the work area.

## Exhaust Fans

If an exhaust fan is going to be effective in ridding the kitchen of cooking odors, heat, and humidity, it must be vented to the outside, and the nearer the fan can be placed to the outside, the better. The ideal location for a fan is on an outside wall directly above the range or cooking area. If the range or cooking surfaces can't be placed on an outside wall, you can install the fan in the ceiling or on an interior wall over the range and connect it by ducts to the outside. Hooded fans do a somewhat better job than those without hoods.

Ducts from the fan to the outside vent should be straight. Bends decrease the efficiency of the ventilating system.

Most kitchen fans make a lot of noise when they are running at high speed; so it is smart to install the largest-size fan available. If you do this, you can run it at a low speed and get the same amount of ventilation as you would with a smaller fan running at high speed.

## Counter Tops

About the best material for counter tops is laminated plastic. It is durable, easy to keep clean, and heat-resistant, and it comes in a wide range of colors. The one area where you should not use this material is right next to the range or cooking surfaces, for the plastic can be damaged by the intense heat from hot pans taken off the burners or out of the oven. A good material to use here is laminated wood, which can also be used as a chopping block.

Laminated wood, of course, can be used for all counter tops, but it is much more difficult to keep clean than laminated plastic. Ceramic tile makes a good, durable counter top, but it is noisy and very hard on china and glassware.

## Cabinets

Cabinets can be a major cost factor in any kitchen remodeling. You can pay $200 or more for each running foot of cabinets—1 foot of base cabinet, 1 foot of counter with top, and 1 foot of abovecounter cabinet—if you want deluxe stuff. This can bring the cost for cabinets in the average-size kitchen to $2,500. On the other hand, you can get good-quality but not fancy knock-down cabinets that you or your carpenter can install for around $50 a running foot. It's just a matter of how much you want to spend. You should, however, avoid using low-quality cabinets, for the drawers won't work properly.

Most people prefer wood cabinets, although metal cabinets of good quality

A built-in desk provides a handy corner in the kitchen for telephoning, planning menus, and writing grocery lists. Shelves of 1- by 10-inch western pine boards hold cookbooks and recipe files. The cupboards behind the louvered wood doors store linens and cookware. [Designer: James W. Morrow, Portland, Oregon  Photo: Western Wood Products Association]

are excellent. One disadvantage of metal cabinets is that they are mass-produced by a relatively few firms and your choice is limited. Wood cabinets, on the other hand, can be custom-tailored to fit your requirements.

Wood cabinets are available in stock sizes, or you can have them custom-made. Stock cabinets are manufactured by a few large firms with national distribution, whose advertisements you may have seen in magazines. The vast majority of stock cabinets are made by regional and local firms with limited distribution. You'll find suppliers for all kinds of cabinets listed under "Kitchen Cabinets" in the Yellow Pages.

Custom cabinets that are designed for your particular kitchen are not much more expensive than stock cabinets of equal quality. This is true if the custom cabinets can be made in a cabinet shop. If they are going to be custom-made on the job, they will cost a great deal. Most suppliers of kitchen cabinets have their own cabinet shops, and so do some large builders and remodelers.

## Ceiling, Floor, and Walls

Washable acoustical tile is a good choice for ceilings because kitchens are noisy rooms and the tile will help absorb some of the sound and make the kitchen a pleasanter place to work in. For flooring you want a relatively soft material that won't absorb stains and grease and will be easy to keep clean. A resilient material such as linoleum or vinyl is a good choice. Prefinished wood also makes an attractive and comfortable kitchen floor. Be careful about selecting a hard, dense material such as brick or flagstone for your floor. Such floors can be most attractive, but they are hard on the feet and legs if you have to spend many hours a day in the kitchen. Carpeting was a popular kitchen floor covering at one time, but although it is soft and absorbs sounds, it is not easy to keep clean.

## Detailed Plans

Once you have decided on your basic layout, have selected the major appliances and equipment to be used, and have the specifications, you should get together with the firm that is going to do the work—builder, remodeler, kitchen specialist—and have the firm make detailed plans for your approval. The firm can use your rough plan as a guide, but it should send a representative to take measurements of the existing kitchen. In a kitchen remodeling, measurements must be accurate to the last fraction of an inch, for if they are not, you will find that all the parts won't fit together or there won't be quite enough space for a critical item. Let the people who are going to do the work be responsible for final measurements.

# 12. Cooling the House

## Central Air Conditioning

The best way to cool a house is with central air conditioning, but this can be an expensive business. The system costs money to install, and it is going to cost money during the hot months to operate it. How worthwhile an improvement central air conditioning will be depends pretty much on where you live. It's obvious that in very hot areas central air conditioning has become as essential as central heat is for colder areas. Within the past few years the zones where air conditioning is the rule rather than the exception have been moving farther and farther north. So it may well be that in your particular part of the country, even if it isn't in the Deep South or the Southwest, air conditioning has become the accepted thing, expecially in better-quality houses.

While climate is the most important consideration, other important factors may encourage you to invest in air conditioning. Noise pollution—from the streets, from the neighbors, from low-flying aircraft—has encouraged many families to install air conditioning just to get peace and quiet in their homes. The poor quality of the air has been a deciding factor for many people, for reasons of health. And there is no doubt that with air conditioning the inside of the house stays a lot cleaner.

The final consideration, of course, is the cost of installation, and this depends entirely on the size, design, and condition of your house and the type of heating system you have. The size of the house is important because the more space you have, the larger the size unit needed to cool it. You can figure that it will take 1 ton of air conditioning (a ton is the unit of measurement used in air conditioning) to cool each 500 square feet of floor space. And each ton of air conditioning will cost $700 or more. This means that if you have a modest-size house with 1,200 square feet, you'll spend more than $1,400 for air conditioning. If you have a big house with 2,000 square feet, your base cost will go up to $2,800.

If you have a relatively new house that has a modern forced—warm-air heating system, your installation costs are going to be on the low side because the cooling unit can be installed to utilize the blower on the furnace as well as the existing ducts and registers. Many such heating systems were especially designed and installed so that they could be used for air conditioning. If you have an older system, the ducts may not be large enough to handle the flow of cool air, and a larger blower will have to be installed.

For houses that are heated by hot water, steam, or electric baseboard units, the design of the house can be the key factor in determining the cost of installation. For a one-story house with an attic or attic crawl space or a basement or basement crawl space, installation of the air conditioner is not too much of a problem. The cooling unit can be put in the attic with ducts running to registers in the ceiling, or it can go in the basement with ducts running to floor registers. In a two-story house matters are more complicated and a good deal more expensive. What usually is done is to install two systems, one in the attic to cool the upstairs rooms and one in the basement to handle the downstairs rooms. The cost of this type of installation can be $4,000 or so. From a standpoint of comfort it is more desirable to have cold-air registers in the ceiling than in the floor or at the base of the wall of a room.

The cost of operating a central air-conditioning system can be high unless steps are taken to reduce heat gain in hot weather to a minimum. And it's more important than ever to reduce operating costs because electric rates keep going up, and while you may not mind the high cost of operating your system the cost may discourage a potential buyer.

To obtain low operating costs for air conditioning, the ideal houses are those that were built for electric heat. These houses have adequate insulation in all vital areas: roof, floor, and walls. They have either storm windows or areas of insulating glass, and they are as tight against heat loss (and heat gain in summer) as houses can be. What's more, they are usually rather compact houses, which means that a smaller-size cooler can be used.

If you are going to install air conditioning in an older house, you must figure in the cost of items necessary to reduce operating costs to a reasonable amount. For example, if the house is not adequately insulated, insulation work may cost around $1,000. If you don't have double glazing, the cost of storm windows for even a modest-size house will be $300 or more. And if you have to increase the electric service capacity to handle the air conditioner, another $400 may be added to your total cost.

The best way to approach the installation of air conditioning is to call in several local air-conditioning firms that handle brand-name equipment. Have each one inspect your house and give you an estimate on the cost of installation plus the annual cost of operation with the house in its present condition. Also get the cost of operation if certain improvements—more insulation, storm windows, double glazing—are made and the cost for making these improvements. Only then are you in a position to know what it is actually going to cost to install the system and how much it will cost each year to operate it.

A good air-conditioning contractor will make a very careful study of your house before deciding on the size of unit you need. He will figure out the amount of heat gain through the roof, windows, and glass areas as well as the amount generated inside the house by people, cooking, bathing, washing clothes, and so on. You want a system that will have the capacity to keep the indoor temperature at around 78 degrees in hot weather and also to remove moisture, but at the same time you don't want an oversized system that would cost you extra money.

You must depend on the contractor to do a good job of installing the system, but there are points to watch out for. One is the location of the outside condenser. It is best if this is placed on the north, or shady, side of the house, for this location will help reduce operating costs. Also don't put the condenser too close to a bedroom as it can be noisy when in operation. And be sure that any ducts that run through areas that are not to be cooled, such as an attic crawl space, are heavily insulated so that the cool air inside the ducts will not be wasted.


Heat Pumps

If you are going to install central air conditioning and also need a new heating system, you may want to install a system that will provide both heat and cooling: a heat pump. In summer the heat pump takes the heat from inside the house and exhausts it to the outside. In winter, it does the reverse: it takes heat from the outside air and puts the heat into the house. The only form of energy it requires is electricity.

Insofar as operating costs are concerned, a heat pump does best in areas where electric rates are relatively low and winters are not severe. In colder regions there won't be sufficient heat in the outside air to provide enough heat for the house; so electric resistance heaters inside the heat pump go on automatically to provide additional heat. These heaters take a great deal more electricity than is required to operate the heat pump, and operating costs therefore rise substantially each time they go on. Heat pumps are most practical in warmer areas and in relatively compact houses that are tightly built and very well insulated.

## Room Air Conditioners

These can be used to cool the entire house as well as individual rooms, but unless they are built into the wall under a window or at some other point, they are not considered a permanent improvement. Therefore, they will not add value to your house, just to your comfort.

## Attic Fans

In areas where nights are relatively cool, an attic fan can do a good job of cooling the entire house so that everyone gets a comfortable night's sleep and there is even a gentle cooling breeze through the house during part of the day. A true attic fan should not be confused with the portable exhaust fans frequently used to pull heated air out of attics or rooms. The real honest-to-goodness attic fan will have a blade up to 42 inches in diameter and should be of a size that will change the air in the entire house every 60 to 90 seconds, depending on the outside temperature. Such fans are permanently installed in the attic floor, in the gable end of the attic, or even in a cupola on the roof when there is no attic crawl space. The cost is only a fraction of that of central air conditioning: around $250 installed.

## Improvements to Make a House Cooler

There are many improvements that can make a house cooler in summer and reduce the cost of operating air-conditioning equipment. It goes without saying that the attic or the underside of the roof should be well insulated because this is the area of greatest heat gain in summer as well as heat loss in winter.

*Roofs.* If you are going to reroof your house, you may want to consider using white or light-color shingles, for they will help keep your house cooler. A white roof absorbs only about one-half the amount of heat from the sun that a dark roof absorbs.

*Glass Areas.* Windows, sliding doors, and fixed glass areas allow a great deal of heat to enter the house. Insulating glass is effective in reducing heat loss in winter but is not effective in keeping out the sun's rays that heat up objects inside the room.

Awnings are very effective in keeping the sun's rays away from glass areas. Awnings of aluminum, canvas, hardboard, or steel should extend far enough on each side of the window so that the sun can't strike the glass from an angle. And the awnings should not have side panels, for these allow air to be trapped under the awning, where it becomes very hot; the heat is then absorbed by the glass.

Another effective way to reduce heat gain through glass is to cover the glass with a special sun film. This keeps out a large percentage of the sun's rays but allows you to see out. Sun film is the ideal solution for large glass areas and sliding glass doors that cannot be protected effectively by awnings.

# 13. Reducing Heating Costs

Among the most desirable improvements you can make these days are those that will reduce the cost of heating your house. Not only will these improvements pay for themselves in a relatively short time with the money they save, but they will also make the house more attractive to a buyer.

Almost everyone knows about the spiraling costs of heating energy: electricity, natural gas, and fuel oil. One of the first questions a buyer will ask is "How much does it cost to heat this house?" And if the cost is excessive, you have probably lost a buyer. What's more, even if the buyer wants to buy, the high cost of heating the house may make it difficult for him to get a mortgage loan. Reputable lenders will hesitate to grant a loan if they feel that the carrying charges on the property may be too high for the income of the borrower. In short, you will find more buyers who can qualify for a loan if your annual heating costs are $500 a year than if they are $1,000 a year.

And just as important as what it costs to heat a house today is what it may cost to heat the same house tomorrow and in the years to come. Many authorities project that by 1980 the cost of natural gas will be three times what it is today and the cost of electricity and fuel oil will be at least twice what it is at present. This means that if it costs $600 to heat a house today, it will cost at least $1,200 to heat the same house in 1980.

There is another good reason for cutting down on the amount of energy needed to heat a house, and that is that one fine day we may find there is some form of rationing or restriction on the amount of energy we can get regardless of what we may be willing to pay. Natural gas and fuel oil are both in short supply and even electricity, when it must be generated by imported oil, may be subject to some sort of rationing.

Those of us who live in the Northeast had a taste of what energy rationing can be all about during the winter of 1973–1974. At that time, as you may remember, there was an embargo on fuel oil from the Middle East, on which the Northeast is dependent to heat houses. So a form of rationing was put into effect. The general idea was that each house would receive 15 percent less oil than it normally required and that it was up to the homeowner to conserve enough fuel so that he could get along on 15 percent less energy. By luck the winter was very mild, and it was relatively easy for people to get along with less fuel than they normally required. But if the winter had been severe, a lot of people would have been in trouble. Guess what kind of luck you would have in trying to sell a house if there were some form of fuel rationing and your house couldn't quite make it through the winter on the amount of fuel or energy it was able to receive.

There are several ways to go about reducing your heating costs. The first step, of course, is to cut down the heat loss from the house structure to the absolute minimum. You can also save energy by improving the efficiency of your heating system so that you get the most heat for the energy consumed. And, finally, you can reduce your dependence on conventional energy— electricity, natural gas, and fuel oil—by installing some form of auxiliary heat such as a solar heat system, a woodburning stove, or an efficient fireplace. If you take all these steps, you'll be in pretty fair shape to cope with whatever happens in the field of energy for heating the house.

## Reducing Heat Loss

Reducing the loss of heat is the most obvious and important step you can take to cut heating costs. You want to reduce the heat loss to a minimum and do this first because even the most efficient heating system in the world will use an excessive amount of energy if it is trying to heat the whole outdoors.

Insulation and storm windows are the key to reducing heat loss. If you would like to learn just how much they can save you in your area, consult your state energy agency or state department of environmental protection. These agencies often have accurate data on the cost of these improvements in your area and on the time in which this investment will be repaid by savings of energy.

## Insulation

An adequate amount of insulation in all the right spots is the single most important way to reduce heat loss. Insulation is so essential, in fact, that one gas utility has offered to pay one-fourth of the cost of installation up to $100 to any customer who insulates the roof of his house, and another gas company will provide interest-free loans for up to 80 percent of the cost of installing insulation. If you use natural gas for heat, check with your gas company to see if it has a similar arrangement.

The chances are that while your house does have some insulation, it does not have enough for today's requirements. Even by the standards in existence before the energy crisis, few houses were properly insulated. Many houses in the colder regions that the builder claimed were fully insulated have only 3 or 4 inches of insulation in the attic floor and perhaps 2 inches in the walls. Almost the only houses that were well insulated were those designed and built for electric heat. But even the amount of insulation in these houses may not meet today's requirements.

Before the energy crisis, 6 inches of mineral wool (fiber glass) insulation in the attic floor or on the underside of the roof was considered adequate for all but the extremely cold regions of the country. Today it pays to have at least 9 inches of insulation for these areas of the house, and in very cold regions it is not uncommon to find 14 inches or more of insulation at the top of the house. We heard of one builder in Connecticut, where winters are cold but not so severe as in some parts of the country, who is putting 9 inches of insulation in the attic floor and claims that the added cost of the material will be paid for in fuel savings within a few months.

The effectiveness of all kinds of insulation in reducing heat loss is measured by the R value, which is given on the insulation or on the package that it comes in. The higher the R value, the more efficient the insulation. Don't judge the effectiveness of insulation by thickness alone. Some insulation materials may have to be many inches thick to furnish the same R value as another material only 1 inch thick. Use the R value in judging insulating qualities.

Just what R value you need depends on where you live. You need a higher R value in the far North than in the South. For example, in Atlanta, Georgia, where winters are relatively mild, insulation with an R-19 value would be adequate for the attic. In a somewhat colder area such as Hartford, Connecticut, you would want an R-24 value, and in Minneapolis, Minnesota, R-30. For accurate and up-to-date information on the recommended R value for your area, consult your state energy agency or state department of environmental protection.

## Types of Insulation

Many different materials are used for insulation, but the most important ones for a house are mineral wool and plastic-foam boards.

*Mineral Wool.* Mineral wool is the commonest insulating material. It is made of slag or glass fibers and is available in batts, blankets, and loose fill (also known as blow-in insulation).

Batts are short lengths of mineral wool, usually about 48 inches. They come in widths that can be fitted between standard-spaced framing. Batts are used most often to insulate the floor of an attic, where they are set between the joists after the ceiling below has been installed.

Blankets are similar to batts but are much longer, up to 50 feet or so. They come with a stapling or nailing flange so that they can be fastened in place between the wall studding or between the floor joists on the underside of a floor or be set in place in the attic just as batts are.

Batts and blanket insulation come with or without a vapor barrier. You should use the type without a vapor barrier only when you are adding insulation to existing insulation. If you are applying insulation to an uninsulated area, use the type with a vapor barrier. Be certain that the vapor barrier faces the warm side of the house, never the cold side. The purpose of the vapor barrier is to prevent the moist air from the house from getting into the insulation. If moist air reaches the insulation, it will condense into a liquid, which will decrease the effectiveness of the insulation. When insulation is installed on the floor of the attic, the vapor barrier should face down, against the ceiling of the room below. When insulating the floor above an unheated area, the vapor barrier should face up, against the floor of the room above.

Loose-fill insulation comes in a bag. Because you can simply pour it into place, it's handy to use for insulating between the attic floor joists. This is the type of mineral wool used by firms that insulate the walls of existing houses by blowing the insulation into the wall cavity. Loose-fill insulation does not have a vapor barrier. If one is required, use polyvinyl plastic sheeting.

*Plastic-Foam Boards.* These boards are made of polystyrene or polyurethane foam. The standard-size board is 2 by 8 feet and ranges in thickness from ½ to 4 inches. Plastic-foam boards have a lot of insulating quality. A 2-inch-thick board, for example, has an R value of about 19. Under normal conditions these boards do not require a vapor barrier. They can be nailed into place or secured with a mastic. They are handy to use where there is insufficient room for the thicker mineral wool and also where moisture may be a problem, as over a masonry wall that becomes damp at certain times of the year.

## Where to Insulate

The most important parts of a house to insulate are the attic floor or the underside of the roof, the outside walls, the underside of floors above unheated areas such as crawl space, and the outside edge of any concrete slab floor. In cold areas it is also wise to insulate the walls of any heated basement, at least down to the local frost line.

*Attic.* The attic is the area of the house with the greatest heat loss in winter and the greatest heat gain in summer. You want to make certain that your attic is very well insulated. You need at least an R-19 value, or a minimum of 6 inches of mineral wool. But as we have said before, check with your local state agencies to find out exactly how much insulation you need in your area.

If there is no flooring in the attic, it's easy enough to find out how much insulation there is between the floor joists: just measure it. And if there is not enough, it's easy to add more. You can use batts, blankets, or loose-fill mineral wool. But if you use batts or blankets, be sure to get the kind without a vapor barrier.

If there is flooring in the attic, the only way you can measure the thickness of the insulation is to rip up a board. And adding any required insulation will not be easy. What you must do is either rip up most if not all of the flooring so that you can add insulation between the joists or call in a firm that can blow insulation between the joists.

Ripping up the floor is the least expensive method if you do the work yourself, but it is a miserable job and takes hours and hours of hard labor. Having a firm do the work is a lot easier on you, but it costs money—about 50 cents or more per foot of area to be insulated.

In some houses insulation is applied between the roof rafters rather than between the floor joists of the attic. This is fine if you plan to convert the attic into a living area, but if you don't, you are losing money and heating energy because what you are doing is heating all that attic space. You will be wise to insulate the attic floor even if there is insulation between the rafters. In this way you remove the entire attic from the area of the house to be heated, and this step alone will save you a lot of money. If at some time you decide to finish off the attic, the fact that the floor is insulated will not make any difference.

If you live in an area where there is snow in winter, you can judge the efficiency of the attic insulation by how fast snow melts from the roof. If snow melts from your roof before it melts from the roofs of houses around you, your insulation is not good.

One problem connected with insulating the attic is that unless the insulation is properly applied and the space above it is vented to the outdoors, the attic may become damp during cold weather. The dampness is caused by moisture vapor coming up from the warm area of the house. Even if the insulation has a vapor barrier, there are generally enough cracks to allow some warm, moist air to reach the attic. Dampness in the attic can be eliminated by venting the space on the cold side of the insulation. If the attic floor is insulated, install vents or louvers at each end wall of the attic and leave them open in cold weather. If the roof rafters are insulated, there should be a vent at each end above the insulation. The usual practice is to leave at least 2 feet of space between the peak of the roof and the insulation and to vent this space at each end. Another way is to install vents along the eaves so that the space between the insulation and the roof boards is vented to the outside.

*Outside Walls.* There are two ways to learn how well, if at all, the outside walls of the house are insulated. One is to run the palm of your hand over the inside surface of the wall in cold weather. If your hand feels cold, the wall is not very well insulated. A more accurate method is to take two thermometers and make a test. Secure one thermometer to the inside surface of the wall with masking tape, and place the other thermometer in the center of the room at about the same height. If, after a few hours, the one on the wall reads 10 or more degrees lower than the one in the middle of the room, the wall is not properly insulated.

The most practical way to insulate the outside walls in an existing house is to have loose-fill mineral wool blown into the wall cavity. In most communities there are firms that specialize in this work and have the equipment and experience to do the job. They will remove pieces of the siding or make small holes in it so that the insulation can be blown under pressure into the wall cavity. They then replace the siding or patch the holes. Insulation can be blown into any wall in which there is a cavity regardless of the type of siding. The siding can be wood, asbestos shingles, stucco, or brick veneer. Of course this method won't work in houses built of solid brick or stone. About the only way brick or stone walls can be insulated is from the inside, by applying sheets of plastic-foam boards over the existing inside walls and then covering them with a new wall surface such as gypsum board.

*Floors.* The underside of floors above unheated space must be insulated. These include floors above crawl space, unheated basements, and under-house garages. You can easily tell if a floor has been insulated by looking at it from the underside. The commonest kind of insulation for floors is a mineral wool blanket, which must be applied with the vapor barrier side facing up. You will find many floors to which insulation has been applied with the vapor barrier side facing down, thus causing a problem with moisture. This mistake occurs because many workers find it a lot easier to install the insulation in this way than in the correct way. If your insulation has been applied this way, take it off and put it on the right way.

*Basement Walls.* In the colder areas of the country it's wise to insulate the walls of a heated basement. It's not always necessary to extend the insulation to the floor, but it should run as far down as the frost line. Plastic-foam boards are suitable for basement walls because they can be applied directly over masonry with a mastic.

*Concrete Slabs.* The perimeter of any concrete slab under a heated area should be insulated to reduce heat loss through the edges of the concrete. It is especially important to insulate a concrete slab if there are heating ducts or pipes in the concrete; otherwise a good deal of the heat in these lines will be drained to the outdoors. You can often tell if a slab is not insulated by the fact that the snow around its edges melts more quickly than it does on the ground some distance away. And in the early spring the grass around the edges becomes green before the rest of the lawn because it gets the benefit of all that heat wasted through the slab.

Either plastic-foam boards or rigid fiber glass boards may be used to insulate the edges of the slab. Neither of these materials will be damaged by moisture or by contact with the soil, and their efficiency will not be reduced by contact with damp earth. First, dig a trench around the edges of the slab to a depth of about 2 feet, and then fasten strips of the insulation to the edges of the slab with a mastic or with masonry nails.

## Cost of Insulation

You can save a lot on the cost of insulating or of adding insulation by doing the work yourself. About the only job you can't do yourself is to blow insulation into walls, for this procedure requires special equipment. But you can do all the rest of the house yourself: the attic or the underside of the roof, the underside of the floors, and even the perimeter of slabs. Insulation takes work but not great skill, and you can get complete installation instructions from your building supply dealer or from the manufacturer of the insulation material.

## Storm Windows

If you have a well-insulated house, the heat loss through glass areas will be about 30 percent of your total heat loss. To cut heat loss from this source, install storm windows. You need a storm window for every window of the heated area of the house, including the basement and the attic if these areas are heated.

The only glass window that does not normally require a storm window is one made of insulating glass (double-glazed window). But in the colder regions of the country, where there are 6,500 degree-days or more annually, the installation of storm windows even on insulating-glass windows and sliding doors can be a wise investment. One manufacturer of sliding glass doors makes triple-glazed units, consisting of three layers of glass with an air space between each layer. These are far more efficient in reducing heat loss than the standard insulating-glass units made of only two layers of glass. If you live in a cold region and are installing a sliding glass unit, you may wish to consider installing a triple-glazed unit.

Before the cost of heating energy began its upward spiral, it was a rule of thumb that properly installed storm windows would pay for themselves in energy savings in about ten years and from then on would return about 13 percent on the investment in reduced fuel costs. Today, in spite of an increase in the cost of storm windows, it takes far less than ten years to save enough energy to pay for the windows, and the annual dividend will be higher than 13 percent.

## Types of Storm Windows

The most popular storm window for a double-hung window is the triple-track aluminum combination unit that is permanently installed and can easily be switched over to a screen in summer. Such windows are excellent for double-hung windows, but they can't be used on casement windows, awning-type windows, and most horizontal sliding windows. For these you should use a storm panel that fits on the inside so that the window sash may be opened as needed. Storm panels are clipped to the sash rather than set into the frame, and they move with the sash when it is opened. They are not as efficient as storm windows on the outside, but they are much better than nothing.

Aluminum combination storm windows come with a baked-enamel finish, usually white, or with a natural aluminum color. The better-grade units with a natural aluminum color are anodized to resist pitting and discoloration through oxidation. Plain aluminum units that have not been anodized soon discolor and may not hold up long under certain conditions. It would be wise to paint such units. If you wish, you may also paint the anodized aluminum units.

One of the best ways to judge the quality of an aluminum combination unit is by weight. A good-quality unit will weigh far more than a less expensive one and will be rather rigid, while a low-quality unit will wobble and even bend when it is handled. A good-quality unit will have glass that weighs 18 ounces per square foot, while a cheap unit will have only 15-ounce glass. And a good-quality window will have thicker weatherstripping than cheaper ones.

Aluminum combination storm windows are made up to fit individual windows. It's important that they be properly installed. They should fit tightly in the window frame, and the joints along the sides and top should be caulked so that there is a tight seal between the edges of the frame and the window frame. There should be no caulking along the bottom edge, but there should be a few small holes or vents so that any water that reaches the window sill will drain off. Without drain holes, water can collect on the sill and damage the paint.

If you have aluminum or steel primary windows in your house, be sure that when the storm windows are installed there is a "thermal barrier" between the frame of the primary window and the frame of the storm window. The purpose of the thermal barrier is to keep the two metal frames from coming into direct contact with each other. If they do, the cold will be conducted to the inside surface of the primary window frame, and a lot of moisture may condense. A thin strip of wood or insulating material can be used for the thermal barrier. This problem will not arise if you have old-fashioned wood-frame storm windows because a wood frame is a poor conductor of cold, but a metal frame is an excellent conductor.

## Storm Doors

Every outside door needs a storm door. The best kind is made of wood or aluminum with an inside core of insulating material. Very lightweight aluminum doors offer some protection for the primary door against wind, but they are so thin that they offer little protection against cold.

## Improvements to the Heating System

An inefficient heating system can waste as much as 50 percent of the fuel or energy it uses. That means that if you have such a system, and a lot of us do, your annual heating costs are about twice as high as they should be. What's more, the chances are that the house is not very comfortable in cold weather, with some areas too hot and others not hot enough.

Even the most efficient heating system in the world, of course, won't perform very well if it is being asked to heat the whole outdoors. So before you go after the heating system, be sure that the house is well insulated and that you have storm windows as well as caulking and weatherstripping.

And before you make extensive and expensive improvements in your heating system, first make certain that it is operating at peak efficiency. Dirty furnace filters, for example, can waste a lot of fuel over a heating season and also reduce the life of the furnace. A filter should be cleaned or replaced when you can hold it up to the light and not see light through the filtering material. A thin coating of soot inside a boiler or furnace can cut its efficiency by one-half, and an improperly adjusted burner also wastes fuel. As a rule, oil burners should be cleaned and adjusted once a year, and the inside of the boiler or furnace vacuumed to remove all accumulations of soot. Gas burners should be adjusted every two or three years.

Because a thin coating of dust on radiators and baseboard units reduces heat output, these surfaces should be vacuumed from time to time. Radiator covers are usually poorly designed and reduce heat output; so if you want maximum heat, take them off. If pipes and ducts run through unheated areas, such as the attic or the basement crawl space, they should be insulated so that the heat is not lost. You can get insulating material for these pipes and ducts at most hardware stores, and you can probably apply it to them yourself.

Needless to say, it is a waste of money to supply heat to any area that does not absolutely need it. Garages, for example, should not be heated in this day and age. There are other ways to keep the car engine warm enough in cold weather so that it can easily be started. A drip stick heater, for example, costs less than $5, and even the more expensive electric engine heaters cost only a fraction of what it takes to heat a garage.

It also pays to close off any room or rooms that are not essential. Many families have found that by closing off two rooms they can reduce heating costs by as much as 15 percent. And you can cut 5 percent or more off your heating costs if you will train small children and family pets not to keep coming inside and then immediately deciding to go outside, holding the door open the while.

Many heating systems are inefficient and waste energy because they are not properly balanced. In a well-balanced system the flow of heat to all areas of the house will be more or less uniform. But if the system is not well balanced, some rooms or areas will get a lot of heat quickly while others will get little heat and at a much slower rate. What usually happens is that the thermostat is turned up to force heat to the colder areas. And once the thermostat is turned above 68 degrees, your fuel costs rise at an alarming rate.

Forced–warm-air and circulating–hot-water heating systems can be balanced without much difficulty. With a circulating–hot-water system there are adjusting valves in the pipes where they come from the boiler. Opening or closing these valves will increase or decrease the flow of hot water to certain areas of the house. With a forced–warm-air system there are dampers in the ducts that can be adjusted to increase or decrease the flow of air to the registers. It's possible to balance either of these systems yourself if you want to save money. You'll have to use a trial-and-error approach and keep adjusting the valves or dampers until you get the desired results. A steam-heat system can be balanced by replacing the air valves on each radiator with adjustable valves. These can be set so that the radiators at some distance from the boiler will get steam before the radiators closer to the boiler and nearer to the thermostat heat up.

There are many other ways to improve the efficiency of a heating system, but they will run into money. Quite a lot of money, in fact. Last winter we asked our plumber how much it would cost just to replace a big old-fashioned steam radiator with a newer, more compact unit. He quoted a price of $250 to $300 for a new radiator, including $50 for the labor to hook it up. And a neighbor of ours paid $100 to have a cold-air–return register installed on the first floor of his house. So before you begin to spend a lot of money, make as certain as possible that the improvements are going to pay off in lower heating costs and a greater degree of comfort.

A good source for suggestions and facts is the outfit that sells you the energy you use: electricity, gas, and fuel oil. Most electric and gas companies and the larger fuel oil delivery firms have engineers who can come over and inspect your house and system. They can then advise you on what you might do to improve the system's efficiency, how much you might save each year, and what the approximate cost of making the improvements would be. You should also call in two or more heating contractors and see what they suggest and what savings might be obtained. The very best source of impartial advice is a heating engineer, but such an expert is not only expensive but hard to find except in larger communities. The following are some ways in which an existing system can be improved.

## Zone Control

If you have a circulating–hot-water or forced–warm-air system, it may pay you to have it split into two or more zones, each zone being controlled by its own thermostat. This can make a good deal of difference in reduced operating costs and in comfort. For example, if the system is split so that one zone is for the living areas and the other for the bedrooms, you can maintain a lower temperature in the bedrooms, where heat normally is not required during the day. Splitting an existing system will require some changes in the piping or ductwork, the addition of another circulating pump or blower, and a thermostat for each zone. The cost will be somewhere around $1,000, but at the rate that fuel costs are going up, it might take only a few years to pay for these changes with what you'll save on heating bills. And there is no doubt that zone control will make for a much more comfortable house during the cold winter months.

## Furnaces and Boilers

In many older houses you find a coal-fired furnace or boiler that has been converted to automatic heat with the addition of a gas or oil burner. By and large these "conversion" units are not as efficient as a unit designed for automatic heat. But the cost of replacing one of these old heaters comes high: $1,000 or so. Again, you will want to get proof that the new equipment will save enough money to pay for its cost in a relatively few years.

You might also wish to consider replacing an undersized furnace or boiler with one that has the capacity to handle the job. Every heating plant has a certain level of maximum efficiency, and if you must constantly force your heater to run above its normal level, you'll use fuel that would not be required if the heater were of the correct size.

## A New Heating System

We have heard that in some areas many homeowners are spending $2,000 or more to switch from natural gas or fuel oil to electricity to heat their houses. They are doing this because of the high cost of gas and oil in their areas and also because of uncertainty about the future availability of these fuels. And we know of one couple that did just the opposite: they switched over from electric heat to an oil-fired forced–warm-air system. When this couple built their house in 1974, they were unable to get oil because the oil company had put a limit on the number of new customers it could service each year. About a year after the couple had been living in their new place, the oil company notified them that they could now have oil if they wanted it. They jumped at the chance in spite of the fact that it was going to cost them $2,500 to put in the furnace. But they had a good reason to make this investmement: their electric bills for heat alone had been running over $300 a month.

If you get the notion that you'd like to switch to a less expensive type of energy and one that you think will be available in the years to come, do some checking. A good source for the kind of information you want is your state energy agency. If it doesn't have the figures that will tell you what the projected cost for the various kinds of fuels will be, it can tell you where you can get them. And the agency can also advise you on the future availability of the various kinds of energy. It can make a lot of sense to spend the money to switch to some other form of heat, but only if you are sure that this form will be less costly in the years to come.

## Auxiliary Heating Systems

In these days it makes a lot of sense to add some form of auxiliary heating system capable of providing a fair degree of heat for the entire house. The right kind of auxiliary system is good insurance against increasing costs of conventional energy and also makes you less dependent on electricity, gas, and fuel oil to provide you with heat. There are three kinds of auxiliary systems to consider: solar heat, woodburning stoves, and fireplaces. You might even wish to install all of them. We know of some vacation houses in New England that are heated entirely by a combination of solar heat, wood stoves, and a fireplace.

### Solar Heat

Installing solar heat might be the smartest improvement you could make because with this system you can get up to 80 percent of the heat you need in winter plus your hot water free from the sun. Think of what that can mean to you when heating bills go up each year. And think of what it can mean to someone interested in buying your house.

The commonest kind of solar heat in use today consists of three basic elements. There is a solar collector made of panels of glass, metal, and insulating material, usually mounted on the roof. The collector traps and absorbs the sun's rays and converts them into heat. Inside the collector are coils filled with a liquid to carry the heat to an underground storage tank, which is also filled with a liquid or, sometimes, with small rocks. The heat in the storage tank is then transferred to the distribution system that carries it to the various areas of the house.

The size of the collector and storage tank depends on the climate, the amount of heat the solar system is designed to produce, and the size of the house. In a relatively cold area, a solar system that is designed to supply about 70 percent of the total heat for a house with 1,200 square feet of floor area requires about 500 square feet of collector and a 1,200-gallon storage tank.

At the present time most solar systems are only 60 to 80 percent efficient.

The rest of the heat needed when there is cloud cover or extreme cold must be provided by other means, such as an oversize hot-water heater, a fireplace, a heat pump, or a forced–warm-air furnace fired by oil or gas.

Solar heating systems are still very expensive, the average installation costing about $6,000. But the projections are that even at this price a solar system will pay for itself in five to eight years, and after that you'll be getting your heat for practically nothing. A system designed just to provide hot water (and hot water takes about 20 percent of all the money you spend on all forms of home energy) will cost relatively little: $1,800 or so.

Solar systems do best in houses that are especially designed for them, but under the right conditions they can be installed in existing houses with good results. The collector must have a southern exposure that is not shaded by surrounding buildings or trees. Most collectors are installed on the roof, but they may be installed in the yard. And the house must have a forced–warm-air heating system, for this can serve as the distribution system for the solar heat and also provide standby heat. If you have an electric heat, steam, or hot-water system, you must put in a separate distribution system for the solar heat. That's an added cost, and a high cost at that. For solar heat a house should also be relatively compact and well insulated and otherwise protected against heat loss.

At the present time, most solar systems are designed by architects and installed under their supervision. But more and more firms, both large and small, are entering this field, and that means that soon it will be possible to purchase a well-designed solar heat system almost as easily as you would purchase a central air-conditioning system. And as increasing numbers of firms get into this field and production of the elements increases, the costs will go down. However, you can be certain that there will also be some shady outfits in the solar heat field as it becomes more popular; so watch your step.

## Woodburning Stoves

A woodburning stove makes a very satisfactory form of auxiliary heat. In the past few years such stoves have become very popular, and there is probably more demand for them today than at any time since the days before central heat. If it is heat and economy of operation you are after, a stove is much better than any fireplace. Even the best-designed fireplace is inefficient in comparison with a wood stove. A fireplace burns a great deal of wood to produce relatively little heat for the house. Moreover, many fireplaces actually waste more heat from the house than they produce. A wood stove uses relatively little wood to produce a vast amount of heat, and as it radiates heat from many surfaces, it can heat a sizable area. A good wood stove costs less than a masonry fireplace, and it can be put almost anywhere in the house, even in an upstairs bedroom.

One homeowner we know told us about his happy experience with wood stoves. He owns a relatively new one-story house heated by electricity. Since his electric bills for heat were running about $250 a month, he decided to do something about it. He bought two well-designed wood stoves. The cost of the stoves plus the chimneys was close to $1,000, but once he got the stoves in operation, his electric bills for heat dropped to less than $50 a month. He pays $50 a month for wood, but he's still saving $150 a month on his heating costs. And he plans next year to cut his own wood during the summer months so that he'll make additional reductions in his heating costs. Both he and his wife are delighted with the wood stoves. The stoves are easy to tend, the fire burns all night if the dampers are properly set, and if the homeowners wish, they can maintain temperatures up to 80 degrees in very cold weather with the stoves alone.

We know of several families in our area, New England, that have installed large woodburning stoves in the basements of their houses. Some of these families have cut their heating fuel costs in half just by running the stoves in very cold weather.

There are many kinds of stoves on the market, from reproductions of the old, reliable Franklin stove, which is a combination fireplace and stove, to reproductions of parlor stoves, potbelly stoves, and stoves that one can cook on as well as depend on for heat. Some of the stoves that are most efficient in providing a maximum amount of heat from the least amount of wood are imported from Scandinavia. These stoves have been designed to heat an entire house in areas where winters are very cold.

The best kind of stove is made of cast iron, which holds and radiates heat much better than ordinary steel. The interior of the stove should contain baffles and heating chambers to utilize a large share of the heat produced by the burning wood. The cost of a good wood stove runs around $400, plus the chimney and installation.

Wood stoves can be put in almost any area of the house as long as they can be connected with an existing chimney or there is a way to connect them to a prefabricated metal chimney. They are light enough to be set on any solid floor, but they do require a base made of some noncombustible material: asbestos board, metal, brick, or stone.

## Fireplaces

Almost everybody wants a fireplace in his or her home; so even if a fireplace is not a very efficient way to provide auxiliary heat, adding one can be a sound improvement. You have to keep a sharp eye on costs, however, for fireplaces can be a very expensive kind of improvement, and if they are, you won't get your money back when you sell your house. For example, it will cost around $1,500 to have a mason build a conventional brick fireplace with a brick chimney for a one- and one-half-story house. If you have the same fireplace built of stone instead of brick, the cost can be several times this amount. And you will also have to pay a carpenter to make the opening in the wall for the fireplace and add the mantle and finish work; this can add another $500 to the cost. It is very doubtful that the fireplace will add $2,000 or so to the value of your house, but it will certainly make it easier to sell the house at a fair market price.

*Masonry Fireplaces.* These fireplaces are usually made of brick or stone and sometimes of concrete block. A masonry fireplace needs a solid foundation; so the only logical place to put it in an existing house is on an outside wall on the first floor. Adding an inside fireplace and an inside chimney to an existing house would cost a great deal of money. Of course, if you are putting on an addition, a family room, for example, and want a masonry fireplace, it can go just about anywhere on the first floor.

A masonry fireplace can be designed in almost any way you want. It can have a conventional single-front opening, be a corner unit, be two-sided or four-way, or be set in the middle of a room with a custom-made metal hood. But if you want a fireplace to provide the maximum amount of heat with the smallest fire, you should have the conventional front-opening type with a back and two sides to radiate heat into the room. Most of the fireplaces built today are not built to provide much heat. They are so deep that most of the heat goes right up the chimney. The two- and four-sided fireplaces don't have enough surfaces to radiate heat. Fireplaces built in this century have been installed for aesthetic rather than practical reasons. Fireplaces built in this country in the early days were made to produce heat. They are very shallow, and the back surface radiates heat into the room.

If you decide that a masonry fireplace is what you want, take the time to track down a mason who really knows fireplaces: many masons do not, and that is why so many fireplaces don't work properly. Either the fireplace smokes, or the fire never burns briskly. Get references and check them out before you allow a mason to build you a fireplace.

If you can't locate someone who is a fireplace pro, you're better off to buy a metal fireplace unit and have it enclosed in masonry. Such units cost about $300. They are carefully engineered and contain all the basic elements: firebox, throat, damper, smoke shelf, and so on. You won't save much money by using one of these rather than a fireplace built entirely of masonry, but you will be sure that the thing works properly. Some metal units, by the way, are designed so that they will circulate warm air into the room or through ducts into adjoining rooms or even upstairs. This type of unit can be a very satisfactory form of auxiliary heater. We have such a unit in our house and also have a couple of registers on the second floor. When we have a fire going, there is a nice flow of warm air upstairs even if the radiators are turned off.

*Metal Fireplaces.* The least expensive way to get a good fireplace is to forget about masonry and use one of the many styles of metal prefabricated units. These units utilize a metal prefab chimney that is light enough to be hung from the house framework or secured to an outside wall with brackets. Metal prefab fireplaces don't need masonry foundations but simply sit on a base made of a noncombustible material. This means that they can be used any where in the house—on the first floor, in the basement, on the second floor, and even in the attic. They can be set in the middle of a room or in a corner or even hung on an outside or inside wall.

Prefab units come in all sorts of shapes and sizes. The most familiar is the cone-shaped unit popular in vacation and contemporary houses. Most of these are made of heavy-gauge steel with a porcelain finish and come in a wide range of colors. There are other units, more conventional in design, that can be used as is or be set into a wall or covered with a veneer of masonry or gypsum wallboard. Metal prefab units range in price from about $300 up, and the total cost of installation with a prefab chimney can be less than $600.

# 14. Improvements to Electric Wiring

You may want to consider making some major improvements in your house electric system if what you have can't handle all your electrical needs, especially heavy-duty equipment such as room air conditioners, clothes dryers, and kitchen ranges. Home buyers more or less expect the wiring in a house to be adequate for their everyday needs, and a house with a wiring system that is not completely adequate is a very dated house. We know of a couple that turned down a perfectly charming old house when they learned that the wiring was not adequate for room air conditioners. Even when it was explained to them that the cost of improving the system wouldn't be high, they were not interested. The chances are that they assumed that if the wiring was out of date, so was a lot of the other mechanical equipment.

It will also be necessary to increase the capacity of the electric system if you plan to install electric heat in the entire house or in one or two new or existing rooms or if you want to install central air conditioning. You may want to make minor improvements in the wiring by adding more circuits or just a wall or ceiling outlet. And you'll become involved in new wiring if you add more living space by building an addition, finishing an attic or basement, or enclosing a porch. Finally, you will certainly want to make improvements in the wiring if the present system is unsafe for one reason or another.

## Electricians

Most communities require that all electrical work that involves the permanent house wiring be done by a licensed electrician. Local building codes also require that all the work be done in accordance with the National

Electrical Code, but some communities have regulations that supersede the National Electrical Code.

You or your electrician will probably have to get a building permit before any extensive changes or additions can be made to the wiring. When the work has been completed, it will have to be checked by the building inspector.

Electricians and electrical contractors are listed in the Yellow Pages. We have found that electrical appliance stores are a good source for the names of good people in a particular area. If you get in touch with someone who has a shop that is not in your community, be sure that the outfit is licensed to work in your town. Because all the work must be done according to the code, about the only difference between electricians is what they'll charge to do the work.

## Increasing the Capacity of the System

The total amount of electric power available in a house is determined by the capacity of the service equipment. This equipment includes the fuse or circuit breaker panel and the main switch. The capacity of the service equipment is measured in amperes (amp) and can be 30, 60, 100, 150, or 200 amperes. The more amperes you have, the more electric power you have.

The 30-ampere service furnishes only 120 volts; you'll know this because only two wires come from the utility pole to the house. The other, larger services supply 120/240 volts, and three wires come to the house from the utility pole.

Major appliances such as hot-water heaters, clothes dryers, and kitchen ranges require the 120/240 volt system; so if you have only the 120-volt, 30-ampere service, about all that it's good for is lights and a few small electrical appliances. You don't find the 30-ampere service very often except in a few older houses in rural areas and in some vacation cottages.

If you try to use more electricity than the service equipment is designed to supply, you will have trouble. The commonest kind of trouble is the blowing of a fuse or circuit breaker when a particular appliance is plugged in or turned on. Sometimes the circuit breaker will not blow, but the equipment doesn't operate properly because it is not getting enough power. Operating equipment on less power than it is designed for can ruin it.

Even if your service capacity is adequate for your present needs, it may not be adequate if you try to install an additional piece of equipment. We have a 60-ampere service, the minimum allowed these days by the National Electrical Code, which is adequate but will not be adequate if we want to install a clothes dryer, an electric range, or even a large room air conditioner.

The only way to provide the additional electric power you may need is to increase the capacity of the service equipment. There are two distinct parts to this job. The first and simpler consists of replacing the present fuse box or circuit breaker panel with one with a larger capacity. If you have a 120-volt system and increase it to 120/240 volts, a third wire must be brought to the house from the nearest utility pole, but this job is usually handled by your electric utility firm.

The second part of the job is not so simple, for it involves adding any circuits you may need. You will need, for example, a special-purpose circuit for each piece of equipment that is permanently installed. The list of equipment would include items like a bathroom heater, a clothes dryer, a sink disposal unit, a room or central air conditioner, a hot-water heater, and a water pump. It might also be necessary or desirable to install additional lighting circuits or appliance circuits in the kitchen and laundry.

All this is going to cost money. It may cost from $200 to $400 to increase the capacity of the service equipment, and it may cost $50 or more for each special-purpose circuit.

## Adding Circuits and Outlets

The cost of wiring is generally figured at so much per outlet, that is, for each wall switch, convenience, or special-purpose outlet or outlet for a lighting fixture. The price per outlet can range from $8.50 to $25, although we recently paid $40 to have an outlet installed on the wall of a stair landing. The price per outlet does not include the lighting fixture.

The price you pay per outlet depends on how much time it takes the electrician to do the job. Costs will be lower per outlet in new construction or on improvement jobs such as a new addition or wiring an unfinished attic. In these cases the electrician can get in while the wall and ceiling framework is exposed and can run the wires and install the outlet boxes with relative ease. Costs can also be relatively inexpensive if the electrician can run the wires up from a basement or down from an attic. But costs can be very high if wires must be fished up through walls and across ceilings, which was the case with our $40 outlet.

If you want to add an outlet to finished space, you'll be wise to be as flexible as possible on the exact location of the outlet. Perhaps moving the outlet a foot or so can make the difference between a $10 and a $40 outlet.

When it is practical, it's a good idea to have two separate circuits to serve each room, especially the kitchen. With this arrangement, if one circuit should fail, you would still have the second one to provide some light and power.

## Unsafe Wiring

The most important improvement you can make to your house wiring system is to make it safe or as safe as any electric system can be made. And the electric wiring in a lot of houses is very unsafe.

In older houses there may be wiring that was installed long before there were adequate wiring regulations, or the wiring may have been installed by someone who had never heard of codes or didn't pay any attention to them. When we were renovating our present house, we called in an electrician to add a couple of circuits. One day he announced that he had found that almost half the wiring in the house wasn't approved house wiring but telephone line wire. He just couldn't believe that this light wire had not set the house on fire years ago.

Some months ago we received a sample of a little gadget designed so that anyone could test an outlet to see if it was properly grounded. We went around testing all the polarized outlets in our place just to see how the device worked. Polarized outlets, by the way, have three rather than two holes in them and are designed for appliances, power tools, and the like that have a three- rather than a two-prong plug. The third hole in the outlet is a ground, and the purpose of the polarized outlet is to protect you from shock if there is a current leakage due to faulty insulation or an exposed wire in the equipment you are handling. Of the fifteen outlets we checked, only six were properly grounded; the remaining outlets afforded no better protection than ordinary two-hole outlets.

It's not just in old houses that you find hazardous wiring conditions. A lot of new houses, for example, have wiring made of aluminum rather than copper, and this can be a serious hazard.

## Inadequate Number of Circuits and Outlets

This is a very common condition, especially in older homes that were wired before there were all the electrical gadgets that you find in most houses today. The way most of us solve this problem is to stretch out the existing system with miles and miles of extension cords plugged into all available outlets. This is a bad solution for two reasons. First, it overloads the circuits, and while the fuse or circuit breaker may not blow, there is a chance that a wire will overheat and start a fire. Second, extension and lamp cords are not designed to carry the heavy loads required by items such as coffee makers, toasters, and room heaters. They may overheat to start a fire or ruin the equipment. Also, the insulation on these cords is not very durable and may not last when exposed to wear such as being run under a rug or carpet.

The only practical way to solve this problem is to install additional outlets and, if necessary, an additional circuit or two. This may or may not involve increasing the capacity of the service equipment.

An up-to-date wiring system should have one 20-ampere general-purpose circuit for each 500 square feet of living space, or one 15-ampere circuit for each 375 square feet of space. You also should have two 20-ampere circuits to provide power for outlets in the kitchen, dining area, laundry, and utility room. Finally, you should have a special-purpose circuit for each major appliance: air conditioner, dryer, and so forth.

## Grounding

If the house wiring was properly installed, the entire system and each outlet are grounded so that if any problem does occur, the fuse or circuit breaker will blow. If any outlet in the system is not grounded, it can cause a fire or produce a dangerous shock. You can have an electrician check your system to be sure that it is properly grounded, or you can do it yourself with testing devices sold at most hardware and electrical supply stores. If your system is not properly grounded, have an electrician attend to it at once.

## Aluminum Wiring

You find house wiring made of aluminum rather than copper in some newer houses. Aluminum is far less expensive than copper and is a good conductor of electricity. But after a period of time the aluminum may pit and eventually break loose at connections, creating a serious condition.

You can tell easily enough if you have aluminum wiring by taking a plate off an outlet and looking at the color of the wires connected to it. If they are a copper color, you have copper. If you have aluminum, the wires will be a silver color. If you do have aluminum wiring, check first with your local building inspector, who should come over and inspect the condition of the wiring. If it is hazardous, the inspector will recommend that you call in an electrician. Sometimes all that needs to be done is to rework some of the connections or replace some of the wires. In other cases a complete rewiring job that might cost $1,000 or more will be required.

# 15. Improvements to the Exterior

"Curb appeal," an expression used in the real estate trade, refers to how a house looks as you see it from the street—from the curb. A house with good curb appeal is one that looks so fresh and attractive from the street that the prospective buyer is practically sold on it before he or she even gets past the front door.

Builders of new housing developments have learned from experience that how a house looks from the outside can be almost as important as how it performs on the inside (more important for some people). Good curb appeal is such a significant sales tool that developers spend time and money to give their houses all the curb appeal they can. They'll spend a lot of time with their architect or designer to work up a front exterior that will be very appealing to most people. They'll spend thousands of dollars to give a model house all the curb appeal they can. They'll paint the front door an inviting color, add an attractive fence to the front yard, put down inviting walks, and add lots of plants and flowers and even good-size shade trees. And they'll check the house each morning to make sure that the grounds are in perfect shape and that there isn't a spot where paint has chipped, hairline cracks have appeared in walks or driveways, or weeds have sprouted in the planters. We once saw a $60,000-a-year sales manager pull an expensive handkerchief from his pocket and use it to wipe bird droppings from a wrought-iron railing at the front entry of a model house.

And curb appeal—that first impression—is as important for a used house as for a new one. If your house has a lot of curb appeal, not only will it be easier to sell but you'll probably get a better price for it than if its curb appeal were poor. There are many things you can do to give a house more curb appeal. Some are expensive; some are not.

## Get Rid of Old Porches

The old-fashioned front or side porch has pretty much gone by the boards these days, simply because there is usually too much traffic and lack of privacy to make sitting on the porch a pleasure. Unless a front porch or even a side porch was built at the same time as the house and is an integral part of the structure, most houses look better without a porch, especially one that was tacked on at a later date.

Old porches often date a house, and they make adjoining rooms dark and frequently damp because they block circulation. And both porches and wood stoops are difficult to maintain. They need constant painting and repair, and the wood can easily be damaged by decay or termites. So it's usually a good idea to get rid of porches unless they are suitable for conversion into year-round rooms.

You generally require a building permit to remove a porch even if you plan to do the job yourself. If you want someone to do the job for you, try a general contractor or a wrecking contractor. And be sure that the price you get includes hauling all the debris away.

## Simplify the Entrance

After a porch has been removed, it is often desirable to change the location of the front door or to add, subtract, or redesign front windows. This can make an enormous difference in the overall appearance of the house. Sometimes just simplifying the entryway itself can give a house a much more contemporary look.

## Add Window Shutters

In most areas of the country window shutters don't serve any real function today, but they do make a lot of houses look better. If you have to buy a large number of shutters, the cost can run high, and that's why you find many houses with shutters just on the front windows, where they count the most.

Stock wood shutters run around $20 a pair. If you use old shutters, you'll either have to strip off the old paint yourself (this is a terrible job) or take them to a furniture-stripping outfit. These places charge about $5 a pair to strip old shutters. Wood shutters must be painted every four or five years. Vinyl plastic shutters require less maintenance than wood shutters and come in a wide range of colors.

Today, most shutters are installed simply by screwing them to the house siding rather than by using hinges, as was done years ago. This makes a lot

An upper-level enclosed porch (top) was removed to improve the front appearance of this house and allow light to reach the upstairs bedrooms (bottom). New siding and roof complete the face-lifting. [*Bird & Son, Inc.*]

Redesigning the entrance to simplify lines was a small but effective improvement to this house (left). Exterior shingles were replaced with narrow vinyl clapboard siding (right). [*Bird & Son, Inc.*]

of sense because shutter hinges and latches are expensive to buy and equally expensive to install. The last time we priced shutter hardware, a set cost about $9, and as we needed nineteen sets, we decided to screw the shutters to the siding.

Whether you choose wood or vinyl plastic shutters, it is wise to stick with the classic type of louvered shutter rather than the solid block or panel type or shutters with fancy cutouts of animals, birds, or marine motifs. Many people feel that these shutters cheapen a house.

## Get Rid of Details That Don't Match the Style of the House

Few things detract more from the appearance of a house than extraneous details that have been added in the hope of "prettying it up" but that are not in keeping with the general style of the house. For example, multicolored aluminum awnings may look all right on a Florida stucco house, but the same thing on a Cape Cod house in New England looks totally inappropriate. Overly fancy doors, too much or too fussy ornamental metalwork on stair rails or as trim, too many different colors on door and window trim, sometimes coupled with patterned brick walls and variegated roofing colors—all these mean an overdressed house, as distracting to the eye as an overdressed matron replete with shiny earrings, clanking bracelets, dazzling beads and brooches, a bouffant hairdo, and rhinestone-trimmed eyeglasses. Neither house nor lady can be seen for the trimmings.

## Build a Breezeway

If you have a detached garage on one side and your house is short and stubby, connecting house and garage with a breezeway will make the house appear longer and larger. The breezeway will also be a great convenience in going from house to garage in bad weather. And it can be screened to serve as a cool patio for sitting or dining space.

The cost of a breezeway measuring 6 by 10 feet will be about $600. If the present garage is some distance from the house, you might consider moving it so that it can be connected with a breezeway. The cost of moving a small structure such as a garage, including putting in new foundations, will be about $500.

## Add Foundation Planting

Adequate planting does more than conceal the house foundations; it helps integrate the house and ground so that the house appears to be part of the environment, not just a foreign object dumped on the property. Evergreen shrubbery is preferred in most sections of the country, with the exception of tropical and subtropical areas, where plants native to the area are preferred. Foundation planting is an art, and to give your house a truly individual look you should study it in some detail and plan carefully. There are many good books on this type of planting, and you can get help from a local nursery or a landscape architect.

When foundation planting alone won't hide exposed concrete and masonry blocks, paint them with an exterior masonry paint either in earth tones or in a soft grayish green. This will help the blocks blend with the natural surroundings. If you wish them to appear a part of the house, paint them the same color as the siding.

## Get Rid of Overgrown Planting

Most relatively new houses don't have enough decent-sized shrubs and trees around them, but many older houses have too many large shrubs and trees. And overgrown planting does not add one bit to curb appeal but makes the house look depressing, dark, and dreary. Too much planting also can make

The exterior of a 150-year-old Greek revival house (left) after extensive remodeling inside and out, including installing a new cedar shingle roof and scraping and painting siding and old shutters, which were found in a barn (right). The small semicircular window was put in when a downstairs lavatory was installed under the front staircase. The owners plan to add an antique fanlight in the gable when a suitable one is found.

the interior of a house dark and often damp. The worst kinds of overgrown planting are evergreens. Because they don't drop their leaves, they keep away light and air the year around.

Nowadays it takes a certain amount of moral courage to go out with a big pruner or an ax and start hacking away at overgrown shrubs or cutting down a fair-sized tree, but this can make a vast inprovement in the property. A few years back we took down a 40-foot blue spruce from the front of our house. It was keeping the light away from most of the east windows, and it wasn't a very attractive tree because the top had been blown off during a hurricane a few years before. Many of our neighbors couldn't believe that we would take down such a big tree that had been there for many years, but after it was down, most of them agreed that its removal vastly improved the appearance of our property.

Rough-sawn shingles were used on this turn-of-the-century carriage house (top), accenting the curving lines of the gambrel roof (bottom). The new shingles used for the exterior walls were dipped a soft green. The old carriage doors were removed, and additional windows were installed on the first floor. The newly designed front entrance and masonry steps and gateposts were enhanced by the abundant use of foundation planting. A new driveway and lawn were also put in. The interior of the house was gutted, and a dramatic spiral staircase leading to a large second-floor living room off the balcony was installed. There are also two bedrooms and a bathroom upstairs. A spacious den, two more large bedrooms, a kitchen, a dining room, and a bath and a half bath are on the main floor. [*Fort Ridge Builders, Inc., Northport, N.Y.*]

## Front Walks

An attractive walk from street to house can add a lot of curb appeal. If you are going to put down a walk, your best choice is flagstone or brick, especially used brick if you can get it. These two materials are infinitely more attractive and inviting than concrete or blacktop. Of course, concrete and blacktop make perfectly adequate walks, but they don't have the charm of brick or stone.

## Front-Yard Fences and Walls

A front-yard fence made of wood is an asset if it is in good condition and is properly maintained. If it isn't, either repair and paint it or take it down.

As a general rule, a chain link fence at the front of the property does not create a favorable first impression of the property. No matter how well chain link fences are installed and maintained, they have a definitely industrial and commercial look. They are fine for the backyard but not for the front of the house.

Brick and stone walls along the front of the property are definite assets. Walls made of masonry block are fine in certain areas, such as Florida and the Southwest, but do not have wide acceptance in other parts of the country.

# 16.  Adding Living Space

Adding living space is one of the most expensive improvements you can make, but it can also be one of the best. You'll benefit from the additional space, and in most cases you can count on getting your money back.

For many home buyers the number of rooms in a house is a key consideration, ranking close to or even ahead of the kind of neighborhood and the general condition of the house. You can have a pleasant house in an ideal neighborhood, but if it is short of living space—if it has only two small bedrooms and a tiny living room and lacks a family room—it is not going to appeal to the vast majority of families. You'll have to wait until you find the one buyer who will be apt to want just that particular size of house.

The number of rooms in a house interests almost every buyer, not just heads of families with dozens of kids. Rooms represent living space, and the more rooms you get for your money, the better, up to a point. If you check the real estate ads in your local newspaper, you'll see that most of them mention the amount of living space in the house, not by the number of square feet but by the number of rooms. You'll find ads reading, "ten rooms," "four comfortable bedrooms," "living room plus family room." It's not the total number of square feet of living space that's important, for few people can visualize 1,800 or 2,000 square feet; it's how many rooms there are.

Comparing the number of rooms in a house is the basic way to determine value. If one house has eight rooms and another has six rooms and they are both in the same price range, it's obvious to most people that the eight-room house is the better buy, other things being equal. You are less likely to run the risk of overimprovement when you add space because only in the strict sense of the word are you making an improvement. What you are actually doing is increasing the size of the house rather than improving one particular area of it.

There is little room for a negative reaction to added space if the addition is handled well. You can see it, and you can measure it, and what you end up with is more living space. Added space is not like a superglorified kitchen or a bath that might appeal to you but might not strike the fancy of someone else, or at least not enough for a prospective buyer to pay extra money for it. Space can only be viewed more or less objectively and positively. Just about everybody appreciates it and wants it.

But you've got to use some good common sense about the kind and amount of space you add. If you have a four-bedroom house and add another bedroom, the chances are you won't get your money back, simply because there is not great demand for a five-bedroom house. And if you add a family room large enough to throw a party for sixty people, you may have trouble finding a buyer with exactly the same needs.

You should also keep in mind that families are becoming smaller. Fewer and fewer couples are having a lot of children. It costs too much money to raise them and send them to college. For years we have considered the average family to consist of two adults and two children, but the way things are going it may be safer to assume that the family of the future will consist of only three members. That means that four bedrooms may be the maximum.

## What Sort of Space to Add

Assuming that your house is short of space, the kind of space you want will be what most other people want. A bedroom is always a good bet, especially if it is located and designed so that it can be a multipurpose room—a study, home office, TV room, or hobby room. If you have a two-bedroom house, the addition of a third bedroom is a very sound investment, simply because there is a good demand for three-bedroom houses. Master bedroom suites that include a bath are very much in demand, especially if they can be more or less isolated from the other areas of the house.

Family rooms are very desirable rooms to add or to create because they are practical and have become extremely popular. Separate dining rooms or dining areas with good access to the kitchen are also good. More and more women are getting tired of having to serve meals either in the kitchen or in the living room; so the dining room is coming back into favor.

## Remodeling

The least expensive way to get more living space is to create it out of what you already have. An attached two-car garage, for example, can be made into a comfortable master bedroom suite with its own bath or into a family room. A breezeway can be enclosed to make a small dining area off the kitchen, and a porch can be enclosed to make it a family room or a second living room. These areas offer the best potential for added space because they are on the ground level, and ground-level space is the best.

A full attic, of course, can be remodeled into additional bedrooms, and the job can be done at a very reasonable cost. But as you've seen, attic bedrooms are not particularly desirable. Basements can be made into family rooms or used for other purposes, but they are the least desirable space you can utilize.

## Putting On an Addition

This is the most complicated and expensive way to add living space, and it's also the best. An addition will cost several times as much per square foot as converting existing space such as the attic, garage, porch, or basement into living areas, but an addition will add substantial value to your property. You may get back only a portion of the money you spend finishing off an attic or a garage, but if you put on an addition and keep costs from getting out of hand, you'll get back your investment without much difficulty.

There are several reasons why an addition can be such a desirable improvement. First, if done correctly, an addition can make a great improvement in the appearance of many houses. Take a rather typical little box of a house and add a wing on one side, and you no longer have a box but a pretty nice-looking house. And if you live in a development where all the houses look much the same, an addition is going to make your house different and larger-looking than the rest.

Another reason why an addition is a good improvement is that it can be planned and tailored to meet a specific need. If you are converting existing space into living areas, you are forced to work with whatever space you may happen to have. If you want to convert the garage into a family room, for example, the family room must be the same size as the garage. It can't be any larger or smaller. If you add bedrooms to the attic, the bedrooms must conform to the attic space. You may be able to get better utilization of the space by adding a shed dormer or raising the roof, but you still have a limited number of square feet to play with. An addition can be custom-tailored to suit your exact requirements.

Moreover, an addition can provide much more convenient space than you can usually get by utilizing existing space. If you need another bedroom, a bedroom addition that can easily be reached from the first floor of the house is far more convenient than one up in the attic. And if you need a family room, a family room addition that opens onto the outdoors and is convenient to the kitchen is far better than a basement family room.

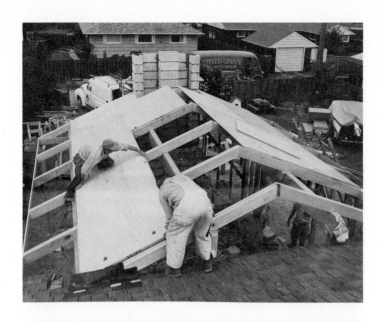

(opposite, top) A family room added to the rear of a house provides a protected terrace that can be reached either from the family room or from the main house. (lower left) Skylight strips in the ceiling provide natural light for the reading area of the family room. (lower right) The fireplace end of the family room. (above) A view of the addition during construction. The fireplace and chimney are of masonry block. (below) Plywood sheathing was applied to the framing after the insulation had been installed. [Western Wood Products Association     Architect: James Macdonald]

But additions do cost a lot of money. A modest-size single-story addition measuring 16 by 24 feet that can make a nice family room or master bedroom with bath will cost about $10,000 before it's finished. You don't want to spend that kind of money unless your house really needs the added space and for a very sound reason. At least you don't want to spend that kind of money if you want to get it back when you sell.

What are worthwhile additions? Well, if your house lacks a family room, a family room addition makes sense. If you need a fourth bedroom and another bath, a master bedroom suite could be a wise investment. We have also seen several additions to provide a decent-size dining room.

## Permission to Build

Whether you can add an addition and where it can be added depend on the amount of land you have. So before you do anything more definite than making a rough sketch of your proposed addition, make certain you've got the land to put it on.

Local building regulations establish building lines, which are fixed distances from the actual boundaries of the property beyond which no building or structure may project. For example, if the local building line is 12 feet, that means that 12 feet is the maximum distance the addition can come to the boundary line. If it's going to project beyond the 12-foot point, you should reduce the size so that it will be within the boundary line, move the location so that it will conform to the line, or try to get a variance.

Many homeowners have spent a lot of money in having detailed plans drawn for an addition only to find out, when they went to get a building permit, that the addition would extend beyond the building lines. In some cases, work on these jobs was under way before it was stopped by the building authorities. The only way to be certain that your proposed addition will conform to local building lines is to check the survey map of your property. This should show the location of the existing house and the distance from it to the building lines. If you don't have such a map, there will be one on file at your local building department.

Most lots are deeper than they are wide. This means that there is usually more space for an addition at the rear of the house than on either side. And as most houses are set rather close to the front property line, there is usually little chance of adding to the front of the house.

If you find that your planned addition does not conform to the building lines and it is the only solution to your space problem, you can go before the local planning and zoning board and try to get a variance. The result is always in doubt; so don't put another nickel into your project until you get a ruling. And be prepared to be turned down, for unless you can prove hardship, the chances are that you won't get a variance.

You may have to change the shape of your addition to make it conform to property lines or reduce its size. And you may have to change its location from the side of the house to the rear. It may be that a two-story addition will provide the space you need and at the same time allow the addition to conform to the amount of land available.

## Location

We asked a builder friend what he considered to be the best place to put an addition, and he answered, "Wherever you've got the land to put it on." And this is true. The amount of land you have available for the addition will be a major factor in determining its location. If the setback lines prevent your building the addition on the front or on either side, you build at the rear or you don't build at all. But assuming that you do have enough space around the house, some areas are better than others.

Putting an addition on the front of the house is the least desirable choice because this makes a drastic change in the appearance of the house. It also brings the house closer to the street, which is not good. An addition at the back of the house is best because it won't be very noticeable. In fact, you may not even know that there is an addition until you go around to the side of the house. And as the addition is not noticeable, you can do things that you can't when you add to the front or sides. You can, for example, put a very modern or contemporary addition at the rear of a traditional house, and it won't make any difference. If you were to add the same style of addition to the front or sides, you'd probably be unhappy each time you passed your house from the street. Another good thing about a rear addition is that you generally have more privacy there than on the sides or front. It's also very convenient to the outdoor areas.

Additions at the side are not desirable if there are neighboring houses close by. And they do make a drastic change in the appearance of the house. You need a good design to tie a side addition in with the main house.

If possible, the addition should be located so that it can easily be reached from the living areas of the house. You don't want to have to pass through the kitchen or a bedroom to reach the family room or bedroom in the addition. And if you can locate the addition so that it can be reached by an existing door, you will save the cost of installing a door.

(top left) Before the addition was built and other improvements were made, this house had a chopped-up and dated look. The owners, a young couple, decided a face-lifting and more space were needed. (top right) A small wing to be used as a family room was added to the house. The couple did all the work themselves with the exception of the architectural plans, wiring, and heating. Hardboard siding was used to match existing siding on the rest of the house, and vinyl-clad double-pane wood windows were used in both the older part of house and the new addition. (bottom left) The underside of the overhang was covered with a slotted hardboard soffit to keep birds from nesting under the eaves and to simplify the appearance. New aluminum gutters were added. (bottom right) With the new wing, the entryway was completely redesigned, and a new brick walk put down. Landscaping with attractive shrubs and plants emphasizes the crisp simplicity of the new design. Note that the appearance of the entire house was improved by the elimination of dark painted panels on the corners and at the entrance. [*Peter Perri/Andersen Corp. and Masonite Corp.*]

## Planning the Project

Only after you have found exactly how much land is available for your addition and where it can be located in relation to the house can you begin to plan the addition. You should have some professional help in planning. It's one thing to make rough drawings that indicate the approximate size of the structure, and you certainly want to have a lot of ideas and suggestions on what you'd like to have included in the plans. But you do need professional help to pull the ideas together and figure the best way to tie the addition in with the main house. Unless the addition is made to blend with the main house, it can be a drawback rather than an asset to the appearance.

*Stock Addition Plans.* A number of firms offer stock plans for various shapes and sizes of additions. You'll find these plans on sale at many building supply houses and offered through ads in home and remodeling magazines. They are fine for giving you good ideas, suggested materials, and kinds of construction, but they don't take the place of plans specifically designed for your particular addition or your house. Very few houses are alike, and even when they are, the land they sit on may be quite different from that of surrounding houses. This makes it virtually impossible to find a stock plan for an addition that will be perfect for every situation. Such plans provide a good starting point, but they must be modified to meet your requirements.

*Home Improvement Contractors.* Many of these firms have stock plans for certain kinds of additions that are modified to suit individual needs. Some firms even offer a standard shell addition that you can finish yourself. Others have on their staffs a designer who can custom-design an addition for you. This can be a good solution if the designer has talent. Not all designers do.

*Architects.* Architects are the best persons to plan an addition for you. Even if you can't afford to have an architect handle the entire operation, it's worth paying a fee of a few hundred dollars for consultation work. An architect may be able to save you the amount of the fee, and you'll certainly come up with a better-looking addition than if you simply have a contractor tack something onto the house. This is an important consideration because while a good addition can enhance the appearance of your house and thus add to its value, a poor addition may do almost the opposite.

*Having a Drawing Made.* You'll be wise to have a drawing made of the house with the addition in place before you go ahead. This is the only way you can know in advance how the completed project is going to turn out. An architect can make a drawing, called a rendering, for you. If you don't use an architect, try to locate a draftsman to do it for you.

## One-Story and Two-Story Additions

If you need to add more than one room to your house, a two-story addition makes a lot of sense. First, a two-story addition will cost a little less than a one-story addition with the same amount of floor space, for when you go up instead of out, you save on foundations, outside walls, and even the roof. This can add up to a lot of money in materials and labor.

Another advantage to a two-story addition is that it takes up less land. This can be important if you have a small lot or if you can't put in the size of one-story addition you need because it would come too close to the building lines. Don't discard the idea of a two-story addition just because you have a one-story house. We recently saw an outstanding addition that consisted of a two-story structure added to a one-story house. The addition had a living room on the first floor and a master bedroom and bath on the second floor.

This type of addition can save several hundred dollars. Placing the addition so that an existing window can be made into a doorway will be less expensive than having to start from scratch and open up a section of a wall.

## Keeping Costs Down

Every square foot of space you add is going to cost you money, perhaps $35 or more per square foot. It's foolish to spend $10,000 or so on an addition and not get all the space you need and can use, but it's equally foolish to spend money on space that you don't really need or space that is wasted because of poor planning.

You can save considerable money if you adjust your plans so that they lend themselves to the use of standard-size building materials with a minimum amount of waste and unnecessary labor in cutting materials to the correct size. For example, the standard-size sheet of plywood sheathing measures 4 by 8 feet. If you have an outside wall that is exactly 12 feet long, it can be covered with three full sheets of plywood without any cutting or 1 inch of scrap. But if you make the wall 14 feet 8 inches long for no very good reason, it will take four sheets of plywood, one of which will have to be cut to size. What's more, you'll have a big piece of waste plywood. If this process is repeated throughout an addition because of the manner in which the job has been planned, you'll end up with a pile of the most expensive firewood

The masonry wall connecting this New England house to its garage is actually the rear wall of a spacious new family room. The room faces a wooded area in back of the house. Light, air, and rear access are provided by double-pane insulating-glass sliding doors. The room was planned without windows on the right side to shield it from glaring car headlights at night and to ensure privacy from the road. [*Photo: Fred Hamilton   Architect: Al Riese, Madison, Connecticut*]

in the county. Always check your plans with a contractor to be sure that you have made as efficient a use of materials as possible.

You should also go over the plans and project with your contractor and get comparative costs on the various ways in which the job can be done. For example, you may find that a concrete slab will cost a good deal less than a conventional foundation with wood floor framing. But if the site for the addition is on a slope or much below the level of the house, so much fill may be needed to provide a suitable base for the slab that you'll save money with a conventional floor. Or you may find that changing the style of the roof will make it easier and less costly to build.

## Shell Additions

The best way to save a lot of money on an addition, of course, is to do a good deal of the work yourself. We don't suggest your trying to do the whole job yourself unless you are skilled at all the various trades and have the time and energy or don't need the addition for years to come. But having a contractor put up the shell of the addition—the foundations, floors, outside walls, roof, windows, and doors—and then taking over the finishing work make a very practical approach. Once the shell is up and the walls and roof are enclosed, you have a weathertight place to work in, and most of the finishing work is something you can do by yourself or with a minimum amount of help.

# 17. Enclosing a Porch or Breezeway

Enclosing an open porch or a covered terrace or winterizing a porch that is already enclosed can be an excellent way to get more living space, and at a good price. If a porch is basically well constructed, you can make it into a year-round room for about $15 a square foot. And if a porch is already enclosed, you may be able to winterize it for $8 a square foot.

Not every porch is worth bothering with. In many older houses, and in some that are not so old, you'll often find crackerbox porches that were tacked on after the house was built with little regard for either the appearance of the house or the way in which the porch was put together. We call a lot of these porches "two-by-four porches," because two-by-fours were the heaviest lumber used in their construction. Usually both the roof and the floor have begun to sag because the framing is inadequate. And the porch may have a definite "tilt" because it is supported by a few decayed wood posts set in the ground. If you have this kind of porch, you are better off if you remove it entirely, for to reconstruct such a shoddy structure would cost more in the long run than starting from scratch. The appearance of the house probably will be vastly improved because its original lines will be apparent and the effect will be cleaner and crisper.

The ideal porch to work with is one that was designed and built at the same time as the house. Porches of this type seldom have a tacked-on look, and they usually are well constructed.

Depending on its size and location, a porch can be put to all sorts of good uses if it is made a part of the main body of the house. Even a small back porch off the kitchen can be converted into the very popular "mud room." If it's big enough, you can add a toilet and lavatory and also let it serve as the home laundry.

A good-size rear or side porch can be made into an extra bedroom, study, TV room, or dining room. Not long ago we saw a house in which a portion of

The open porch at the side of this house (left) was seldom used. The owners therefore decided to enclose it for added living space and year-round use. New outside wall framing was installed across the top and bottom of the porch, and stock sliding windows with insulating glass also were installed (right). The new clapboard siding matches the gable end of the house. [*National Woodwork Manufacturers Association*]

the side porch had been used to make space for a much-needed second bathroom. (In our present house the kitchen is located in what was once a screened-in side porch.) If the porch adjoins the living room, the wall between the two can be removed to create one large room. This is also something you can do if you have a covered terrace at the rear of the living room.

A great thing to do if you have a two-story house with a porch that has a flat roof is to make the roof into a second-floor deck. This can be a nice private place for sunning or just sitting, and it adds another outdoor living area to your house.

A front porch doesn't offer as many possibilities as a rear or side porch. Because the front porch is usually the front entry to the house and opens directly into the living area, it doesn't work as a bedroom. In any case it is never good to have a bedroom at the front of the house because it would lack privacy and get a lot of street noise. But converting a front porch is an excellent way to get a larger living room: just take out the wall between the two. If you want to go to the added expense of moving the front entry, a front porch can also make a nice family room or dining room.

Front porches usually make the front living room dark and dingy, and this is one reason why many people rip them off. But if you combine the porch with the living room and add a lot of glass at the front, you'll have a nice, bright living room.

## How Much Will It Cost?

The cost of enclosing and winterizing a porch depends on a lot of factors. One is how the porch is to be used. It will cost more if you decide to combine the porch with an existing room—the living room, for example—than if you keep it as a separate room. The reason is that if you combine the porch with another room, you must remove a section of the exterior house wall. This is a bearing wall that carries the load of the floor above, the roof, or both. If you remove a section of this wall, a wood or steel girder must be installed to handle the load, and the girder can cost many hundreds of dollars. But if you keep the porch as a separate room—bedroom, family room, or dining room—you need not bother with a girder, for the outside wall can be left in place.

Costs will also rise considerably if you decide to alter the basic design of the porch. Many porches have shed roofs, which do not always furnish sufficient headroom for a finished room. And the roofs often add little to the architecture of the house. Changing a shed roof to a pitched roof with a gable end can vastly improve the appearance of the porch and also supply additional headroom, but it will add to your costs.

And your costs naturally are going to depend on the condition of the porch. If all the framing is sound and the quality of construction is good, you will be ahead of the game. But if much of the framing has been damaged by decay and insects, you must spend a lot of money. Before you spend much time on an old porch, have a contractor check its condition.

There are times when it can make sense to put money into fixing up a beat-up old porch rather than ripping it off and putting on an addition. As the porch is an existing structure, you'll probably have less trouble in getting a permit to enclose it than you would to get a permit to rip it off and build an addition. This would certainly be the case if the existing porch was put on before the present building lines were established and it projects beyond the lines. As long as the porch exists, it can remain, but if you pull it down, any addition you put on will have to conform to the building lines.

## Scope of the Work

You should discuss all details of the work with a contractor and get a rough estimate on the job. Some of the areas of greatest importance are discussed below.

A small porch (opposite, top left) was enclosed to enlarge a living room. The generous use of large sliding windows allows full enjoyment of a woodland view (top right). The room opens directly onto the remainder of the flagstone terrace (opposite, below). A steel beam was installed to hold up the roof after the removal of a structural bearing wall. The house seems much more spacious. A sketch (below) shows details of construction. [*National Woodwork Manufacturers Association*]

DARKENED AREA WAS THE
PORCH. PLAN SHOWS SPACE
GAINED BY ENCLOSING IT, AND
REMOVING THE TWO WINDOWS.
THE LIVING ROOM NEARLY
DOUBLES IN SIZE AND USEFULNESS.

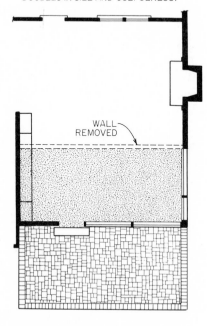

WALL
REMOVED

SKETCH SHOWS HOW BEARING WALL WAS REMOVED
AND STEEL BEAM INSTALLED TO SUPPORT RAFTERS
AND JOISTS; TWO-BY-FOURS FINISH JOB.

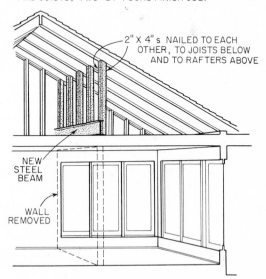

2" X 4" s NAILED TO EACH
OTHER, TO JOISTS BELOW
AND TO RAFTERS ABOVE

NEW
STEEL
BEAM

WALL
REMOVED

*Foundations.* You need good foundations for a porch, but you do not necessarily require a solid masonry foundation wall. Such a wall can cost a lot of money and piers of masonry or wood can be perfectly adequate. The piers should rest on a solid foundation or footing made of poured concrete, and there should be enough of them to provide adequate support. Wood posts should be made of pressure-treated wood so that they will resist decay and attack by insects. If you wish to enclose the crawl space for the sake of appearance, this can be done with a curtain wall of asbestos board or a similar material that will not be harmed by moisture and will not require a lot of maintenance. The underside of the porch floor should be insulated, and any heating and water pipes should also be insulated to prevent freezing and heat loss.

If you do decide to have a masonry block foundation wall installed, be sure that there are vents on all three sides and that one vent is large enough so that someone can get into the crawl space. And the ground under the porch should be covered with heavy-duty plastic sheeting to keep the dampness of the earth from getting into the crawl space. Plastic sheeting can be just as effective as a more expensive concrete slab floor.

*Heating.* You can heat an enclosed porch either by using the existing house heating system or with electric heat (baseboard or wall panels). Check with your contractor to find the least expensive method. If the contractor recommends electric heat as the least expensive method, be sure that your electric service entrance has also been checked to make certain that it has the capacity to handle electric heat. If it does not, you must have a larger service entrance installed, and this can add $300 or more to your costs. And if the contractor says that it will be easier to heat the porch with your house heating system, make sure that the system has been checked to determine whether it has the capacity to handle this additional load without having to run full tilt. A furnace or boiler that must run at maximum capacity will not last as long as one that does not have to be forced.

If you are combining the porch with the living room, don't assume that the existing registers or radiators in the living room are adequate to handle the added space. You may need to add a register or radiator to maintain a proper degree of comfort. If you are enclosing a covered terrace with a flagstone floor, electric heat is probably the most sensible approach, for it is usually very difficult to bring in either forced–warm-air or hot-water lines.

*The Roof.* You might want to consider basic changes in the roof if they won't cost a great deal. If there is not quite enough headroom, for example, you might want to raise the roof a few inches. Or if the roof is a poorly designed

Space was added to the bungalow (top) by enclosing the side stoop and front porch. The old shingles were removed, and new vinyl siding was applied. The horizontal lines of the siding increase the apparent breadth of the house (bottom). [*Bird & Son, Inc.*]

An enclosed deck adds interest, light, and year-round use
to a bedroom. Exposed framing makes an interesting
architectural detail. Note the
electric heater enclosed in
the box seat in the bedroom.
[*Western Wood Products
Association Architect: Dan-
iel Solomon, AIA Photo:
Joshua Freiwald*]

shed type, you might consider having it converted into a more attractive pitched roof with a gable end. If the porch has a flat roof and you want to use it as an upstairs deck, find out how much it will cost to reinforce the roof so that it can become a solid deck.

You should also inspect the porch roofing to be sure that it is in good shape. For some reason porches often have roofing made of the least expensive and durable material available, and you certainly want a good roof for your money. The underside of the roof should be insulated; other-wise, the porch room will become very hot in summer and will waste a lot of heat in cold weather.

*Walls.* The best kind of siding to use is that used on the main house. Of course, if your house is built of brick or stone, you'd do better to switch to a wood siding that will blend in with the rest of the house. We don't recom-mend that you use stone, which is costly, and brick is not satisfactory

Casement double-pane windows are most suitable for enclosing a porch or breezeway, for they provide a maximum amount of light and air. [*Anderson Corp.*]

because new brick will not blend in with the old brick of the house but stand out like a sore thumb.

If you need to install windows, and you will unless you already have an enclosed porch with good windows, use the best windows you can afford. And remember that while windows let in light, they also let in street sounds, and they can reduce the amount of usable wall space. If you are making a bedroom out of a porch, it's wise to use windows of the awning type. These can be set high up on the wall and will provide light and ventilation, but they don't use up a lot of valuable wall space. They also provide greater privacy than windows set at eye level in the wall.

# 18. Exterior Painting

A fresh coat of paint can do wonders for almost any house. The right kind of paint job can make a nondescript house look good and a good house look even better.

Paint can be a very inexpensive way to improve the architecture of a house. It can be used to reduce the importance of unattractive features by "painting them out." Dormer windows that are out of scale or an oversize chimney can be made to seem less dominant by painting them the same color as the roof. If the exterior of the house is composed of several different kinds of materials (wood, brick, stone, stucco), you can pull them together by painting everything the same color. And paint can be used to emphasize the good features. For example, if you have an older house with attractive trim around windows or cornices, painting them a different color from the siding makes them stand out and demand attention.

Although a fresh paint job may not always add much value to your house, you can be pretty certain that if the old paint is in poor condition or its color is a poor choice, it will detract from the value. In fact, many real estate brokers will suggest that a seller invest in a fresh coat of paint in cases of this sort. We know of one little house that didn't sell, primarily because both the siding and the woodwork were painted a dirty brown. The broker finally convinced the owner to spend a few hundred dollars and have the place painted white, and it sold almost immediately at the asking price.

Every material used for house siding can be painted with good results if the correct type of paint is used. You can paint asbestos shingles, unfinished or factory-finished aluminum siding, vinyl siding, bricks, masonry blocks, stone, stucco, hardboard, and all types of wood siding: clapboard, shingles, plywood.

All forms of wood siding must be painted or coated with some sort of protective finish such as a wood stain, clear stain, or wood sealer. About the only kind of wood siding that does not actually need a protective coating is redwood, but even redwood will not weather evenly and may become stained and discolored by dirt. It's worth giving even redwood a clear coating of a wood sealer.

In theory the nonwood types of siding such as aluminum, stucco, and brick need not be painted. Many owners of houses made of these materials don't paint them because once they've started painting, they must repaint every few years, and this runs up maintenance costs. But if painting can improve the appearance of the house, and it often can, we think it's worth the cost.

## How Often to Paint

You can figure that a good-quality paint job will last from six to eight years. After this length of time, the paint film becomes so thin that it's time for another coat. If you have wood siding and put off repainting too long, the wood will begin to be exposed. When this happens, you'll need two coats of paint, a primer and a finish coat, and this increases your costs.

Of course, not every paint job will last as long as eight years. Certain bright colors fade more quickly than others, and while the paint film may still be good, the color has a washed-out look. You may also have to paint more frequently if you live in an area where there are a lot of industrial fumes that can discolor and ruin paint.

## Exterior Paints and Finishes

Many different kinds of paints and finishes are used for outside work. The choice of which ones to use depends on what is being painted, the type of material, the condition and type of the existing finish, and the effect you wish to achieve.

When homeowners have their houses painted by a professional, they often leave the choice of the paint or finish up to the painter and feel that all they have to do is to select the colors. This is a mistake because while some painters know all about the advantages and disadvantages of the many finishes, others do not. Many painters use just one kind of paint regardless of other conditions, and this can often lead to future problems. So whether you are painting the house yourself or having the job done by a professional, you should know a little about the various finishes available.

## Opaque Paints

We'll begin with paints with an opaque finish, that is, with enough pigment to hide completely the surface over which they are applied.

*Linseed Oil Paints.* These are commonly called "house paints." They are thinned with solvents such as turpentine or mineral spirits and so have a strong odor until they dry. And they dry rather slowly. You don't want to apply these paints when there is a chance of a late-afternoon shower, and you don't want to use them when there are a lot of flying insects about. Because linseed oil paints can be harmed by moisture, they are not the best paints to use over masonry such as brick or stucco. And you don't want to apply them even to wood if the wood is damp or may absorb moisture at some future time. But these paints do have some distinct advantages over other types of house paints. They cover very well and adhere to surfaces in varying conditions. For example, they can be applied over old paint that is badly chalking or has become very worn. And oil paints can be applied to such surfaces with a minimum of surface preparation and without the need for a primer.

We didn't use an oil paint a few years ago, and the omission cost us a lot of time and money. We have a large outbuilding on our place, and the old paint was in very poor shape—chalking and so thin in spots that the wood was showing through. And a lot of the paint was cracked. Because we had a few gallons of latex house paint around, we decided to use it rather than buy a linseed oil paint. It took us hours to prepare the surface, and then we had to apply a coat of latex primer and a finish coat. The job took days and days. If we had used a linseed oil paint, all we would have had to do would be to give the old surface a wire-brushing and then slap on a single coat of paint.

*Latex Exterior Paints.* These are far more popular than linseed oil paints. They are easy to apply, you can clean brushes and other painting tools with water, and they dry in less than an hour. Latex paints can be applied over a damp surface and can be used on all forms of masonry as well as on wood.

One of the chief advantages of latex paints is that they breathe and allow moisture behind the paint film to flow through and escape outdoors. This reduces the possibility of the paints blistering and peeling. But the advantage is realized only when the latex paint is applied over a latex primer that has been applied directly to the bare wood. If you apply a latex paint over an old paint that is blistering and peeling, the condition will continue. So if you have been having trouble with blistering and peeling paint, don't let anyone tell you that you can correct the situation by applying a coat of latex paint. The only way latex paint will do any good is first to strip off all the old paint and then to prime the wood with a latex primer.

Latex paint can be applied over other kinds of paint provided the old paint is in good condition. But if the old paint is heavily chalking, badly worn, or filled with cracks, a latex primer must go on before the finish coat of latex. However, latex is an excellent paint to use for new work and for repainting over an old finish that is in good condition.

*One-Coat House Paints.* These are linseed oil or latex paints with additional amounts of pigment to give them greater hiding power. Don't let the name mislead you, however, because it does not mean that you can slap a coat on bare wood and get by with just one coat. All ''one-coat'' means is that if the surface has previously been painted or has been primed, you'll need only one coat. But this holds true for most regulation exterior paints of good quality. Unless you are making a drastic change of color, the chances are that you can get by with just one coat. We recently decided to change the color of our house from white to slate gray and did it with just one coat of latex paint. It was a good-quality paint, and that generally means a lot of hiding power.

*Linseed Oil Emulsion Paints.* These are relatively new, and we have not had experience with them. They are supposed to combine some of the advantages of linseed oil paints and latex paints. They can be applied to damp surfaces, and they hold well over most old paints.

*Pigmented Oil Stains.* These stains are often used on wood shingles and wood shakes, but they can also be used on plywood and other kinds of wood siding. They contain less pigment than ordinary house paints; so while they add color, they do not conceal the texture of the wood grain. Oil stains are easier to apply than paint, especially over a rough surface, and they generally don't last as long as paint. On the other hand, it's easy to slap on another coat if it is required. Another advantage in using a stain is that it will not blister and peel, as paints will under certain conditions.

But stains can be applied only to bare wood. If you apply them over old paint, the result will be about the same as if you had used a very thin coat of house paint.

*Masonry Paints.* Latex is the best kind of paint to use on all forms of masonry walls except those made of slag or cinder blocks. Cinder blocks contain

A much crisper, more up-to-date appearance was achieved by painting this 1920s house (left) a darker color and adding new shutters (right). Aluminum storm sashes were also installed. Additional foundation planting completes the fairly modest exterior renovations, which make a big difference in the overall effect. [Lisanti]

particles of iron, and if you use a water-thinned paint on them, rust stains will appear. Use an oil-base "stucco paint" on these materials. You can also use this paint on old masonry that is never damp.

*Trim-and-Shutter Paints.* These paints have an enamellike finish and dry to a high gloss. They are either a latex or an alkyd-base type of paint; both types are good. The paint used for the siding often is also used for the trim (windows, doors, cornices), but this is not a good practice. You need a hard, durable finish on these areas, which get a lot of wear, and a trim-and-shutter paint is made for this very purpose.

## Natural Finishes

While paint and even pigmented stains contain a good deal of pigments, natural finishes contain very little so that they allow the natural color of the wood to show but at the same time provide a protective coating. Some types of natural finishes form a surface film, while others penetrate the wood pores. One thing to remember about natural finishes is that they don't hold up as long as paint or a pigmented stain. It is the pigment in the finish that helps it to resist destruction by the sun's rays. The greater the amount of pigment, the longer the finish will hold up. Paint with a lot of pigment may last from six to eight years, but a clear finish may last only one year before it must be replaced.

*Exterior and Spar Varnish.* This finish is sometimes used on trim and frequently on the front door. It is a very poor kind of finish to use for exterior work. Because it contains very little pigment, it soon breaks down from exposure to the sun. What's more, because it is a film on the surface of the wood, it must be removed before a fresh coat can be successfully applied. If any of your exterior woodwork is coated with varnish, you'll be wise to paint it unless you want to spend time and money removing the old varnish every year or so and applying a fresh coat. If the old varnish is still in good condition, you can paint right over it, but if it's badly cracked and scaling, strip it off.

*Penetrating Clear Sealers.* Sealers are much better than varnish if you want a natural finish for outside woodwork. Unlike varnish, which forms a film on the surface of the wood, a sealer penetrates the wood pores. This means that when the sealer begins to break down, you don't have to remove it. Just wipe the surface clean, and apply a fresh coat of the same sealer.

## Condition of the Surface

Today's paints and finishes are generally excellent and can do wonders, but they won't do well if they are applied over a surface that is in an unsatisfactory condition. If there is something wrong with the old paint, you must correct the condition before putting on a fresh coat. If you don't, you are wasting money.

## Old Paint Blistering and Peeling

This is probably the commonest of all paint problems, and it can occur on new houses as well as on very old ones. The condition is easy enough to spot because the blisters on the paint film are obvious, and when the paint begins to peel, the bare wood is exposed.

The reason that paint blisters and then peels is that there is moisture in the wood under the paint film. As the moisture is drawn out of the wood, it lifts the paint film off the wood, creating a blister. If you split a blister, you'll often find drops of water. In time the blisters will split of their own accord, and the paint will peel from the siding.

Blistering and peeling are caused by moisture in the wood that has been painted. How did moisture get to the wood? There are many reasons. In a new house it may be that an oil-base paint was applied to damp siding. If this is the case, the blistering and peeling will occur over most of the wall surface. Moisture can also reach the siding through cracks and seams around window and door frames or at the joints between the siding and the cornice. Water that flows off improperly hung gutters or leaky downspouts can also cause blistering. In all these cases the blistering and peeling will occur close to the source of the trouble.

Often this paint problem is caused by moisture from inside the house flowing through the walls to the wood siding. In cold weather the moisture content of the air inside the house is considerably higher than that of the colder outside air. Moisture vapor is a gas, and it flows from warm to cold. As it is a gas, it can pass through ordinary building materials such as plaster or gypsum wallboard and wood. What happens is that the moisture vapor flows through the wall and condenses into a liquid when it strikes the cold sheathing or wood siding. In time it seeps through the siding and lifts the paint film off.

Blistering and peeling due to the condensation of moisture vapor most frequently occur on walls around rooms with a high moisture content such as bathrooms and kitchens. But the condition can occur on any wall.

There are several ways to tackle this problem. One is to decrease the humidity in the house during cold weather or to use exhaust fans to remove the moist air from kitchens and bathrooms. Another approach is to install some sort of vapor barrier on the inside walls that will prevent the moisture vapor from getting into the wall. A couple of coats of wall enamel make a good vapor barrier, and so does a coat of aluminum paint followed by a coat of flat wall or enamel paint.

Another approach is to install small vents in the outside walls so that the moisture vapor can escape to the outdoors before it has a chance to condense into a liquid. These vents are sold at most hardware stores and lumberyards and are not difficult to install.

Latex house paints are less likely to blister and peel than oil-base paints because the latex paints breathe and allow the moisture vapor to flow through them. This advantage holds true only if the latex paint is applied over a latex primer that has been applied to the bare wood. If you have an oil-base paint that is blistering and peeling, it won't help matters to put on a coat of latex. What you must do is to strip off all the old paint, apply the latex primer, and then add the finish coat of latex.

## Alligatoring

This is a condition that you find in many older houses. It consists of deep cracks in the many coats of paint so that the surface has a texture about the same as the skin of an alligator. There is only one way to handle alligatoring, and that is to strip off all the old paint right down to the wood. This can be a very time-consuming or expensive operation. You might find that it will cost less to apply aluminum or vinyl siding over the old siding than to strip off the old paint and repaint.

## Checking

This is the name for small cracks in the top coat of paint. Checking is not as serious as alligatoring. Scraping or sanding may remove the hairline cracks, or they can be filled in with exterior spackle.

## Chalking

Many house paints are designed so that they chalk, for chalking helps to keep the surface clean and also reduces the thickness of the paint film, making it more suitable for repainting after a period of time. But if the chalking is abnormal and the paint seems to be washing away, that's another matter. You should not apply a latex house paint over this sort of surface. Either use a latex primer first or just an oil-base paint.

## Selection of Colors

Most of us stick with the color originally used when repainting, and for good reasons. First, you know in advance just how the house will look when it's finished—about the same as it was before the fresh paint was applied. Also, if you use the same color as before, you can do the job in one coat. If you change colors, you may need two coats, and that runs up the cost. But if you are not perfectly satisfied with the present color or if you feel that it is not a particularly popular color, you may be smart to make a switch.

If you want a safe color, select white. Almost everyone likes white houses.

White stands up well without fading. The only real drawback to white is that it does show dirt and grime easily, and this is a problem if you live in an area where the air is full of dirt and fumes. Gray is a good choice and does not show dirt as easily as white. The same holds true for red and brown. Blue and beige are also good house colors. Yellow and pink are tricky house colors. They fade rather quickly, and not everyone likes them.

It's a good idea to drive around and look for houses painted in the colors you are considering before you make a final choice. And if you don't find any houses with the color you have selected, you had better look for something else. It may make it easy for people to find your house if it's the only pink one in the entire county, but it may make it difficult to sell the house until you have given it a fresh coat of paint in a more generally accepted color.

## Getting the Job Done

The major cost of having a house painted is for labor. The last time we had our house painted, the job cost $850. Only $150 of this amount went for paint and miscellaneous supplies; the remaining $700 went for labor. It's obvious that you can save a tremendous amount by painting the house yourself. If you have a typical medium-size one-story house and the surface is in pretty fair shape, you can do the entire place in a few weekends. And if you have a very large house, there is no law that says you have to do the entire job all at once. A neighbor of ours has a big old house that he is painting himself. He is taking his time. He paints one side each year, and eventually he'll get the whole place done.

You can also save a good deal of money by doing some of the work yourself and hiring a painter to do the rest. A lot of people with a two-story house don't like the idea of painting while standing on a high ladder. So they hire a painter to do the top half of the house, and they do the lower portions themselves. There are others who do all the necessary preparation work themselves and leave the painting to a painter.

If you decide to have the entire job done by a professional, then it's important that you spell out all the details of the work before you agree to a price. Go over the proposed work carefully with the painter so that there will be little room for doubt as to what is to be done and what you'll be getting for your money. Some of the areas you want to cover are as follows:

1. *Surface Preparation.* This includes the sanding, scraping, spackling, and priming necessary to ensure a good paint job. If window glass needs putty or if joints require caulking, these should be included in the estimate. There are many painters who will give

you a good price on a job and then, when they begin work, explain that the price does not include all the required preparation work or that it includes only going over the walls with a wire brush.

2. *Scope of the Work:* Painting a house can mean different things to different people. You may assume that it will include painting the siding, trim, window sashes, shutters, gutters, and ornamental ironwork. You may even assume that it includes painting the detached garage, fence, or foundation walls. But to the painter who is doing the job, it may mean just painting the siding, windows, and trim. The way to play it safe is to list every element on the outside of the house that is to be painted and include this list in your letter of agreement or contract with the painter. It would also be wise to include a list of items that are not to be painted. We made such a list at the suggestion of the man who painted our house because he had found it a good way to avoid misunderstandings.

3. *Brand and Color of Paint:* Your agreement should state the brand of paint to be used and the color. If you are changing colors, you should find out in advance whether one or two coats will be needed to do the job. The only sure way to find out is to apply the paint to the surface and see how it turns out. And this is the only sure way to know how a particular color is going to look when it's on the siding or trim. It's worth paying a few dollars for a quart of paint to make a test before you go ahead and paint the entire house. And it's especially important to make a test if you are using a custom-mixed paint because once you've ordered several gallons of this paint, you cannot return it if you don't quite like the shade or the color. We did this when we painted our house, and it saved us a lot of money and made for a better choice of color than we had originally specified.

4. *Be at Home When the Painters Come:* This is good advice because unless you are around the house, the chances are that something you don't want to happen will happen. A lot of painters, for example, forget to put drop cloths over all the foundation plants, and some of the shrubs get spattered with paint. Even the best painters get some paint where it is not wanted—on the walks or the front steps, for example—and if you are not there to see that the paint is wiped up immediately, it may be around for a good many years. And painters do miss a few spots. The men who painted our

house were very good and very careful, but even so they managed to paint one piece of corner trim the same color as the siding and not the color specified for trim. They came back the day after we had noticed the error and corrected it, but some painters might take a year before they got around to doing such a small touch-up job.

## The Time of Year for Painting

Early fall is the ideal time for painting in most parts of the country. The days are not too hot or too cool, and there are few insects to get stuck in the fresh paint. The next best season is late spring, which is the traditional time for painting. Summer is not a good time for outside painting because unless the work is done early in the morning or late in the afternoon, the paint may dry too quickly.

Oil-base paints require dry weather. They should not be applied over a damp surface, and they take at least overnight before they dry and won't be harmed by water. Latex paints may be applied over a damp surface, and they dry in less than an hour. But be careful about using a latex paint outside if there is a chance of a sudden shower. We have heard of cases in which most of the latex paint on an entire wall was washed off because of a summer shower that struck before the paint had set.

# 19. Roofing and Siding

## Roofing

A new roof on your house can do a lot more than keep out the rain. You'll be happily surprised at how much it can improve the appearance of the house. A new roof is like a fresh coat of paint on the outside walls: it helps make the house look fresh and new. So don't think of a new roof as just a basic improvement that must be made to keep out the rain. The right color of roof will have added benefits. For example, a white or light-color roof reflects heat away from the house; so this is a good choice if you live in a very warm climate. A light-color roof can also make a small or low house seem larger, and a dark-color roof can make a tall house appear lower than it actually is.

Don't put off getting a new roof until the old one fails and begins leaking like a sieve. One of the mistakes we made after buying our house was to take the chance that the old asphalt shingles on the roof would last a good many more years. We didn't even bother to check the roof carefully and went ahead and spent our money on other improvements. Then one day we had a bad wind and rain storm, and after the wind had finished ripping up those brittle old shingles, we had a dozen leaks in the roof. A neighbor of ours took a chance on a built-up flat roof, which started to leak right after he had finished decorating the walls and ceilings of the room below. The water ruined all his hard work. So if you are ready for a new roof, get it before you make any other improvements.

But be equally certain that you do need a new roof, because even a new roof can leak and small leaks can easily be repaired. Don't be sold a new roof just because one or two asphalt shingles are torn or missing or improperly nailed wood shingles have come loose. And don't let someone sell you a new roof when the real trouble is that the flashing around the roof valleys and chimney is at fault. New roofs cost money. Under more or less ideal conditions in which a minimum of preparation work is required, reroofing a small house with standard-quality asphalt shingles will cost more than $500. When we had our house reroofed in 1972, the cost exceeded $1,400, and today that price would be a bargain. On the other hand, once a roof is at the end of its usefulness, there is no point in wasting time and money trying to patch it or in spending money on one of the so-called miracle coatings advertised by some outfits.

The way to determine if you need a new roof is by its age or its condition or both. The vast majority of houses built in the 1950s and early 1960s have roofs made of standard-quality asphalt shingles, and these are good for about fifteen years. Shingles used on the more expensive custom-built houses may have a life expectancy of up to twenty-five years. But if you have a typical development house and it's more than fifteen years old, you are probably about due for a new roof.

You can also get a fair idea of the condition of your roof by inspecting it from the ground with a pair of field glasses. This is a better way than going up on the roof because walking about on a roof is likely to damage the roofing material. Check the roof from the south side, which gets the most exposure from the sun and is likely to show the greatest signs of age. Look for areas where the protective mineral granules have disappeared from the surface of the shingles, exposing the black felt mat. You may also find accumulations of these granules at the base of the downspouts connected to the roof gutters. The loss of the granules means that the shingles have dried out and are becoming brittle. It is time to think about a new roof.

Wood shingles have about the same life expectancy as the better-grade asphalt shingles—twenty to twenty-five years. You can tell when wood shingles are almost worn out because they begin to curl up at the edges and even split lengthwise.

Although asphalt and wood shingles have a life expectancy of not much more than twenty-five years, certain kinds of roofing materials will last considerably longer, although they may require repair from time to time. Slate shingles, for example, will last almost indefinitely. If some of the slates are broken or come loose, they can be replaced or reset. The same is true of the tile used on many houses in Florida and the Southwest. But be certain that the roofer you get to repair these roofs has had experience with them. Many roofers who are well qualified to handle asphalt and similar kinds of materials don't know anything about slate or tile and can do more harm than good.

## Reroofing with Asphalt Shingles

If you have a pitched roof, which most of us have, the most popular material for reroofing is asphalt shingles. These are available in a variety of colors and textures, and you should look over samples before you make your final selection. Until rather recently the quality of shingles was based on their weight. Today weight is not such an important factor in determining the life of shingles, which often are made of lighter but more durable materials than in the past. Manufacturers of good shingles provide guarantees or warranties that give the life expectancy of a particular grade of shingles. Because a major factor in reroofing is the cost of the labor, it's worth using the best-quality shingles you can afford, for the difference in price between shingles good for fifteen years and those good for more than twenty-five years is not great.

*Roofs Suitable for Asphalt Shingles.* Asphalt shingles can be applied to any roof that has a pitch of at least 4 inches or more per horizontal foot. It is sometimes possible to use asphalt shingles on low-slope roofs, but other materials are more satisfactory for these installations.

You can apply asphalt shingles directly over old asphalt shingles, and you can have them applied over old wood shingles without having the old shingles removed. In fact, it's better to leave the old wood shingles in place. Aside from the fact that it will cost money to rip them off, they add a certain amount of insulating value to the completed roof. But you should not apply new asphalt shingles over an old layer of asphalt that has previously been applied over wood shingles. If you do, the roof surface will be very wavy, and the new shingles may come loose because the nails have gone into the old shingles rather than the roof boards. If you have a layer of asphalt over wood shingles, they must all be ripped off.

Asphalt shingles cannot be applied directly over wood shakes, for shakes are very rough and uneven and the job will not turn out well. Have the old shakes ripped off.

*Cost.* The price of installing asphalt shingles is quoted at so much per square, which is 100 square feet. The price per square depends on the quality of the shingles and the amount of preparation work. If there is just a single layer of old asphalt shingles and the flashing around the chimneys and valleys is in good shape, the cost per square will be relatively low. If you have a layer of old asphalt over wood shingles, however, the cost per square will be very high. In this case it is usually necessary not only to rip off both

(top) Examples of some of the many textures available in asphalt roofing shingles. (center) Three examples of good roofing workmanship. The skilled application of shingles is important to the total appearance of a house; thus it is advisable to use established roofing firms. [*Asphalt Roofing Manufacturers Association*] (bottom) Good-quality asphalt shingles are long-lasting and require little maintenance. Properly applied, they are wind-resistant. They carry a label of the Underwriters Laboratories, Inc., for fire and wind resistance.

UNDERWRITERS LABORATORIES INC.®

LISTED
**PREPARED ROOFING MATERIAL SHINGLES – CLASS A**

DEGREE OF RESISTANCE TO EXTERNAL FIRE
AND FLAMMABILITY LIMITS
IN ACCORDANCE WITH UL STANDARD 790
DEGREE OF WIND RESISTANCE
IN ACCORDANCE WITH UL STANDARD 997
WHEN APPLIED IN ACCORDANCE WITH
INSTRUCTIONS INCLUDED WITH THIS ROOFING
**ISSUE No. A-00000**

layers of the old roofing but to install a solid plywood deck as a nailing base for the new shingles. This work can triple the cost of reroofing.

This is the sort of problem we encountered in our house when the roof began to fail. The roof consisted of roof boards set a few inches apart. The old wood shingles had been nailed to the roof boards, and when the asphalt shingles were added over the wood shingles, they, too, were nailed to the roof boards. This was as far as we could go in this fashion. If we wanted a new roof, both old layers of roofing would have to be ripped off because it would be impossible to nail new roofing in place and get the nails into the roof boards.

We had two options. One was to use asphalt shingles. This would involve not only ripping off the old shingles but also replacing the roof boards with a solid deck of plywood because roof boards are not suitable for asphalt shingles. The other approach was to rip off the old roofing and then use wood shingles, which could be nailed to the roof boards without the need of a solid plywood deck. We got bids from several good roofers on both approaches and finally decided on wood shingles. Even though these cost a good deal more per square than top-quality asphalt shingles, the final cost of using them would be less. But we live in an area where wood shingles are still popular and there are no codes to forbid them. In many areas their use is forbidden because of the fire hazard.

## Selecting Shingles and a Roofer

As we have said, the difference in cost between standard and top-quality shingles is not great, and there is no question that a roof with a twenty-five-year guarantee can be a strong sales feature when you sell your house. So get the best-quality shingles you can afford. And be sure that you get self-sealing shingles, for these can take high winds without damage. Most major asphalt shingle manufacturers make self-sealing shingles, which have an Underwriters Laboratories label on the package stating that they are wind-resistant.

The people who handle most of the roofs these days are roofing and siding firms, and you'll probably find a good many of them in your area listed in the Yellow Pages. Many firms stick to one brand of shingles, but if you press them to use another brand, they'll generally do it.

It's wise to call in three separate roofing firms to offer bids on your job. Be sure that they are all bidding on exactly the same kind of job. It makes a good deal of difference in the price if one roofer is basing his price on using standard shingles while another plans to use the top grade of materials. It also makes a difference if one roofer does not include replacing worn flashing while the other does. And it can make a whale of a difference in the cost if one roofer figures on taking a chance and applying new shingles over two layers of old shingles while the other plans to rip away the old shingles before installing the new.

You may also find that each roofer estimates a different number of squares of shingles to be installed. Sometimes the difference is just an honest mistake, but sometimes it's not so honest. One roofer may estimate low in the hope of getting the job. Then, after the job's under way, he'll announce that it will cost a couple of hundred dollars more than the estimate because more shingles are required than he anticipated. Other roofers will figure on using more squares than are actually required so that they can make a bigger profit. If you call in three roofers and each of them figures the job at a different number of squares, someone is not telling the truth.

Before you sign a contract with any roofer, check his references. You want to make sure that he does good work, cleans up when he has finished, and is reliable and honest.

## Scope of the Work

Your contract with a roofer should describe in detail the scope of the work he is to do. If you are reroofing over a single layer of asphalt shingles, there probably won't be any special problems, and all you need to be sure of is that the shingles are applied in strict accordance with the manufacturer's directions.

If you are putting asphalt shingles over old wood shingles, however, several things should be done to ensure a good job, and these should be spelled out in the contract. First, any loose wood shingles should be nailed down, and any missing ones should be replaced. If some of the shingles are badly warped, they should be split and the two halves nailed down. If this is not done, the warped wood shingles will prevent the asphalt shingles from lying flat, and you'll have a very uneven-looking roof when it's finished.

If the old wood shingles are badled curled or turned up at the butts, the finished roof will be uneven. One way to handle this situation is for the roofer to nail tapered strips of wood along the butt edges of the wood shingles to produce a relatively smooth surface. For a top-quality installation, the wood shingles should be cut back along all the edges for a distance of about 4 inches and a 1-inch by 4-inch strip nailed in place. This produces a clean, smooth edge. As all this preparation work requires added labor, you want to make sure that it is covered in your agreed-on price.

In case you have had to rip off all the old shingles and install a plywood deck, be sure that the roofer covers the deck with a layer of 15-pound asphalt-saturated roofer's felt. This will prevent the danger of the shingles'

A dilapidated duplex (top) becomes an attractive single-entrance dwelling (bottom) with the addition of a new roof, new vinyl siding, and shutters. The front exterior was completely redesigned, and dual front doors were replaced with an entry porch. Columns and a demibalcony help unify the front. The interior also was completely redesigned by opening up walls and removing staircases. A foyer was added inside the front entrance along with a center staircase. [*Bird & Son, Inc.*]

buckling if they are applied over a wet deck as well as damage to the shingles from saps and resins in the wood. The felt also ensures a more weathertight job. Many roofers don't bother to put on the felt because it takes additional labor.

## Your Contract with the Roofer

The contract should spell out in detail the brand, quality, and color of the shingles to be used as well as the scope of the work involved. It should give the total cost of the job and the method of payment. The contract should also contain some sort of guarantee from the roofer to cover the installation of the roof. The guarantee you get from the shingle manufacturer covers only the materials, not the workmanship. If your roof fails because of improper installation, you must go to the roofer to get satisfaction.

Your roofer should show proof that he carries liability insurance to protect you in the event of injury due to the roofing operation. And he should also carry some form of property insurance to cover any damage to the house and grounds. This can be very important if it is necessary to rip off the old shingles before the new ones can be installed. Most roofers, of course, don't rip off the entire roof at one time. They rip off a relatively small section and then install the new shingles in this area before moving to the next section. If they must leave a portion of the roof unprotected overnight, they cover it with heavy plastic sheeting. Even so, a sudden shower or driving rain might allow water to get into the house.

The roofer should state in writing that he'll clean up all debris left from the work. This can be very important when ripping is involved, for ripping can make a horrible mess if the roofer and his men are not careful or don't take the time to pick up every piece of old roofing from the grounds and in and around planting.

## Wood Shingles

These cost more than top-quality asphalt shingles and require more labor to install. They should last about as long as top-quality asphalt shingles, or about twenty-five years.

It's possible to add to the life of wood shingles and also to give them color by staining them with a shingle stain. The best way to do this is to dip the shingles into the stain before they are applied. If you stain the shingles after they are in place, only the exposed portions of the shingles will be stained.

Wood shingles can be installed directly over old wood shingles, but they should not be applied directly over old asphalt shingles. The best policy is to rip off the old asphalt shingles and have holes drilled in the solid wood deck to provide ventilation for the underside of the wood shingles.

## Residing

Residing the exterior of the house is a very popular home improvement these days. As a matter of fact, it's hard to look through the real estate pages of a local newspaper, listen to the radio, or watch television without learning of one or more firms in your area that specialize in the installation of one or more types of siding.

The great appeal of residing is that if you use one of the prefinished materials, you won't have to paint the siding for a good many years. The manufacturers of many siding materials provide a guarantee of up to twenty years or so, and even then the siding may not need to be painted unless the sun has caused the colors to fade badly. In the meantime, the siding requires no maintenance except a hosing down if it becomes dirty.

Residing is a practical solution if the paint on wood siding is in such poor condition that it must be removed before new paint can be applied. Hiring someone to strip all the paint off a house can cost a great deal, and doing it yourself can take forever. Moreover, any type of new siding applied over the old siding will help to make the outside walls tight and eliminate drafts and heat loss.

The right choice of siding can improve or make a dramatic change in the appearance of a house. For example, if you have a stucco house, you can give it a new look by covering the stucco with another type of siding material. If you have a house that seems too short for its height, you can make it appear longer by covering the outside walls with horizontal siding.

New siding can do a lot, but there are things that it can't do. Many homeowners, for example, reside because the paint on the existing siding blisters and then peels. Now this condition is caused by moisture inside the walls. You can cover the old paint with a prefinished type of siding, and while the finish on the siding won't be harmed by the moisture in the walls, the moisture is still there and will eventually cause trouble. You want to find out how the moisture is getting into the outside-wall cavity and correct matters before you go ahead and cover up the symptoms with new siding. If you don't locate the source of the moisture and correct the fault, eventually you may get damp spots on the interior surfaces of the walls, decay in woodwork, and even an infestation of termites.

For reducing heat loss through the outside walls, new siding is no substitute for standard-thickness wall insulation. If you don't have insulation in

A good example of what new siding can do for a house. In this instance, vinyl clapboard was installed over the worn old siding (top). The only other major improvements were the addition of gutters and the removal of the small window next to the front door (bottom). [*Bird & Son, Inc.*]

the outside walls, don't let a siding man tell you that if you put on new siding, you won't need it. The thin backup boards used with certain types of siding fall far short of the insulation value needed for an outside wall in areas where central heating is required. If you need insulation in the walls, have it blown into the wall cavity, and have this done before the siding is installed. Just before residing is the perfect time to have insulation blown into the walls. Because the existing siding will soon be covered up, the insulation firm can drill holes and take out sections of siding as required without spending a lot of time patching and repairing after the work is finished.

An important point to bear in mind if you reside your house primarily to reduce the need for painting is that unless the trim around doors, windows, corners, soffit, and cornices also is covered with new siding, the trim will still have to be painted every six years or so. On many houses the cost of painting the trim can be far higher than painting the siding. This is especially true if you have an older house with a lot of fancy woodwork, or gingerbread. And applying new siding over trim is an expensive job compared with installing siding on the wall surfaces. Many homeowners have saved money by having a lot of the trim removed when residing, but before you do this, think long and hard: you might be removing the best features of the house.

New siding can be applied over any existing siding material. In the case of wood, the new siding goes right over the old; so this is the least expensive type of installation. If the outside walls are of masonry (stucco or brick), the usual practice is first to install wood furring strips over the masonry and then to secure the new siding to these strips. As this method of application increases the thickness of the walls considerably, it may be necessary to build out the trim around windows and doors. This is an added expense, and you want to find out how much it will cost before you decide to reside.

Many older houses were resided with what is called "insulating siding." This abomination was supposed to resemble brick, stone, or wood shingles but never quite made it. The stuff looks dreadful and makes a house with the best lines in the world look like a tar-paper shack. Before new siding is installed, the old insulating siding should be ripped off so that the new siding can go right over the original wood siding.

## Siding Materials

The most popular materials for residing are aluminum and vinyl. Both aluminum and vinyl siding look very much like wood clapboards, and some types resemble wood shingles or vertical boards with a V joint. Once the siding has been applied, most people automatically assume that it is the traditional wood and can tell the difference only by very close inspection.

Aluminum and vinyl siding won't rust, and the finish won't blister or peel. When you figure that it costs $800 or more to paint the siding on a modest-size house every six or eight years, it's easy to see that aluminum and vinyl siding can pay for themselves in lower maintenance in a relatively short time. Obviously, also, the low-maintenance aspect will be attractive to many buyers.

Both these materials come in a variety of standard colors. The finish on aluminum siding is baked-on enamel, while the colors of vinyl siding are built into the plastic during manufacture. Most manufacturers of aluminum and vinyl siding also produce materials suitable for use as trim.

Steel siding is relatively new and has much the same advantages as aluminum. The one disadvantage it has in comparison with aluminum is that if the baked-on finish is scratched, the exposed metal must be touched up with paint at once to prevent rusting.

While aluminum, vinyl, and steel all make suitable siding materials, the success of the job depends finally on the application. Most applications are made by firms specializing in roofing and siding. If the application is poor, the siding not only will look terrible but may buckle because of expansion and contraction. Although the manufacturer of a particular siding may guarantee it for a good number of years, the guarantee applies only to the siding material, not to the application. You must be sure to get a firm that not only does excellent work but also will guarantee the actual application of the siding (and be around to back up the guarantee).

Other common kinds of siding materials are made of wood or a wood product such as hardboard. Hardboard comes in sheets or as clapboards. It is made of pressed wood fibers and is available in colors or wood tones. Cedar shingles, redwood, and plywood are also suitable for siding but are used primarily on new rather than old houses.

## Cost of Residing

The price of siding is usually quoted at so much per square, or 100 square feet. The average cost of aluminum, vinyl, or steel siding installed is between $150 and $200 per square. But it is not just the number of square feet of siding that determines the final cost of residing. There are other items that can add to the final price, and you want to be sure you know what they will cost before you decide to reside.

If you want the trim covered, for example, this will cost extra. And as we pointed out earlier, unless the trim is covered, you will still have to spend time or money to paint it every six to eight years. The cost of covering the trim with aluminum, steel, or vinyl varies with the amount of trim and the design, but it can easily amount to $1,000.

The amount of work required to prepare the surface for the new siding and necessary carpentry work will also determine the final cost. If you have a stucco house, for example, wood furring strips must first be attached over the stucco to serve as a nailing base for the new siding. And in many houses the trim is not thick enough to take another layer of siding. This means that all the trim must be built out by fastening strips of wood to the exposed surfaces. This can cost a large sum if you have a large house with many windows, doors, and so on.

A good siding man will make a very careful inspection of your house before he gives you an estimate on the job. He'll measure the house to determine the number of squares of siding required. He'll also measure windows and doors, soffits, cornices, corners, and the like to determine the amount and cost of the trim. And he'll make note of how much preparation work is involved. His estimate will cover all these items and be specified in the contract.

# 20. Garages, Carports, and Driveways

## Garages and Carports

A garage or a carport can be a highly worthwhile improvement, especially if it is built to do more than just provide a place to park the car. An oversize garage or carport, for instance, can be an ideal place for the storage of bulky recreational gear, garden and lawn equipment, outdoor furniture, and other items that can't conveniently be stored in the main house.

In warm climates, either a garage or a carport is a good spot for the home laundry (washer and dryer) or a workshop. Other homeowners plan a carport so that it will do double duty in the summer as a covered terrace. Either a carport or a garage can be a good spot in which the kids can play in bad weather, and a sizable two-car garage can, of course, be converted into a rental studio apartment if zoning regulations permit.

In cold areas, a garage is particularly desirable as protection from snow and freezing winds. In hot climates, a carport is preferable, for while it shields the car from the sun, it also allows air to circulate, thus keeping the interior of the car from becoming overheated. If you have ever stepped into a car that has been sitting in a closed garage all day with the hot sun beating down on the roof, you'll know why a carport is more desirable than a garage in the hot sections of the country.

A carport is also the best solution if you have a very small lot, for you can build an open-ended one over a portion of the driveway. In that way, you won't lose any of your valuable lawn or garden. The total effect, in fact, is much lighter and airier than a regular structure. A garage, being solid, must be much more carefully placed.

## Location

Local setback regulations may be the main factor in determining the location of either a garage or a carport. As a general rule, these regulations will allow car storage facilities to come closer than a dwelling to the actual lot lines.

Check with your local building department, and have it show you on a survey map of your property where you have space for either a garage or a carport.

Usually there is more space in the rear of a house than at the sides, and this is the reason that you so often find a garage or a carport added at the rear. A rear location can be a good one for a number of reasons. First, as the structure will not be visible from the street, it does not have to be carefully designed and built to harmonize with the architecture of the house, as is the case when you build at the side. You get more privacy at the rear, and this means that if you have a carport or leave the garage door open, the contents of the structure will not be exposed to prying eyes, possibly those of a potential thief looking for a bicycle, lawn mower, or even a car. The disadvantage of a rear location is that it may require a lot of driveway, which will cost money and take up some of your valuable land.

A side location probably won't require much more driveway than you already have and is generally more convenient, as it will be close to the front or side door of the house. But the structure must be carefully designed so that it will harmonize with the architecture of the house. If you have a traditional house, for example, a very contemporary-looking carport is not going to add to the overall appearance of your property. There are a few other points to keep in mind about a side location. If you place a garage (or a carport with a solid wall) on the north, or prevailing-winter-wind, side of the house, it will help protect the house from the cold winds and keep your heating costs down. But if you place it on the south, or prevailing-summer-wind, side, it will block cooling breezes. A garage or solid-wall carport will also block some natural light from certain areas of the house. An open carport, on the other hand, permits a maximum amount of light and air movement.

An attached garage or carport is, of course, more desirable than a detached one, provided that it can be added to the house without blocking light from one or more rooms. If the structure must be detached, build it as close to the house as possible. And it's a good idea to connect the structure to the house with a breezeway, especially in colder climates.

## Storage

The rule here is to build as much storage into your garage or carport as you can afford and have space for. One of the major complaints about practically every house is that there is not enough storage space for all those bulky items that have become part of our daily lives: power mowers, garden tractors, snow blowers, outdoor furniture, garden tools, skis, snowmobiles, bicycles. And remember that while you may not have all this assorted junk, a family looking for a house may well have all these items and more, and it will be looking for a place where they can safely be stored. A garage or a carport is the ideal place.

The best kind of storage space is a storage shed or bin that is included in the design of your carport or garage. If you have a good-size storage bin, you won't have to clutter the garage with all this equipment, and everything will be out of sight even if the garage door is left open or you build a carport.

A good storage bin should be about 4 feet in depth, and it can run the entire width or side of the structure. It should be fitted with solid doors that can be locked, and you should have a pickproof lock and not depend on a padlock for security.

We prefer a storage bin with doors on the outside so that you can get into it easily without having to move the car out into the driveway. Outside doors can be an important feature where children are concerned, because children can't put their equipment into the bin unless they can get into it with relative ease and without having to ask an adult to move the car. You don't get quite the same degree of protection against possible theft with outside doors as you would if the doors opened into the garage. That's assuming, of course, that the garage doors are always closed and locked. It doesn't, of course, make any difference in a carport, which has no doors.

## Dimensions

The minimum dimensions for a one-car garage or carport are 13 feet 2 inches by 23 feet. For a two-car garage you need at least 23 feet 10 inches by 23 feet. These dimensions allow you just enough room so that you can get in or out of a car when it is parked. They don't provide any storage space except for articles placed on racks on the ceiling.

## Design

Regardless of where a garage or a carport is located on the property, it should be designed so that it will harmonize with the general style of the house. If you have a rather conventional or traditional house, do not try to put up a carport made of aluminum or steel framing with a roof of colored reinforced fiber glass panels. A structure like this may look fine in Florida and the Southwest and with certain contemporary houses but not with traditional ones.

A rustic-looking carport is simple to construct and is not expensive. If desired, the structure could be closed in to make a two-car garage. [Photo: Alma McArdle]

## Features to Be Included

Before you get estimates on either a garage or a carport, make a list of all the features you want included so that you'll get a true estimate of the cost of the work.

*Floors.* Poured concrete makes the best kind of floor but will cost more than blacktop. Unlike blacktop, concrete will not be damaged by oil or gasoline dripping from the car, and if it is painted with a concrete floor enamel, oil and gasoline can be wiped off without leaving stains. Also, a concrete floor makes a much more attractive surface if you are using the carport as a play area for children or as a covered terrace.

A drain is not necessary for the floor of a carport, but you should have one in the floor of a garage, especially if you live in an area where there is heavy snow so that snow melting from the car can flow off the floor.

*Windows.* Plan to have enough windows in a garage to provide good natural light and ventilation in hot weather. And you should have plenty of windows if you are going to have a laundry or a workshop in the garage.

*Electricity.* You will need electricity in a garage if you want to install an automatic garage door opener, but you will also want it in both a garage and a carport to provide lights at night. Light fixtures should be wired to a three-way switch so that they can be turned on and off either from the carport or garage or from the house. You will also want outlets to provide power for such items as a battery charger and a drip stick heater for cold-weather starting. And the garage or carport makes a good spot for an exterior outlet box to provide power for electric garden tools.

*Plumbing.* If you are going to use your carport or garage as a home laundry, you need to bring in supply and drain lines from the main house. You may also want to do this if there is a chance that at some later date you may wish to convert the garage into a living area, either a bedroom and bath or a rental unit.

## Cost

A good-quality frame two-car garage will cost in the neighborhood of $5,000, while a one-car garage will cost about $3,500. The cost of a custom-made frame carport will generally run about $1,000 less than a garage, although you can get a steel-supported carport with a corrugated aluminum roof for about $500 if you put it up yourself.

## Driveways

Today a good driveway plus adequate off-street parking is as essential to a house as a good roof or a good heating system, maybe even more essential for some people. We heard of one buyer who wouldn't bother to look at a house because he smashed the tail pipe of his expensive car while going up a poorly graded driveway.

A good driveway is essential not only because it's a convenience and a safety factor but also because it is one of the first things about your property that people coming to the house will notice. If your present driveway is in poor condition, poorly situated, or dangerous, improving it will be a wise investment for you and for your property.

The ideal driveway is as straight and as short as possible. You won't add value to your house by making the driveway unnecessarily long or curved, unless this is the only way to reach the garage or parking areas. Otherwise, a long driveway just eats up money. It costs money to build, money to maintain, and, if you live in a cold area, money or time to plow.

A good driveway should not be close to trees and shrubs, the corner of the house, or high ground that might block the driver's view, especially when backing up. This is especially important if there are small children about, for they have a habit of darting out onto the driveway, often with serious results.

It is also important that the entrance of the driveway from the main street have good visibility in both directions. If there are trees, shrubs, or high ground that can block vision, get rid of them or move the driveway.

## Off-Street Parking

More and more communities are requiring adequate off-street parking, but you may want to add it in any event. It's a convenience to your visitors and will provide better security for your own cars than leaving them on the street at night. A parking place for two cars will require an area of about 20 by 24 feet. You can often create off-street parking by enlarging the end of the existing driveway.

## Turnarounds

These can be a great convenience and a safety feature, especially if the driveway opens onto a busy main street or if there are obstructions which block vision when you enter the street and which cannot be removed. Parents in particular are impressed with a turnaround because backing a car filled with children onto a busy street can be a nerve-shattering experience. Turnarounds, of course, take up space. The minimum area for a standard car is 18 by 10 feet, which must be added to one side of the driveway. But it's worth the money and land it requires.

## Types of Driveways

Asphalt or blacktop is the most popular surfacing material for driveways, and it is generally accepted as standard construction these days. It is moderate in cost: about $2 a square yard installed. If it is properly installed and pitched so that water drains off to the sides and if it is correctly maintained, it should last almost indefinitely.

Of course, blacktop does have disadvantages. It's not the most attractive material in the world, and it can become uncomfortably hot in summer. It also radiates heat into the house. The typical blacktop driveway is not designed to handle heavy trucks and can be seriously damaged by them. If your driveway is going to be used by heavy garbage or fuel oil delivery trucks, it will be worth paying extra to have it made thick enough to handle these loads. We know one man who rushes out of the house twice a week to haul his refuse cans to the street so that the garbage truck won't come up his driveway.

Blacktop has to be maintained if it is going to last. It can be damaged by oil and gasoline from cars and by frost. The best way to ensure the long life of a driveway is to treat it with a blacktop sealer once or even twice a year. A good rule to follow is to apply a sealer when water falling on the driveway is absorbed by the blacktop rather than running off.

Concrete makes an excellent driveway that requires little if any maintenance and can take heavy loads, but it's so expensive that it's seldom used these days. It will cost around $5 a square yard.

Crushed stone or gravel makes an attractive and low-cost driveway, but it has many drawbacks. Unless the soil under it is treated with a weed killer, weeds and grass come up through the stones. It is not a good material if the driveway is on a slope because rain will wash the gravel down and cars coming up will tend to throw the gravel back with considerable force. A window in our car was broken by a piece of gravel thrown out by the tire of a car going up a gravel driveway in front of us. Finally, a gravel driveway is difficult to keep clear of leaves, grass clippings, and other debris, not to mention snow.

Bricks set in sand on top of a bed of gravel make a good-looking driveway and one you can put down yourself. Bricks do best on a pretty level surface. They won't hold well on a slope, and they also become slippery in wet weather. But they are most attractive. We saw a brick driveway in a development home a few years ago and learned that it had been put down by the owner right over an existing blacktop driveway. It made that house look far more attractive than the houses around it.

## Contractors

There are good, reputable driveway contractors in every community. You should get estimates from several before you sign up with one. And if you have any doubts about a contractor, check him with your better business bureau or department of consumer protection. There are still a few slippery characters in the blacktop driveway business; so you must watch your step unless you know the reputation of the firm. A blacktop driveway is only as good as the firm that puts it down. When the surface is first applied, you can't tell the difference between a first-class job and a shoddy one, but it won't take much time before a shoddily built driveway begins to disintegrate. By that time you've paid for it, and the people who put it down may have left town for good.

# 21. Swimming Pools

Only a few years ago, many real estate brokers and appraisers took a rather dim view of swimming pools as an improvement that added value to property. The general feeling was that unless you lived in an area where pools were the rule rather than the exception, you might find that adding a pool not only did not increase the value of your property but could sometimes make it more difficult to sell, even if you were willing to throw in the pool for nothing. Although there are still some buyers who won't pay an extra dollar for a pool, by and large swimming pools have become an accepted improvement. So, if you have the right kind of pool and have had it installed at a fair price, it may well add a good deal of value to your property.

But do not put in a swimming pool simply as an investment. Unless you and your family really intend to use and enjoy it for many months of the year, there are a lot of other and better ways to spend your home improvement dollars. For many families the pool is the focal point of outdoor living and is in almost constant use for many months of the year. Other families have put in a pool, used it for a short time, and then lost interest, and the thing just sits there taking up space in the backyard.

You should also keep in mind that a pool is going to require a certain amount of maintenance. A pool must be prepared for the cold weather, it must be cleaned from time to time, and the pool along with pump, filter, and so on will require repairs. If you live in the colder regions, you may need a heater if you want to use the pool for a longer period than July and August, and pool heaters cost money to install and to operate.

## Investigating Pools Before You Buy

Swimming pools cost money. The average home in-ground pool costs around $6,000. Even a small round aboveground pool that you might pick up for the kids to splash in will probably end up costing you close to $500 plus a lot of hard work. Before you invest in any kind of pool, you should do a lot of investigating in order to know what you are getting into and to protect your investment.

The place to start is your local building department because every community will require you to have a building permit before you install a pool, and the installation must conform to local building regulations. These regulations include the type of pool you can install, the method of construction, and the distance from the pool to your property lines. They may require you to install an approved type of fencing around the pool. Even the electrical work that may be needed to operate the filter pump and pool lights must conform to the new and very strict electrical codes that recently have been adopted because of the hazard of mixing electricity with water.

It is your responsibility to know about these local regulations and to make certain that whoever installs the pool does the work in strict accordance with them. For if a pool is installed in violation of any of the regulations, you will have to pay extra to have the violations corrected, get the people who installed the pool to correct them free, or not use the pool. Do not assume that everything is fine because a pool dealer tells you that the work will conform to the codes. Give the pool plans and specifications to the building department, and get a ruling on them before you sign an agreement.

A swimming pool will increase your property tax; so it pays to put in a less costly pool even if you can afford something more expensive. And remember that it's not just the pool itself that will increase your tax but the decking and fencing around it.

We know of no rule of thumb on the cost of a pool in relation to the value of a house; so you must depend on common sense to tell you how much you can invest in a pool and still hope to get back your money, or at least a good part of it, when you sell. One thing is sure: if your house is valued at around $35,000 and you put in a $10,000 pool, it is very doubtful that you'll get $45,000 for the entire package when you try to sell. It's usually safest to install a pool that is more or less in the same price range and of the same size as those in other houses in your general area.

## Types of Pools

There are three basic types of swimming pools: the below-ground pool, the on-ground pool, and the aboveground pool.

*Below-Ground Pools.* Below-ground pools are just that: they are set below or entirely in the ground. They are generally made of poured concrete, Gunite, or a vinyl plastic liner over a frame of treated plywood or metal.

Poured-concrete pools are the most expensive kind and are seldom found except in the homes of the very wealthy. A well-made poured-concrete pool will last almost indefinitely, but it does require painting every few years and may also need repairs.

Gunite, a process in which concrete is sprayed over a metal form, is somewhat less expensive than poured concrete and produces a very similar kind of pool. One great advantage to Gunite over all other methods of construction is that it allows you to build a pool in a variety of shapes: oval, round, kidney-shaped, free-form. Gunite pools can be relatively inexpensive in the warmer sections of the country such as southern California and Florida because temperatures do not get below the freezing level and there are many firms that specialize in this type of pool construction.

The commonest and least expensive below-ground pool is the one with a vinyl plastic liner. Since the pool must conform to the standard size and shape of the liners, your choice of size and shape is somewhat limited. A good-quality plastic liner that is properly installed will last ten or more years and can then be replaced for a few hundred dollars. If holes occur in the liner, they can be patched easily without having to drain the pool.

The below-ground pool is the most expensive because of the necessary excavation work. If you want a pool deep enough for diving, you must make an excavation well over 8 feet deep. And you should be sure in advance that you can go that deep without problems. If you hit ledge rock, you have a problem, and the same holds true if you strike water. It's wise to have test bores made if you are not certain of soil conditions. You also want to make sure that the excavation will not damage the roots of valuable trees. And, needless to say, you should be sure that it will be possible to bring earth-moving equipment to the pool site. Trying to make the excavation by hand would be a very costly operation, provided that you could find anyone to do it.

*On-Ground Pools.* The on-ground pool, set partway above and partway below ground, is a good solution for those who want most of the advantages of a below-ground pool but don't wish to spend quite so much money or can't put in a below-ground pool because of soil conditions or other factors. This type of pool is made with a frame of treated plywood, steel, or aluminum with a vinyl plastic liner. You can set it so that half of the pool is below ground and the remainder above ground. If you have a sloping site, you can set one end of the pool at ground level and allow the other end to extend above ground to almost the full height of the pool. And you can obtain sufficient depth for diving with this type of pool. We have seen some very attractive on-ground pools that had most of the advantages of an in-ground pool but cost a good deal less money.

This pool is screened from the street by a 6-foot fence of 1- by 4-inch resawn cedar boards. The posts are 4- by 4-inch Douglas fir. Low-growing shrubbery and low-maintenance gravel are used as ground cover. [*Photo: Western Wood Products Association*]

*Aboveground Pools.* The aboveground pool consists of a vinyl plastic liner supported by a frame of aluminum or steel and sits right on the ground. It requires no excavation but does need a firm and level area.

The aboveground pool is a common sight around most suburban neighborhoods. The most familiar is the relatively small and inexpensive round pool, usually blue, that is set up for the kids. But these pools do come in much larger sizes and different shapes. You can do a lot of swimming in the larger aboveground pools, but as they are only 4 feet deep, they are not suitable for diving.

Aboveground pools are relatively inexpensive, and they can be put up in a hurry. A trained crew can assemble a good-size one in a day or two. It can be installed without disturbing the landscaping, and, what's more, it can easily be taken down and moved. However, unless you can give an aboveground pool a built-in look, it is not an improvement in the literal sense of the word.

You can make an aboveground pool quite attractive by using decking and planting. We know an architect who put in an aboveground pool on his property because ledge rock made it impractical to install any other type. He put a wood deck around the pool, used a curtain wall of native stone to conceal the metal framework, and ended up with a pool that looked like $10,000 but had cost him about $2,000. So if you are looking for a pool at a moderate cost, look first at aboveground pools.

Once you know what kinds of pools are permitted in your area or on your particular lot, you can decide which of the approved kinds of pools you want to install and get some estimates on the cost. In-ground pools of poured concrete, Gunite, or vinyl plastic over a wood or metal frame are usually installed by swimming pool builders and contractors. These firms usually have their own earth-moving equipment to make the excavation. You can find these firms listed in the Yellow Pages.

Some swimming pool builders also install the on-ground type of pool. These pools may also be purchased from swimming pool dealers who sell aboveground pools. You will also find aboveground pools on sale at discount houses, variety stores, department stores, mail-order houses, shops that specialize in outdoor furniture, and, of course, swimming pool shops and centers.

Most of these stores won't install the pool for you or may not even suggest anyone who can install it. All they do is sell you a package, more or less complete, and it's up to you to figure out how to get the pool installed. If the package is not complete—if some parts are missing or don't work—it may be a long time before you take your first swim.

## Buying a Pool

There are a lot of different elements to a modern swimming pool, and that means there are a lot of things that can go wrong with it. The only way you can protect yourself is to buy a pool from a reputable outfit that will guarantee the entire pool. This means that the firm will guarantee not only the workmanship in the installation but also the materials and equipment such as the vinyl liner, pump and filter, and heater. If you don't use a firm that guarantees the total pool, you may have to go to the manufacturer for satisfaction if something goes wrong, and this can be a headache.

If you are having a pool installed by a pool contractor or pool builder, shop around at local outfits that have been in the pool business for a number of years. Many of them will be members of the National Swimming Pool Institute, a trade organization concerned with, among other things, improving the ethics of the swimming pool business. Some pool builders handle pools that are nationally advertised.

You should get from pool builders the names of some of their customers in your area and check with them to see if they are completely satisfied. Also

This walkway of two-by-four Douglas fir laid flat, set on 4- by 4-inch posts with an understructure of 3- by 6-inch and 4- by 6-inch fir, is a good solution to lawn-maintenance problems, for it requires no upkeep. Note the sparse oriental-style landscaping that minimizes gardening chores. [*Architect: Charles H. Scrogin   Photo: Western Wood Products Association*]

ask the pool contractors if they have done any work for local architects and landscape architects. These are very fussy people, and the builders they select to install pools for their clients are usually very good. These builders may also be the most expensive.

Good pool builders won't give a firm estimate on a job until they have visited the site and know something about the terrain and soil conditions, the size and design of the pool, and what you will want in the way of decking, equipment such as heaters, and so on. And good builders will have their own crews and equipment and not turn a major portion of the work over to a subcontractor.

You really must watch your step in buying an aboveground pool. This type of pool can be a fine pool, but there is a lot of hanky-panky in this end of the pool business. In fact, you probably have to be more careful in buying a $2,000 aboveground pool than in buying a $20,000 in-ground pool.

A lot of aboveground pools are sold through outfits that are very strong on selling but weak on everything else including honesty. These outfits advertise pools at very low prices and then switch you to something far more expensive when you have nibbled at the bait. They often charge you far more than the pool is worth or than you could get it for from a reputable dealer. They'll promise you everything and deliver very little.

The only safe way to buy an aboveground pool is through a reputable local dealer. If you are not sure how reputable a dealer is, check with your better business bureau or your state department of consumer protection.

## Installing a Pool Yourself

You obviously can save a good deal of money by installing an on-ground or in-ground pool yourself. But it is a lot of work and takes a lot of time. Don't be fooled by the pool ads that say "Buy today and swim tomorrow." A friend of ours recently installed an 18- by 32-foot aboveground pool. He's a pretty hard worker and has had a lot of experience with major projects, but it took him the best part of three months to complete the pool. And he needed to round up six strong friends to help put the vinyl liner in place. Another homeowner spent an entire summer putting in an on-ground pool. We once spent a Fourth of July weekend helping a neighbor set up a little round pool for his kids, and it was hard work.

# 22. Terraces, Decks, and Fences

Outdoor living is the "in" thing these days and is likely to continue to be so for years to come. And outdoor living usually means a terrace, patio, or deck.

When you add an outdoor living area to a house, you get a lot for your money. You get an attractive place to relax, to sunbathe, and to entertain, a place for family dining, and a good play area for the children. To a certain degree adding an outdoor area is like adding another room to your house, and at a very low cost. We know of many families that get as much use out of their outdoor area as they do out of their living room even though they don't live in a particularly warm climate.

If you don't have an outdoor living area, you should consider adding one. You'll probably get a great deal of use and pleasure out of it, and the chances are you won't lose money on your investment.

## Location

The best spot for an outdoor area is the south side of the house. Since it gets sun the year around, you'll enjoy maximum use of the area. You'll be able to start using it in early spring and continue using it right on into fall. And it will be a good spot for the children to play in even in winter if the sun is shining.

An eastern exposure also is good because it will get plenty of sun in the early morning but will be relatively cool in the late afternoon during the summer months. For those who like to sunbathe, an eastern exposure is the ideal. An outdoor living area that faces north will get good sun during the summer but will be uncomfortably cool in spring and fall.

A western exposure is very poor, and you should avoid it if possible. The area will be fine in the morning, but in the afternoon, when it is most likely to be used, the hot sun can make it very uncomfortable. We have a wood deck that faces west because it offers a good view of the river at the rear of our property. For several years we could not use the deck in the late afternoon until the sun had gone below the horizon. Fortunately for us, a maple tree has now grown tall enough to provide good shade for the deck during the afternoon; so we are finally getting use out of the deck. If it wasn't for that tree, we would probably have put up an awning to provide shade.

It's good if you can set your outdoor living area where it will get the cooling summer breezes but will be protected by the house, fence, or shrubs from the prevailing winter winds. You should also try to place your outdoor living area where it will get the maximum privacy, and this is usually at the rear of the house. In some instances, however, one or the other side of the house might be a better choice. Fencing, shrubbery, and trees can help provide privacy for the outdoor area, but these can increase your costs. So, if possible, try to find a natural location that is suited to your needs and won't be too close to your neighbor's backyard.

It's good to get your area as close to the kitchen or dining area of the house as possible, especially if you plan to serve meals or entertain on the terrace or deck. If there are sliding glass doors at one end of the living room, this would be a natural location for the outdoor area, and the area will make the living room appear larger than it is.

## Size and Shape

There are no set standards for the size of an outdoor living area. It will be up to you to decide how large to make it in order to meet your needs. If you only want a spot in which to sunbathe or to sit quietly alone and read, then you can get along with an area measuring 4 by 8 feet. If you want enough space for normal family activities—sitting, sunbathing, family dining, and entertaining a few guests—an area measuring 12 by 12 feet would probably afford ample room. But if you like to throw big parties, you'll need a lot more space.

Don't build too small, but also don't build too big. We have done both and so can speak from experience. Our deck is 24 feet long, but it's only 8 feet wide, and that makes the space a little too tight if we have more than six people at the table. We would have been much better off to make the deck 10 feet wide. We also have a flagstone terrace measuring 24 feet by 24 feet, and that's too big. We don't give big parties, and so we seldom use the terrace. It is not a particularly inviting place for six or eight people; it needs a lot of people.

An outdoor living area is more interesting if it has an irregular shape or is built with two or more levels. However, the least expensive design is a square or a rectangle, and we feel that multilevel decks and terraces can be hazardous for the young as well as the old.


## Screening

If you live in an area where there are annoying insects, you won't get much use out of your outdoor living area in the evening unless you screen it. There are all sorts of devices and chemicals that are supposed to keep insects away from outdoor living areas, but as far as we are concerned, none of them is 100 percent effective. If you don't wish to screen the entire area (and there is not much point in screening what you don't actually use), invest in a little screen house that you can take down in the winter. Houses of this type provide a nice insect-free place in which to sit in the evening.


## Terraces and Patios

We prefer to have a terrace built on the level of the surrounding lawn. Then, if you are entertaining a large crowd of people, they can move easily from the terrace onto the lawn. And it's easier to trim the edge of the lawn if it is flush with the terrace than if it is below the level of the terrace.

A terrace should be pitched slightly away from the house so that water will flow away and not toward the house. A pitch of 1 inch to every 12 feet is adequate unless you live in an area where summer cloudbursts are common. The joint where the terrace meets the house should be flashed with metal so that water from rain or melting snow cannot damage the house structure.

It is best not to use either light- or dark-color materials for a terrace unless it can be shaded from the sun. Light-color materials such as poured concrete that is left unfinished can give such a glare when the sun is out that you will not be able to sit or stand on the terrace. And the rays of the sun will be reflected from the terrace into the house, making it that much warmer inside. Dark-color materials such as blacktop, on the other hand, absorb heat from the sun. That means that after a time the terrace will be uncomfortably warm if not hot. And the heat will be retained by the material so that even after the sun has gone down the terrace will give off heat.

**This exposed aggregate terrace is more attractive than an ordinary concrete slab. The small deck offers a transitional step down from the house to the terrace.** [Western Wood Products Association]

## Materials

The cost of a terrace depends not only on its size but on the materials and the type of construction. About the most expensive terrace is one made of flagstone set on a base of poured concrete. This combination makes a splendid terrace, and if the stones are coated with a clear masonry sealer before the terrace is used, they will be protected from grease and food stains and you will have a terrace that will last for years. As flagstones are neither dark nor light but earth-color, they don't reflect the sun's rays or absorb heat to a great degree.

But the cost of a flagstone terrace with a concrete base is very high. Without a concrete base a flagstone terrace is less expensive. The stones are set on a 1-inch bed of sand over a 3-inch bed of gravel that has been well compacted. This type of construction isn't quite as durable as flagstone set in concrete. The sand and gravel, though well compacted, will move about after a few years, and the stones may become uneven or begin to wobble. But if you can save some money, having to level up a few stones every year or so may not be a high price to pay. You also have a problem with weeds growing in the joints between the stones. This can be handled with a weed killer, but we prefer to encourage grass, moss, or some other low, creeping plant to grow between the stones. You can put down flagstones over a sand-and-gravel base yourself without much difficulty.

A particularly handsome low-cost terrace, and one that you can put down yourself with even less trouble than flagstone, is made of brick. Like stones, bricks neither reflect nor absorb a large amount of heat from the sun. They weather to a pleasant color and are very durable. And you can lay them in many different patterns. One disadvantage of bricks is that they are rather absorbent; so if you don't coat them with a clear sealer, they will stain easily. Also, if they are in the shade, they may become coated with algae or moss, which makes them slippery. Bricks may also be laid over a concrete base in the same manner as flagstones, but we prefer the slightly uneven surface achieved when they are laid over sand and gravel.

Another good do-it-yourself type of terrace or patio is made of precast paver blocks, often called "patio blocks." These are readily available at most building supply houses and garden centers. They come in different sizes, thicknesses, and colors and can be set like stones and bricks over a sand-and-gravel bed. In our opinion they are not as desirable as stones or bricks, but many people like them.

Poured concrete makes a very durable terrace, but you get a fierce glare from it when the sun is out. Of course, if the terrace will be in the shade all the time, there is no problem. Concrete also stains easily, and the stains are difficult to remove. The best thing to do with a concrete terrace is either to paint or to stain it. This will cut down on the glare and also help reduce staining, but it entails a certain amount of maintenance because the stain or paint will have to be renewed every few years.

A more desirable type of concrete terrace is one made with exposed aggregate concrete. In this type of construction, small pebbles, marble chips, or the like are scattered over the concrete slab before the concrete hardens.

They are pressed into the concrete, and when the slab has set, mortar is applied around the pebbles so that only the top surfaces are exposed. This type of construction gives an interesting texture to the terrace and also reduces the glare, but it is more expensive than an ordinary concrete slab. Pouring a concrete slab or installing an exposed aggregate terrace is not something for the average do-it-yourselfer unless you have had experience in this sort of work and have friends who will help you with it.

It's easy to make a terrace by using gravel, pebbles, marble chips, and the like. All you need do is to put a border around the area—two-by-fours treated with a wood preservative and set on edge will do—and then pour the gravel or other substance right over the earth. You'll be smart first to put down black vinyl plastic sheeting, which will prevent grass and weeds from coming up among the pebbles. A gravel terrace is fine if the terrace is a small one used by one or two adults for sunbathing or just sitting. But we don't recommend it for a large terrace because it's difficult to keep clean of grass clippings, leaves, and food particles, and it does not make a good surface for outdoor furniture.

Blacktop or asphalt is sometimes used for terraces, but we don't like it. It's hot and not one bit inviting.

## Wood Decks

A deck, while more expensive than most terraces, has several advantages over them. First, a deck can be installed without regard for the terrain around the house. A terrace needs level ground. If the ground slopes, it will have to be made level, and this requires grading and some sort of retaining wall. And there are many lots in which the grade is so steep that it is impossible to make a level site for a terrace. A deck, on the other hand, can be set on the steepest slope. Some friends of ours have at the rear of their vacation house a deck with its outside edge about 18 feet above ground, on a level with the tops of the surrounding trees. Our own deck is about 8 feet above the grade. But you need not have a sloping site for a deck. We've seen a good many decks that were set on level ground just a foot or so above the grade.

We have found decks to be somewhat cooler than terraces. Natural wood does not reflect heat or absorb it. And the spacing of ¼ inch or so between the deck boards provides for the circulation of air. A wood deck dries off faster after a rain than most masonry terraces.

There are, of course, some disadvantages to decks. If you live where there

A hilly, unused backyard corner (left) was transformed into a popular setting for entertaining and relaxing (right). Constructed entirely of economical garden grades of California redwood, this pleasant scene features multilevel decks that serve as informal seats or as plant display areas. [*Designer: John Matthias   Photo: Ernest Braun; California Redwood Association*]

are heavy accumulations of snow, a deck must be built to withstand the weight of the snow, and this can be expensive. For most decks four-by-fours are suitable for supports, but in heavy snow country poured concrete or steel supports plus very heavy framing are often required to support the decking. And unless you use the expensive clear all-heartwood redwood, a deck does require more maintenance than a terrace.

Our deck is made of red cedar decking, and the framing is of Douglas fir. Every couple of years we must give it a coat of a deck stain that serves as a wood preservative. It takes about 4 gallons of stain to do the top and underside of the deck as well as a couple of days of hard work to apply the stain. One thing you should never do or allow to be done, by the way, is to paint a wood deck. Paint will not protect the wood from decay but will often encourage it. The only type of finish you should use on a deck is an exterior stain containing a wood preservative. And unless you are using the clear all-heartwood redwood, the stain should be applied to each piece of wood before it is installed. We have learned that even architects have allowed decks to be painted with unfortunate results.

There is another point to watch for. Be sure that only galvanized nails are used in deck construction. Steel nails rust and not only leave stains in the wood but eventually will fail.

## Handling Construction

If a deck is to be set just a few inches above ground, you may be able to build it yourself. As a matter of fact, one lumber manufacturer makes deck panels that you can assemble yourself to produce any size deck that strikes your fancy. These prefabricated deck panels are available at many lumberyards and building supply houses.

But if the deck is going to be set any distance above ground—more than a foot or so—you will be wise to have the work done by an experienced carpenter or contractor. In many communities decks are considered to be part of the house structure, and you must therefore obtain a permit to build one. The deck then must be built in accordance with local building codes. These codes specify the grade of lumber that may be used, the size and spacing of supports and framing, and everything else necessary to ensure the safety of the deck.

## Railings

Many codes insist that if a deck is more than 2 feet above grade it must have a railing. We feel that a railing is smart even if a deck is only 6 inches or so above the ground, because someone accidentally stepping off it can be hurt. And if there are small children around, it's a good idea to add some sort of protective screening so they can't crawl out between the rails.

And be sure that the railing is solid. You can bet your bottom dollar that a lot of people will use it as a seat or lean against it with all their weight. And the higher the deck is above ground, the more chance there is that people will sit and lean on it. For our money the best type of railing has vertical supports that are an extension of the vertical supports for the deck framing. That's what we have on our deck. The four-by-four vertical supports run from the ground and serve as top supports for the railing. Another good method is to have the supports for the railing bolted to the joists or beams under the decking. Some decks have railings for which the supports are toenailed into the decking and joists, but this is a dangerous kind of construction. A good way to handle railings is to combine them with seating. Build benches into the railing as a single unit.

This deck with a chalet look was set on posts to extend outdoor living space for a house on a sloping hillside. Such a deck could also enhance the view from the second floor of a house on a flat lot. [*Landscape architect: John Herbst, Jr., & Associates   Photo: Western Wood Products Association*]

## Decking

Decking is usually made of one-by-four, two-by-four, and two-by-six lumber. There should be a space between each board equal to the thickness of a large nail, or about ³⁄₁₆ inch. Don't let anyone build you a deck with no spacing between the deck boards. You would have trouble with water standing on the deck, and eventually the wood would decay.

Deck boards are generally installed facedown, but two-by-fours are sometimes set on edge. This type of construction produces a good deal of structural strength and may reduce the amount or size of the framing required, but we don't consider it a good practice. Debris collects between the boards, and as the seams are almost 4 inches deep, the stuff doesn't fall through but gets stuck. Pretty soon all the seams are filled, and you have to clean them out by hand with a knife or a sharp pointed tool. A friend of ours has such a deck, and she spent an entire weekend on her hands and knees prying assorted gook out of the seams.

If there is a nice tree where you plan to build your deck, you need not take it down—you can let it pierce the deck. If you do, make sure that you leave enough room between the deck and the tree so that the tree can sway and grow. Remember that the higher the deck is off the ground, the more the tree will sway.

## Fences

Building a fence can be a good investment, for there are many ways in which a fence can be used to improve your property. A low ornamental fence— split-rail, corral, picket—along the front, for example, can enhance the appearance of the house and lawn just as an attractive frame can improve the picture that it surrounds. And if it's the right kind of ornamental fence, it can also keep small children and pets off busy streets.

A solid wood fence along the front of a lot will help deflect street and traffic noises away from the house, and a similar type of fence along the north side will protect the house from chilling winter winds and make it warmer and easier to heat. A fence is just what you need to get privacy for outdoor areas, both large and small. And a fence can provide shade and protection from the wind. A louvered or basket-weave fence will give privacy and shade but allow cooling breezes to pass through it.

Fences are excellent, of course, for concealing the less attractive areas around the house such as the back or side utility yards and the children's play area. If you have a small lot, a fence along the back will screen off your neighbor's backyard. As this fence can benefit him as much as it benefits you, he may be willing to chip in on the cost of putting it up or help with the maintenance. There's a lot of truth in the old saying "Good fences make good neighbors."

Before you begin planning a fence, check with your local building department. Most building codes require that a fence be set a given number of feet from the property lines and may also specify the maximum height as well as the style and construction. You should also check your deed, for some deeds contain restrictions on fencing. We know of many developments in which all fences except those required around swimming pools are prohibited. In other cases, only certain kinds of fences can be built.

As fences are made of wood and the price of lumber continues to climb, they are becoming more and more expensive. It's hard to buy even a simple split-rail fence for less than $5 a foot, and a solid high fence can run well over $10 a foot. So don't use more fencing than you need to achieve the desired result.

This deck is placed at the family room level, eliminating a step down from the sliding glass doors. Benches of two-by-four fir are supported by railings of two-by-fours with a two-by-six cap. Note that the rail supports are bolted to the deck framing. [*Western Wood Products Association*]

If you want an ornamental low fence at the front of the house, keep it to a height of 3 feet, which is perfectly adequate. Even a fence for privacy, shade, and protection from the wind usually need not be more than 6 feet high. And you don't have to fence off an entire area to get the results you need. A fence 8 or 10 feet long may be ample to provide privacy, shade, and wind protection if it is put in the right spot.

You can buy the more familiar kinds of fencing—split-rail, stockade, basket-weave, picket—by the foot or by the 8-foot section at many lumber-yards, building supply houses, mail-order houses, and local firms that manufacture and install fencing. If you want something a little different and more specialized such as a louvered, solid board, or herringbone fence, usually you must have it custom-built by a carpenter or build it yourself.

## Woods for Fencing

Redwood is very popular for fencing because it has an attractive natural color and is resistant to damage from decay and insects such as termites. It's important to remember, however, that only the more expensive all-heart-wood grades of redwood contain enough of the natural chemicals to provide

**This stepped-back openwork fence provides privacy for the front yard but lets in cooling breezes.** [*Western Wood Products Association*]

them with the necessary degree of resistance so that they can be placed in direct contact with the earth without using a wood preservative. The less expensive sapwood grades of redwood don't contain enough chemicals to give sufficient protection; so if they are set in direct contact with the earth, they require a preservative.

Red cedar is also highly resistant to decay and insects and is often set in direct contact with the earth without a preservative, but we don't recommend this practice. Red cedar makes an attractive stockade fence, and rough-sawn cedar boards are also popular. Douglas fir, white pine, spruce, and larch are all used for fencing, but these must be treated with a wood preservative if the wood is in direct contact with the ground.

The most critical parts of any fence are the posts. These are set into the ground and often are set in concrete. The posts are the first part of a fence to fail unless they are properly treated against decay and attacks by insects.

**A solid fence of redwood provides maximum privacy for this small outdoor area and keeps out sounds as well as wind.** [*California Redwood Association  Photo: Ernest Braun  Designer: John Matthias*]

Unless you use all-heartwood redwood for the posts, buy posts that have been pressure-treated with a wood preservative. Posts of this kind are available at some (but not all) lumberyards and building supply houses. Many people set posts into the ground after giving the ends a coat of wood preservative. This is better than nothing, but it is not nearly so effective as using posts that have been pressure-treated with a preservative so that the preservative enters every cell in the wood.

Fence posts are usually made of four-by-four stock set 8 to 10 feet apart, but if a fence is considerably more than 6 feet high or is subject to very strong winds, heavier stock or closer spacing may be necessary. The stringers that run between posts and serve as a nailing base for the fence boards are usually made of two-by-four stock, while the fence boards are about 1 inch thick.

Posts for a 6-foot-high fence usually must be set about 2½ feet deep. To give them maximum support, set them in concrete, or use an anchor cleat at the base.

All elements of a fence should be assembled with either aluminum or hot-dipped galvanized nails, which will not rust or corrode. Steel nails should never be used, for they will leave rust stains in the wood and eventually will fail.

## Finish for Fences

Fences can be either painted or stained. Certain types of fences, picket fences, for example, almost call for paint, white paint at that. With other fences, it's a matter of personal choice. We prefer stains on fences because stains are easier to apply, the correct stain will also serve as a wood preservative, and stained fences are easier to maintain than painted ones. We have a rough-sawn cedar fence on our property, and we coated it with a gray-pigmented bleaching stain when it was first installed. It has weathered to an attractive driftwood color, and every three or four years we slap on another coat of the same stain. It takes us only about one hour to coat the fence, which measures 6 by 18 feet.

Whether you use a stain or a paint, it's wise to apply the first coat to the wood before the fence is assembled. Not only is it easier to do the job before the fence is up, but you can coat every inch of the wood.

If you are going to paint a fence, use a good grade of house paint. Either a latex or an oil-base paint will be fine. Apply the primer to the wood before the fence is assembled.

Many different types of stain are suitable for fencing. A clear water repellent is good if you want to protect the wood from discoloration and from being stained by dirt. This is a good choice for redwood, for while this type of wood can often be left unfinished, it will sometimes weather unevenly and it does absorb dirt. If you'd like a driftwood color to the fence, use a wood-bleaching stain. Stains of this type contain a small amount of gray pigment and thus give an immediate driftwood color to the wood as well as allowing it to take on this color naturally. Other pigmented stains can be used to provide color to a fence while allowing the texture or grain of the wood to show.

# 23. Termite Control

It may seem to be stretching a point to consider termite extermination a home improvement project, but actually it is not. Termites can do a whale of a lot of damage to a house structure, and most potential home buyers are concerned about termites, especially if the house is not new. As a matter of fact, the less people know about houses, the more apt they are to ask about termites. But even experienced homeowners will ask if a house has been infested, and it's not uncommon for a potential buyer to offer to pay for the cost of a termite inspection on condition that if termites are found in the house, the seller will pay to have them exterminated and make good any damage they have done.

So if you have a written report from a reliable termite control firm that your property is free of termites or if they have been eliminated and all damage has been repaired, this assurance may not add to the value of your house, but it will certainly make it easier to get closer to your asking price.

Termites are commonest in the warmer states, but today they can be found in all states except Alaska. It is often difficult to tell if a house is infested because there are few visible signs. Termites build their nests in the damp ground below the frost line, and sometimes the nests are 12 feet below the surface.

## How Termites Live and Work

The termite colony is a very complex society consisting of the queen, soldiers that guard the nest, reproductives that swarm at certain times of the year to start new nests, and, most important of all, workers, the fellows that do the damage. Termites live on the cellulose found in wood, and it is the job of the workers to bring cellulose to the nest to feed the members of the colony. Termite workers are blind, can't stand light, and like other members of the colony, must live in a relatively damp environment. They work twenty-four hours a day and can discover wood many feet away.

The workers often begin feeding on wood that is in the ground near the house—old tree stumps, bits of wood left over from construction, untreated wood posts set in the ground, and the like. When they exhaust this supply, they look for ways to reach the house woodwork. One way they do this is to build earthen tunnels about ¼ inch wide over foundation walls, posts and piers, and even pipes so that they can get from the ground to the wood without being exposed to light. The little tunnels are very ingeniously designed to provide a perfect environment for the termite workers.

Once the workers reach the woodwork, they work on the inside, never on the outside. Given enough time, a group of termites can eat the core out of a heavy timber so that only the outside shell remains, with no visible sign that the timber has been seriously damaged.

These tunnels are one of the evidences that termites are present. The fact that you don't find them does not necessarily mean that termites are not at work, for they may have found other ways to reach the woodwork. The presence of tunnels, however, is a sure indication that some boring is going on within. Look for these little tunnels at any point where there is a connection between ground and the house woodwork. And don't be concerned only with the foundation walls. If there are cracks or open seams in the basement floor, you may find tunnels going up along metal posts and pipes.

At certain times of the year, usually in spring and early fall, the termite reproductives swarm and eventually start a new colony. The reproductives have wings and often are confused with flying ants. You can tell the difference because the termite reproductives have two pairs of wings of almost equal length, while the ants have one long and one short pair. Also, the termites are straight-bodied, while the ants have an hourglass shape.

When the reproductives swarm out of the nest, they often come up through cracks and seams around door and window frames. They fly around for just a short time, then drop their wings, and go back into the ground. You'll sometimes find a pile of these discarded wings, and when you do, it's a sign that there are termites about.


Treatment

The method used to exterminate termites is chemical treatment of the soil around the house. The chemical (often chlordane) forms a barrier that the workers can't cross. When this occurs, the workers in the house woodwork soon die because they must get back to the damp earth every twenty-four hours. Meanwhile, members in the colony die of starvation because the workers can't bring food.

This treatment is very effective as long as the chemicals remain in the soil. In time, of course, they will leach away, and if they are not replaced, a fresh group of termites may arrive. The one problem with the chemical barrier is that it must be complete. If one area about or under the house is left untreated, the cure will not be effective.

## Termite Control Firms

In most cases the best way to handle termites is to call in a qualified termite control firm. Such firms are listed in the Yellow Pages under "Extermina-tors." Try to deal with a local outfit that has an established office in your area. Most of these firms will be members of the National Pest Control Association. They should be happy to give you the names of homeowners in your area for whom they have worked. If you want to check further, talk to your local better business bureau or your county agent.

A reputable termite control firm will make a free inspection, and if it finds termites, it will give you a written estimate of the cost of getting rid of them, It will also give you time to study the estimate. Although termites can do a lot of damage, there is no reason to panic and rush ahead to get rid of them at any cost. A week or so, while you consider an estimate and perhaps get other estimates, is not going to make much difference.

Most reliable firms today will offer some form of guarantee that will protect you for a year against the reappearance of termites. Some firms also offer a low-cost insurance plan so that if termites reappear and do damage, the insurance will pay for the cost of repairs.

The cost of termite control varies with the size and construction of the house. A typical price can run between $200 and $450 for the initial treatment. You can expect to pay about 10 percent of the initial cost for each annual inspection and treatment if required.

# 24. A Rental Unit

A rental unit is one kind of improvement that is almost certain to pay for itself, and you won't have to wait until you sell the house to get your investment back. If you live in an area where there is a steady demand for year-round rental units or in a resort area where you can get a good price for a seasonal rental and if you can convert existing space into such a unit or apartment, you can expect to get your money back in a relatively short time, perhaps in three, four, or five years. After that almost all the income will be profit. You will, of course, have to pay taxes on your rental unit, and there will be upkeep and repairs, but these costs are tax-deductible. Also, when you get around to selling, the fact that the property has an income-producing unit can be an attractive sales feature to many potential buyers. And finally, because the rent income can help defray some of the carrying charges on the property, you'll have more buyers who will qualify to get a purchase loan.

Exactly how soon you'll get back your investment in a rental unit depends on how much it costs to create and what rent you can charge. The general rule is that the unit must pay for itself within nine years, but obviously it's best to have a setup that pays for itself in much less than nine years.

There are some disadvantages to having a rental unit right in your own backyard, so to speak. First, the life of a landlord is not always easy, especially when you are close at hand. A tenant naturally expects certain services in exchange for rent, and these services are your responsibility. If a fuse blows, a drain stops up, or a window sticks, you can expect a knock on your door or a phone call from your tenant at almost any hour, day or night, asking you to come and fix matters. And you and your family may not find it agreeable to share your property—parking areas, grounds, and so on. In short, you give up a certain amount of freedom and privacy when you become a resident landlord. But in spite of the disadvantages, if you have the right kind of apartment and can get the right sort of tenants, having a rental unit can be a smart investment and a good hedge against inflation and also provide certain tax advantages.

## Checking Out the Market

Before you do anything else, check out the rental market in your area. At the present time with high building costs and tight money, the rental market by and large is very good, since many people who might otherwise buy a house are forced to rent. But conditions vary with the locality, and they may change in the course of a year or so.

One of the best sources for information on rental units is a local real estate broker who handles rentals. Ads for rentals in the real estate pages of local newspapers also will give you an indication of the demand, and you can learn a good deal about housing trends from the local chamber of commerce. Here are some key questions to be answered before you proceed further:

1. *What's the Demand for Small Rentals?* You should find out what the demand is today and what the forecast is for the future. If industry is moving into an area, the demand for rentals should be good, but if industry is departing, that's another matter. Also see if you can find out from local officials if there are plans for the construction of large apartments or condominiums. Either of these might present a problem because an apartment in a modern complex that possibly includes a swimming pool and other amenities might be more appealing to a lot of people than an apartment over a garage, provided there is little difference in price. On the other hand, many people don't want to live in a big complex. In any case, it doesn't hurt to check it out.

2. *What Type of Rentals Are in Demand?* If the demand is for small efficiency apartments—living room–bedroom with a pullman kitchen and a bath—you are in luck, because this is the kind of apartment that you are most likely to be able to provide, and it's also the least expensive and generally the most practical to construct. If the demand is for units with separate bedrooms, you'll need a lot more space, and your costs will go up. And, of course, in some areas there is a demand only for rental houses, and this leaves you pretty well out in the cold.

3. *What Kind of People Are Renting?* Almost everybody who has a rental unit wants to rent it to a schoolteacher, but there just aren't

that many single schoolteachers about. In any event, according to many homeowners who have rental units, the ideal tenant is a single person with a good-paying and steady job in the general area. Usually older persons and more mature couples are less of a problem than younger ones, but a lot depends on the people themselves. One thing you want to avoid is transients, people who rent for just a few months and then move along to another job in another area. Tenants of this sort are responsible for a lot of wear and tear on the property. You have to clean, freshen, and sometimes repaint the place each time it is vacated. Not only is this a nuisance, but you lose money between tenants.

## Checking Zoning Regulations

If everything has checked out thus far, your next step is to check with the local zoning board to find out if rental units are allowed in your particular area. What you want to learn is whether your house is in a zone that permits multifamily dwellings. If it is not in such a zone, you can't make an apartment unless you can get a variance. How you go about doing this is discussed in Chapter 2, but with a proposed rental unit there are other questions for which you should have answers. The board will want to know how many people will live in the apartment, whether they will cause any sort of disturbance, what facilities you will provide for off-street parking, how much rent you expect to charge, and just about anything else they feel might have a bearing on the matter. And your immediate neighbors will be interested in your project and may speak out against your application unless you've been able to convince them that your project will not reduce property values in the neighborhood.

## Checking the Building Codes

You should also check the local building codes to find out about special requirements for a rental unit. Some of these requirements may also be covered in the local zoning regulations. The codes will specify the minimum number of square feet of living space that you must provide in a rental unit, the fact that it must have a complete kitchen so that it cannot be considered a furnished room, the number of windows, and even the quality of materials that must be used. There may be other regulations designed to protect the safety of the tenant. For example, if the apartment is on a second floor, the code may require that there be two staircases, both inside the building. Even a ground-floor unit will probably be required to have a front and a rear exit as fire protection. And if you go ahead with your project, be sure that you or your contractor follows these codes to the letter, because if you don't, you won't get a permit for occupancy. That would leave you with a rental unit that you would not be able to rent.

## Other Considerations

Some of the following points may come up in your dealings with the zoning board or the building department, but if they don't you had better look into them before you go too far with your plans.

1. *Security.* If your tenant can reach the apartment through a private entrance, you need not be concerned with security, but if the tenant must go through part of your area of the house, you will be concerned. The tenant will have a key to your front door, and you can never tell where a key may end up.

2. *Capacity of the Septic System.* If you have a town or city sewer system, this is no problem, but if you have your own septic system, it can be, because the system may not be large enough to handle the rental unit. It may cost $1,000 or more to put in a larger system.

3. *Off-Street Parking.* In many areas you must provide suitable off-street parking for your tenant. If your present parking facilities are not adequate, you will have to increase their size, which will not only cost money but reduce the size of your lawn, plantings, and so on.

## Location of a Rental Unit

There may be several areas on your property that suggest themselves as possible locations for a rental unit.

*Basement.* Unless one side of a basement is on grade so that it opens out onto the ground, do not consider the basement. First, most local codes won't allow you to have a basement apartment if the entire basement is below grade. Second, most people won't live in such a basement. If one side of the basement is on grade and you can install glass or sliding doors to open it up to the outdoors, you can have a very charming unit, especially if you put in a small patio or terrace, but otherwise a basement does not make a particularly desirable spot for a rental unit.

*Attic.* If there is enough floor space and enough headroom in your attic, an apartment can be put in quite inexpensively, but the stairs should be located so that the attic can be reached without having to go through other rooms of the house. Safety codes may insist that you provide two means of egress, which means that you may have to add an additional flight of stairs. Also, attic apartments, because of the number of stairs involved, are not easy to rent, especially to older people.

*Garage.* A two-car garage or other sturdy outbuilding makes the best location for an apartment because it gets the tenant outside the main house. Even if yours is an attached garage, the partition wall can be insulated to achieve some degree of sound control.

The standard two-car garage is a good size for a studio apartment, which would include a small but complete kitchenette suitable for light housekeeping and a bath. What's more, if the garage was well built to start with, it's not a costly area to finish. Few garages have finished walls and ceilings, and so it's relatively easy to install wiring, plumbing, and new windows and doors.

*Unit in the House.* If there is a lot of unused space in the house, several rooms can be partitioned off to make a rental unit. The first floor is best because you can provide the tenant with a private entrance. In addition, this location eliminates any problem with safety codes for fire-safe stairs and the like. The ideal arrangement, as far as cost is concerned, takes advantage of existing plumbing lines in the house system.

## Material for a Rental Unit

Materials and products to be used in a rental unit should be selected with great care because they are apt to be subject to considerable wear and tear. Try to keep costs down because if you buy the top of the line in every instance, your construction costs are going to be so high that it will be years before you get your money back. On the other hand, if you use shoddy stuff, it will break down or fall apart, and you'll be either constantly fixing it or having to replace it.

*Appliances.* The best rule to follow is to buy the bottom line of good standard-quality appliances. Most of the major appliance manufacturers produce several models; the one with the minimum number of features is the least expensive. At the top of the line is the deluxe model, usually with all sorts of special gadgets. Buy the least expensive model you can get, but buy it from an authorized dealer so that you can get warranties and guarantees and be sure of obtaining good service and parts when needed.

Don't try to save money by buying secondhand appliances. Some years ago my wife and I put together a rental unit, and to save money we bought several used appliances. They lasted only a short time and then had to be replaced with new equipment. In the meantime, our tenant was constantly complaining. In the end we paid more for the old stuff and repairs than if we had bought new appliances in the beginning.

Complete kitchenette units consisting of cabinets, sink, range, and refrigerator are popular for rental units because you can get a complete kitchen in a very small amount of space. But these units can become a problem when they need servicing, for unless there is a local dealer who specializes in selling and servicing the brand of equipment you have, getting it fixed when something goes wrong can be a headache.

*Other Equipment.* Follow the same rule for other fixtures and mechanical equipment in your rental as for appliances: buy standard units made by quality outfits. And be smart and get this type of equipment from a local dealer who can provide service when you want it and will also provide guarantees.

*Walls and Ceilings.* The best material here is gypsum wallboard, and the best finish is paint. Wallpaper costs far more than paint, and when it becomes badly damaged or stained, as it can quite rapidly in a rental unit, it will have to be replaced. Paint, on the other hand, doesn't cost much and can easily be renewed at low cost.

*Flooring.* Vinyl asbestos is the least expensive flooring and does a good job. But if you are making an apartment in the attic or in rooms above your own living area, use wall-to-wall carpeting so that you won't hear your tenants walking about.

# 25. Selling a House

Before you put your house on the market, you had better find out if you are going to be able to afford to buy another one. And we don't mean a better one—we mean just a house. Of course, if you have to move because of a change of jobs or for some equally valid reason, you don't have much choice, but if you just want to move because you feel you can afford something better, could use more space, or can make a big profit, go slow. For even if you sell your house for considerably more than you paid for it, you may find that you still can't afford to buy anything better, if as good.

Inflated building and housing costs and high interest rates on home mortgage loans have tossed many accepted theories about buying and selling a house out of the window. Yesterday if you sold a house and came out with $15,000, representing your equity and some profit, you were in pretty good shape to put up 10 or 20 percent as a down payment on a considerably more expensive house and still have money left over for the savings account. Today, with some lenders asking for a down payment of as much as 40 to 50 percent and getting as much as 9 percent in interest, $15,000 doesn't buy much of a house.

There are many cases of families that figured that this was just the right time to sell their houses because they could get such good prices for them. After signing contracts to sell, they discovered that they were going to have to settle for far less desirable houses for themselves than the ones they had just sold. So, before you get ready to sell, remember that even if you are going to get a big price for your house, the person whose house you are going to buy is also going to get a big price—from you.

The smart approach to this dilemma is first to get a realistic figure from an appraiser or broker as to what sort of price you can expect for your house. Don't put it on the market yet. Figure out how much money you'll get from the sale after you have paid off the balance of the mortgage and the costs connected with the sale. Next see how much will be available as a down payment on another house. Then see how much of a mortgage you can get with this payment. Check first with the bank or other lender that has the mortgage on your present house, for it is the one most inclined to give you a good deal. But also check with a few other local banks and savings and loan associations to see if they can do any better. Once you've found out how much house you can buy with the money you have, start looking around to see what, if anything, is available in this price range. If you find that you can get something better in a new or used house (considerably better, we might add), go ahead if you still want to. Remember, though, that you probably will also be paying a much higher interest rate on your next house.

There are two ways to go about selling a house. You can find a buyer yourself, or you can call in a licensed real estate broker to find the buyer. If you sell the house yourself, you keep all the money; if you use a broker, you have to pay a commission. The average commission will be about 6 percent of the sales price, which means if a house is sold for $40,000, the broker receives $2,400 in commission.

## Working with a Broker

In spite of the money you have to pay a broker, there are advantages to using one, especially when mortgage money is tight. A good real estate broker can often arrange to get financing for a prospective buyer which neither the buyer nor you could arrange on your own. Brokers make it a practice to know the bankers in their area, for they realize that financing is the key to making a sale. If a prospective buyer requires financing, brokers will twist every arm in the county to get an adequate mortgage loan so that they can complete the sale. And a good broker can sell a banker on granting a prospective buyer a mortgage loan with the same zest that he or she sold the prospective buyer the house.

Brokers do more than just help get financing for a sale. They will help you determine the right asking price for the house and also suggest the rock-bottom price that you should accept. Since they know the market, they may suggest a higher price than you would have thought of asking. They can tell you what minor improvements to make so that the house will sell quickly. They will make appointments with prospective buyers to show the house, and they'll do all the wheeling and dealing to get you the best price they can. While it is to their advantage to do this, they do want to sell the house and not have it sit on the market; so they'll be realistic when it comes to the actual selling price.

A note of caution here: sometimes a broker, in order to get the listing for your house, will tell you that you can get much more than you actually can. If the house is priced too high, it may sit on the market for months while a lot of serious buyers pass it up and buy something else that they can afford. If you suspect that the price set by the broker is out of line, it will pay you to ask a real estate appraiser to estimate the true value. You can then make an educated decision as to which price to use.

A very important point to remember in setting the price on a house is that the higher the figure, the fewer buyers there will be who can qualify for a mortgage loan. Each time you add another $100 to your price, the down payment on the house will go up, and so will the monthly payments. Adding just $500 to your asking price can reduce the number of potential buyers considerably.

If you want to sell your house as quickly as possible, your best bet is to deal with a broker who is a member of the local multiple-listing service. This service, known as MLS, provides all member brokers with basic information about the property. While your broker has the primary responsibility for the sale, other brokers in the area will also be showing the house under his or her supervision. Under this arrangement you give your broker what is called an "exclusive listing." This means that your broker is the exclusive agent for the property and will get the commission for the sale whether the buyer comes through his or her office or through another broker's office. If the property is sold through another MLS broker, each gets a percentage of the commission. This is called "co-brokering"; the brokers make their own arrangement as to what percentage each receives. But this part of the transaction is really no concern of yours. What is your concern is that the contract you sign with the broker states exactly what commission he or she will receive. It should also specify how long the broker shall have the listing: 90 days, 120 days, or some other period.

Giving one broker an exclusive listing is far better than a so-called open listing with which many brokers will be involved, getting in each other's way and in your hair. With the exclusive listing you have just one broker in charge. Your broker will coordinate appointments with other brokers in the MLS so as to bring buyers to see the house at your convenience. In addition, your broker will often advertise the property at his or her expense.

If you sign a contract giving a broker an exclusive listing and you sell the house without his or her help, you don't have to pay a commission. But if you sign a contract that gives your broker the *exclusive right to sell*, he or she will get a commission even if you find the buyer and your broker does nothing at all. And if you don't pay, your broker can bring suit against you to collect the commission.

Once you've selected a broker, you should go over the house with him or her so that he or she can see exactly what is to be sold. Point out all the good features, and by all means show records of recently made improvements and repairs because these can be very useful sales tools. The more the broker knows about your house, the more satisfactory will be his or her answers to a prospective buyer's questions. If a broker is obliged to answer the most obvious questions regarding the condition of the house with "I don't know" or "It looks all right to me" or "I'll have to ask the owner," the more disenchanted the prospective buyer is going to become. And be sure that everything you tell the broker is correct.

You should also make it very clear to the broker exactly which items are included in the selling price and which items are not. Items that are physically attached to the house and cannot be removed without damage to the structure are usually considered fixtures and are deemed part of the house proper. Some other items are considered nonfixtures and may or may not be included, depending on the decision of the seller. A built-in range, for example, would be a fixture because if it were removed, a hole would be left in a wall or cabinet. A free-standing range, on the other hand, could be removed without damage to the house; so it would be a nonfixture. A window air conditioner is usually considered a nonfixture, while the same type of unit set into the wall under a window would be a fixture. The point is that you want to make sure that when the agreement for sale is drawn up, both you and the buyer know exactly which items are considered fixtures and which are not. If you don't, you may get into a legal hassle because you've removed an item that the buyer considered to be part of the deal. We got into this very situation some years ago when we sold a house and, as we were moving out, gave the roof TV antenna to a neighbor. When the new owner arrived, he found the antenna missing and claimed that it was a fixture and was included in the deal. Rather than get involved with an attorney, we gave him a new antenna.

A local broker will naturally know a good deal about the general area and the neighborhood: the quality of the schools, the location of shopping centers, recreational facilities, and so on. But if there are other advantages or assets that the broker may not know about, tell him, because these can be important to a buyer.

When you commission a broker to sell your house, he is in your employ, and his first obligation is to protect your interests. On the other hand, the broker is anxious to sell the house; so if he finds an interested buyer, he will act as the middleman, doing his best to bring the two of you together on price and other essential considerations. If he feels that the price offered by a buyer is fair though lower than your asking price, he will tell you and perhaps suggest that this might be the best deal you could make within a reasonable time. You don't have to go along with him, but you should keep in mind that if you hold out too long, your property gets shopworn. The longer a piece of property is on the market, the more difficult it is to sell, simply because when buyers learn that it's been around for many months, they naturally think that something must be wrong with it.

Once a broker has found a buyer and has your approval, he will have the buyer and you sign an agreement of sale, which is a binding contract between the two parties. This is the most important document involved in the sale of real estate, for it spells out (or should) all aspects of the transaction. While the broker may draw it up, you should have it inspected by your attorney before signing.

## Selling the House Yourself

Although you'll save money by selling the house yourself, it's not easy, and it may take a lot longer to find the right buyer than if you have a broker. It can be especially difficult to sell your house if you are off the beaten path because unless you do a lot of advertising in local newspapers, you aren't going to attract many buyers. On the other hand, if you live in a busy neighborhood that is attracting home buyers, a "For Sale" sign on the front lawn may be all that's needed to bring in prospective buyers.

You must be prepared to put up with a lot of inconvenience if you sell a house yourself. Most people shop for a house on weekends or in the evenings, and that means that if you are anxious to sell, you must stick close to the house and to the telephone. And you'll often waste a lot of time and energy showing the house to people who are really house "shoppers" rather than house "buyers."

Before you decide what price to ask, have your house appraised by a real estate appraiser. The figure the appraiser will give you will be the fair market value. This may be substantially lower than what you consider your house is worth because most owners tend to overvalue rather than undervalue their own property. In any event, once you know the market value of your house, you can decide on an asking price, which should be a few thousand dollars more than the market value or the rock-bottom price you will settle for. You always want to begin asking for more than you'll settle for so that you will have room to negotiate with the buyer. Real estate is one of the few remaining areas in which people expect to bargain over price. Some property, of course, is offered at a firm price below which the seller won't go, but in most cases there will be bargaining, with the seller going down a bit and the buyer coming up.

*Advertising.* An ad in the classified pages of the real estate section of local or nearby city newspapers is about the most effective way of letting prospective buyers know that your house is on the market. Depending on the type of house, the price, and type of person to whom you think your house would appeal, choose the newspaper or other publication that you think this kind of person would read. Before you write your ad, study the ads of real estate brokers to see what features they are stressing: number of rooms, location, school facilities, fireplaces, garages, and so on. Many newspapers have trained personnel who can help you write a good classified ad, but you should be able to give them a list of what you consider to be the most attractive sales features of your house.

*Consulting an Attorney.* As you will not have a broker to draw up the various papers connected with the sale, you should have a local attorney. It is particularly important to have an attorney draw up the agreement of sale, for this is a contract between you and the buyer and sets down all the terms of the purchase. Unless this agreement is complete and is carefully worded, you can run into difficulties.

*How to Help the Buyer Buy.* If mortgage money is in tight supply, your problem may be not finding a buyer but finding one who can get a mortgage loan to make the purchase. Over the past several years there have been many cases of homeowners who were simply unable to sell their houses at any kind of reasonable price because buyers could not get a loan to make the purchase. A few months ago some lenders in our area were granting loans only to regular depositors and even so were willing to finance only 50 percent of the market value. That means that if you wanted to buy a house for $40,000, you had to make a down payment of $20,000, a sum most people just don't have.

There was a time when many lenders would allow a buyer to "assume" the existing mortgage so that the seller could get his money. The buyer would then have to put up only the difference between the remainder of the mortgage and the total cost of the house. But lenders don't do this today. They can make more money by lending on short-term high-interest loans or by drawing up a new mortgage at a higher rate of interest.

If you are looking for income rather than cash from the sale of your house, you can, of course, take back a mortgage from the buyer or give him a second mortgage to help cover the cost of the purchase, provided the lender who is giving the first mortgage agrees. But when most of us sell a house, we want to get all our money out so that we can buy another house. And the only way to do this is to find a lender who is willing to give the buyer an adequate mortgage loan. You may be of some help here.

Before you put your house on the market, talk to the lenders in your area to learn about the availability of mortgage money. Find out how much they would be willing to lend a qualified buyer on your house. You should start with the lender who presently holds the mortgage, for this lender knows the house and you. But check with other lenders. If you get advance information on what sort of mortgage terms a buyer might expect to get, this not only will help you decide whether now is the ideal time to sell but will also help you avoid wasting time on a buyer who probably can't get all the financing he needs. And, naturally enough, being able to steer a qualified buyer to a lender who will give him a mortgage is going to help you sell your house that much more easily, and at a good price.

# 26. House Inspection Chart

Today more and more people are calling in house inspection services to check over a house and property before they buy. These services are relatively new but are becoming very popular, for they are probably the best way for a potential buyer to learn the exact condition of a house. If you are buying a house, you will be wise to consider doing the same.

The house inspector, usually an engineer, architect, or contractor, is con-. cerned with what is wrong with the house and not with its market value. Inspectors do not as a rule estimate what it will cost to make necessary repairs or improvements, nor do they do the work themselves. What they do do is to provide the potential buyer with a detailed and objective report on the condition of the property as a whole. Depending on the size of the house and its location, the fee can be from $50 to $100 or more.

It's impossible to say just how much effect an adverse report would have on a potential buyer, for there are many variables, but it is obvious that you will have a far better chance of getting your price, and more quickly too, if your house is in a condition to warrant a favorable report.

The following chart lists some of the major items that an inspection service will look for. It can be a helpful guide to you, too, in deciding where your house might need attention.

# HOUSE INSPECTION CHART

## Site:

1. *Evidence of flooding:* Yes \_\_\_\_\_ No \_\_\_\_\_

2. *Trees and shrubs planted too near foundation:* Yes \_\_\_\_\_ No \_\_\_\_\_

3. *Trees near building that will require maintenance:* Yes \_\_\_\_\_ No \_\_\_\_\_

4. *Type of sidewalks:* _____ No sidewalks: \_\_\_\_\_

   a. Condition: Good \_\_\_\_\_ Fair \_\_\_\_\_ Need repair \_\_\_\_\_

5. *Type of driveway:* Blacktop \_\_\_\_\_ Concrete \_\_\_\_\_ Gravel \_\_\_\_\_ Dirt \_\_\_\_\_

   a. Condition: Good \_\_\_\_\_ Fair \_\_\_\_\_ Needs repair \_\_\_\_\_

   b. Parking facilities: Adequate \_\_\_\_\_ Inadequate \_\_\_\_\_

6. *Terrace, deck, or porch:* Yes \_\_\_\_\_ No \_\_\_\_\_ Which \_\_\_\_\_

   a. Type of terrace: Flagstone \_\_\_\_\_ Concrete \_\_\_\_\_ Brick \_\_\_\_\_ Other \_\_\_\_\_

   b. Condition: Good \_\_\_\_\_ Fair \_\_\_\_\_ Needs repair \_\_\_\_\_

## Exterior of House:

1. *Type of roof:* Asphalt shingle \_\_\_\_\_ Wood shingle \_\_\_\_\_ Other \_\_\_\_\_

   a. Age: _____

   b. Condition: Good \_\_\_\_\_ Fair \_\_\_\_\_ Needs repair or replacement \_\_\_\_\_

2. *Gutters and downspouts:* Yes \_\_\_\_\_ No \_\_\_\_\_

   a. Type: Aluminum \_\_\_\_\_ Copper \_\_\_\_\_ Vinyl plastic \_\_\_\_\_ Other \_\_\_\_\_

   b. Condition: Good \_\_\_\_\_ Fair \_\_\_\_\_ Need repair or replacement \_\_\_\_\_

3. *Siding:* Wood \_\_\_\_\_ Brick veneer \_\_\_\_\_ Vinyl \_\_\_\_\_ Metal \_\_\_\_\_ Other \_\_\_\_\_

   a. Condition: Good \_\_\_\_\_ Fair \_\_\_\_\_ Needs repair or replacement \_\_\_\_\_

4. *Finish on siding:*

   a. Type: Paint \_\_\_\_\_ Stain \_\_\_\_\_ Factory finish \_\_\_\_\_

   b. Condition: Good \_\_\_\_\_ Fair \_\_\_\_\_ Needs paint or stain \_\_\_\_\_

   *c.* Evidence of moisture: Yes _____ No _____

   *d.* Paint blistering or peeling: Yes _____ No _____

5. *Outside doors:*

   *a.* Type: Panel _____ Flush _____ Other _____

   *b.* Condition: Good _____ Fair _____ Need repair _____

   *c.* Weatherstripping: Yes _____ No _____ Needs new weatherstripping _____

6. *Door locks and latches:*

   *a.* Type: Solid brass _____ Brass plate _____ Other _____

   *b.* Condition: Good _____ Fair _____ Need repair or replacement _____

7. *Storm door and screen:* Yes _____ No _____ Need repair or replacement _____

8. *Windows:*

   *a.* Type: Double-hung _____ Casement _____ Other _____

   *b.* Condition: Good _____ Fair _____ Need repair or replacement _____

9. *Storm windows and screens:* Yes _____ No _____

   *a.* Type: Combination _____ Wood _____

   *b.* Condition: Good _____ Fair _____ Need repair or replacement _____

## Electrical System:

1. Power source: Underground _____ Overhead _____

2. Capacity of service entrance: _____ amp

3. Volts: 110 _____ 110/220 _____

4. Adequacy of service: Ample _____ Adequate _____ Inadequate _____

5. Number of circuits: 15 amp _____ 20 amp _____ 30 amp _____ 60 amp _____ others _____

6. Location of distribution panel: _____

7. Overload device: Fuses _____ Resettable circuit breakers _____

**Heating:**

1. *Type of system:*

   a. Forced–warm-air: \_\_\_\_\_

   b. Hot-water radiant in-floor slab: \_\_\_\_\_

   c. Hot-water radiators: \_\_\_\_\_ Baseboard units \_\_\_\_\_ Convectors \_\_\_\_\_

   d. Steam: \_\_\_\_\_ Large, old-fashioned radiators \_\_\_\_\_ Newer, small radiators \_\_\_\_\_

   e. Electric baseboard: \_\_\_\_\_

2. *Heat source:*

   a. Electric \_\_\_\_\_

   b. Fuel oil \_\_\_\_\_

   c. Gas \_\_\_\_\_

   d. Liquid petroleum \_\_\_\_\_

3. *Condition of furnace or boiler:* Good \_\_\_\_\_ Adequate \_\_\_\_\_ Needs repair \_\_\_\_ Must be replaced in near future \_\_\_\_\_

4. *Noise level when operating:* Low \_\_\_\_\_ Moderate \_\_\_\_\_ High \_\_\_\_\_

5. *Condition of pipes or ducts:* Good \_\_\_\_\_ Fair \_\_\_\_\_ Need repair \_\_\_\_\_

   a. Insulated \_\_\_\_\_ Not insulated \_\_\_\_\_

6. *Location of thermostats:* Good \_\_\_\_\_ Adequate \_\_\_\_\_ Poor \_\_\_\_\_

7. *Heater venting:* Good \_\_\_\_\_ Adequate \_\_\_\_\_ Poor; must be repaired or replaced \_\_\_\_\_

8. *Annual cost of operation:* Average \_\_\_\_\_ High \_\_\_\_\_ Low \_\_\_\_\_

**Insulation:**

a. Sidewalls: Yes \_\_\_\_\_ None \_\_\_\_\_ Thickness or R value \_\_\_\_\_ Type \_\_\_\_\_

b. Floors: Yes \_\_\_\_\_ None \_\_\_\_\_ Thickness or R value \_\_\_\_\_ Type \_\_\_\_\_

c. Roof: Yes \_\_\_\_\_ None \_\_\_\_\_ Thickness or R value \_\_\_\_\_ Type \_\_\_\_\_

d. Attic floor: Yes \_\_\_\_\_ None \_\_\_\_\_ Thickness or R value \_\_\_\_\_ Type \_\_\_\_\_

## Plumbing System (Fresh-Water System):

1. *Source:* Public water _____ Private well _____ Shallow well _____ Deep well _____ If private well, has water been tested for bacterial count? Yes _____ No _____

2. *Quality of water:* Hard _____ Soft _____ Requires water conditioner or softener _____

3. *Type of water pipe:* Copper _____ Galvanized iron _____ Other _____

4. *Diameter of service line:* _____

5. *Branch-line size:* _____

6. *Leaks:* Yes _____ No _____

7. *Hot-water lines:* Insulated _____ Not insulated _____

8. *Hot-water heater:*
   a. Capacity: _____ gallons
   b. Recovery rate: _____ minutes
   c. Heat source: Electric _____ Gas _____ LP _____ Oil _____
   d. Condition: Good _____ Fair _____ Needs replacement _____

## Plumbing System (Sewer System):

1. *Sewage disposal:* Municipal _____ Septic tank _____ Cesspool _____
   a. Capacity of septic tank: _____
   b. Date of last cleaning: _____
   c. Capacity versus load: Good _____ Fair _____ Inadequate _____

2. *Type of underground line:* Cast iron _____ Clay tile _____ Other _____
   a. Condition of lines: Good _____ Fair _____ Poor _____
   b. Is leaching field sufficient for load? Yes _____ No _____
   c. Does method of disposal conform to local regulations? Yes _____ No _____
   d. Does sewage leach into: Drinking water source _____ Stream _____ Other water _____

e. Do local codes allow year-round occupancy? Yes _____ No _____

Remarks _____

_____

## Foundation, Crawl Space, Basement:

1. *Foundation walls:* Poured concrete _____ Concrete block _____ Cinder block _____ Stone _____ Other _____

   a. Condition: Good _____ Fair _____ Poor _____

   b. Drainage (outside walls): Good _____ Fair _____ Poor _____

2. *Crawl space:* Yes _____ No _____

   a. Ventilation of crawl space: Good _____ Fair _____ Poor _____

   b. Floor of crawl space: Dirt _____ Concrete _____ PVC over dirt _____

3. *Indication of termites:* None _____ Yes _____ Possible _____

4. *Decay in wood sills:* Yes _____ No _____ Possible _____

5. *First-floor framing:* Good _____ Adequate _____ Undersize _____

6. *Basement:* Dry _____ Damp _____ Wet _____ Sump pump _____

7. *Basement:* Finished _____ Unfinished _____ Usable as living area _____

## Bathrooms:

1. *Number of full baths:* _____ Location _____

2. *Number of half baths:* _____ Location _____

3. *Condition of fixtures:* Good _____ Fair _____ Should be replaced _____

4. *Water pressure:* Good _____ Fair _____ Poor _____

5. *Ventilation:* Windows _____ Exhaust fan _____ Vent _____

6. *Lighting:* Good _____ Fair _____ Poor _____

7. *Ceiling:* Good _____ Fair _____ Needs repair or replacement _____

8. *Walls:* Sound _____ Fair _____ Need repair or replacement _____

9. *Floors:* Good _____ Fair _____ Need repair or replacement _____

10. *Heating facilities:* Good _____ Fair _____ Inadequate _____


## Kitchen:

1. *Size:* _____

2. *Condition:* Renovated _____ Antiquated _____ Other _____

3. *Layout:* Good _____ Fair _____ Poor _____

4. *Storage:* Good _____ Fair _____ Inadequate _____

5. *Counter space:* Good _____ Fair _____ Insufficient _____

6. *Condition of counters, cabinets:* Good _____ Fair _____ Poor _____

7. *Counters, cabinets need:* Painting _____ Refinishing _____

   Replacement _____

8. *Electrical circuits and outlets:* Adequate _____ Inadequate _____

9. *Walls:* Good _____ Fair _____ Poor _____

10. *Ceiling:* Good _____ Fair _____ Poor _____

11. *Flooring:* Asphalt tile _____ Vinyl Tile _____ Sheet flooring _____

    Carpet _____ Wood _____ Other _____

    a. Condition: Good _____ Fair _____ Poor _____

12. *Condition of kitchen sink:* Good _____ Fair _____ Must be replaced _____

    a. Single sink _____ double sink _____

13. *Major appliances:* New _____ Acceptable _____ Antiquated _____

14. *Stove fueled by:* Gas _____ Electricity _____ LP _____ Other _____

15. *Dishwasher:* Yes _____ No _____

16. *Garbage disposal:* Yes _____ None _____

17. *Exhaust fan:* Yes _____ None _____

    a. Location: Over stove _____ In window _____ Other _____

**Garage:** Yes _____ No _____ Carport _____

1. *Attached:* Yes _____ Detached _____

2. *Size:* One-car _____ Two-car _____ Suitable for compact only _____

3. *Storage in garage:* Good _____ Adequate _____ Poor _____ None _____

4. *Overhead garage door:* Yes _____ No _____ None _____

5. *Floor:* Dirt _____ Concrete _____ Other _____

6. *Lighting and electrical outlets:* Good _____ Poor _____ Comments _____

7. *Slope of floor for drainage:* Good _____ Poor _____ None _____

# Index

# Index

Acoustical tile, 93
  for basement ceilings, 103–104
  for kitchen ceilings, 131–132
  limitations of, 103
Additions, 17–19, 171–182
  costs of, 176, 180–182
  deciding on room type, 172
  efficient use of materials in, 180–181
  as an investment, 173
  location of, 177
  permits for, 176–177
  vs. raising the roof, 87
  and remodeling, 172–173
  resale value and, 171–172, 174
  shell, 182
  taxes and, 26
  two-story, 180
Advertisements, 67–68
  real estate, 17, 264
Agreements (see Contracts)
Air conditioning:
  central, 133–135, 159
    costs of installation and operation, 133–134
    estimates for installation and operation, 135
  as an investment, 16, 17
  room, 136, 159
Aluminum frames for swimming pools, 229–231
Aluminum siding, 215–217
  painting, 193, 194
Aluminum wiring, 160, 161
American Institute of Architects, 41, 42
Appliances:
  kitchen, 127–128
  for rental units, 257–258

Appraisal of neighborhoods, 9–15
  adverse influences, protection from, 13
  appeal to market, 14
  appearance of properties, 14
  compatability, 13
  employment stability, 10–11
  movement of buyers into area, 14–15
  police and fire protection, 14
  recreational facilities, 12
  schools, 11–12
  shopping, 11
  taxes, 12–13
  utilities, 13
Arbitration, precommitment of companies to, 50, 60, 62
Architects:
  budget for a project and, 42–43
  costs of, 41–43, 179
  plans for an addition and, 179–180
  rough plans and, 32
  specifications and, 36, 42
  training and ability of, 40–41
  when to use, 43
Asbestos shingles, painting of, 193
Asphalt driveways, 224
Asphalt shingles, 206–209, 213
Asphalt terraces, 240
Attic(s), 87–93
  bathrooms in, 88
  ceilings of, 94
  dormers, 75, 88–90
  fans in, 136
  fire exits from, 94
  floors in, 92–93
  heating of, 92
  improvements on, and taxes, 26
  insulation of, 90–92, 141, 142

Yellow Pages, 49–50, 131, 158, 209, 231, 251

Zoning board, 13, 255
  variance of, 24, 177, 255
  zoning decision appeals to, 24, 177

Zoning regulations, 23, 219
  definition of, 21
  neighborhood stability and, 13
  rental units and, 13, 21, 23, 24, 219, 255
  variance of, 24
  zoning board appeals and, 24